M000311113

THE DISGUISES OF THE DEMON

SUNY Series in Hindu Studies

Wendy Doniger, Editor

THE DISGUISES

OF THE

DEMON

The Development of the Yakṣa
in
Hinduism and Buddhism

Gail Hinich Sutherland

State University of New York Press

Published by
State University of New York Press, Albany

Printed in the United States of America

For information, address the State University of New York Press,
State University Plaza, Albany, NY 12246

Production by Christine Lynch
Marketing by Dana E. Yanulavich

Library of Congress Cataloging-in-Publication Data

Sutherland, Gail Hinich, 1945-
The disguises of the demon : the development of the Yaksa in Hinduism and Buddhism / Gail Hinich Sutherland.
p. cm. — (SUNY series in Hindu studies)
Includes bibliographical references and index.
ISBN 0-7914-0621-0 (alk. paper). — ISBN 0-7914-0622-9 (pbk. : alk. paper)
1. Yakṣas (Hindu deities) 2. Yakṣas(Buddhist deities)
I. Title. II. Series.
BL1225.Y27S88 1991
294.5'216—dc20 90-39203
CIP

10 9 8 7 6 5 4 3 2 1

For Dimitri

CONTENTS

ABBREVIATIONS xi

ILLUSTRATIONS xiii

ACKNOWLEDGMENTS xv

INTRODUCTION 1
Approaching the yakṣa 1
The problematic function of demons in Indian ethical paradigms 2
My approach to the material 4

CHAPTER 1. THE YAKṢA AND THE WATERS 7
Introduction 7
Iconography and method 7
Yakṣa beginnings in Buddhism and Jainism 9
Iconography and metaphor 19
Mythological background 20
Nature cosmology 20
The essence of the waters 21
The demiurge in the waters 23
Trees, water, and fertility 24
Trees in Buddhist tradition 26

The lotus 29
Pots of plenty 32
Makaras 35
The *nāga* 38
The magic fish 43
Local waters 46
The family of demons 49
Introduction 49
Yakṣas and rākṣasas 54
Piśācas 59
Gandharvas 59
Kinnāras or *kiṁpuruṣas* 61
Kubera 61
Introduction 61
Kubera and the *lokapālas* 65

CHAPTER 2. THE YAKṢA IN HINDUISM 69
Vedic Sources 69
Varuṇa 76

CHAPTER 3. TRIAL BY WATER IN HINDU AND BUDDHIST TEXTS 85
Introduction 85
The testing *nāga* 86
The testing yakṣa 88
The Bodhisatta and the yakkha 93
Varuṇa as yakṣa 96
Trial by water continued: moral conclusions 99

CHAPTER 4. THE YAKṢA IN BUDDHIST AND JAIN REPRESENTATIONS AND THOUGHT . 105
Buddhist cosmology and myth 105
The Buddhist cosmos and the demonic 108

Transformation and conversion 109
The fluid, physical, and moral forms of the demons 110
Humans, gods, and demons 112
Outwitting the yakkhas 115
Monstrous yakkhas 118
Kings and yakkhas 120
The yakṣa in Jainism 127

CHAPTER 5. YAKṢĪS 137
Introduction 137
The Buddhist yakkhinī 138
Yakṣīs as *śakti*s 146

CHAPTER 6. THE *MEGHADŪTA* 149

CONCLUSIONS 157

NOTES 169

BIBLIOGRAPHY 191

ABBREVIATIONS

AV, Atharva Veda

Br, Brāhmaṇa

JAOS, Journal of the American Oriental Society

Mbh, Mahābhārata

Md, Meghadūta

P, Purāṇa

Rām, Rāmāyaṇa

ṚV, Ṛg Veda

SN, Samyutta Nikāya

Up, Upaniṣad

ILLUSTRATIONS

1. Parkham Yakṣa
2. Yakṣa from Mahārāshṭra
3. Yakṣī from Besnagar
4. *Caurī* Bearer from Didarganj
5. Yakṣī from Besnagar
6. Yakṣī from Mathurā
7. Bhārhut yakṣī
8. Yakṣa on a Medallion from a Pillar Base (Bhārhut)
9. Dwarf Yakṣa from Pitalkhora
10. *Kīrttimukha*
11. Kubera

ACKNOWLEDGMENTS

The idea for this project began to take shape in an art history course at the University of Chicago taught by Carol Bolon. The seeds of that inspiration have been diligently, faithfully, and critically tended by Wendy Doniger (O'Flaherty) through all stages of their development. I am grateful for her comments as well as for those of Carol Bolon and Frank Reynolds. Any inadequacies, misconceptions, or errors to be found in this book, however, are entirely my own and do not reflect the directions of my advisers.

Research funds for this project were generously provided by the American Institute of Indian Studies, which supported a year of study in India during 1984–85. That that year constituted a personal watershed in many ways, they could not have anticipated. Nevertheless, my thanks are enthusiastic for both the research support and the personal benefits. I wish to express gratitude to the Committee on Southern Asian Studies at the University of Chicago for a grant that helped immensely in 1985–86.

I wish to thank the research facility and photography archive at the American Institute of Indian Studies (AIIS) in the Chief Court House in Ramnagar, Varanasi, for the photographs that appear in this book and for permission to use them. I am especially grateful to Mr. V. R. Nambiar, the director of AIIS in Ramnagar, for his prompt response to my request and for all of the help and attention he gave me when I was staying in Varanasi.

A special thank you is due to Virendra Singh, his wife, Sushila, and their beautiful children. Virendra was both an excellent Hindi teacher and a potent purveyor of *śakti*. The unforeseen direction that my life took was no doubt due to his *pūjā*s.

Immeasurable thanks are due to my parents, Irma and Brian Jones, who generously sacrificed emotionally and financially to help me through graduate school. My husband, Peter, has been a source of loving support and encouragement during the researching, writing, and revising of this book. The drawings in this book were patiently and skillfully done by him. I am thankful for his contribution of them and also for his tremendously thorough and incisive reading of the manuscript.

The real "silent partner" in this entire venture has been my son, Dimitri, who has accompanied me through the various stages of my academic and professional life. It has been our close relationship, along with his unflagging affection and enormous tolerance for change and rigor, that have sustained me throughout. For all of those reasons, this book is dedicated to him.

INTRODUCTION

Approaching the Yakṣa

The yakṣa[1] is an ancient deity and powerful mythological figure, depicted widely in early Buddhist, Jain, and Hindu sculpture; mentioned in a variety of literary contexts; and treated extensively in the mythology of the Hindu Epics and Purāṇas and in the Buddhist Jātakas. In 1931, the art historian Ananda Coomaraswamy published his two-part investigation of the yakṣa,[2] tracing its development in the literature from an amorphous concept of the numinous to a sort of demigod who functions in male or female (yakṣī/yakṣiṇī) form as a primeval symbol of fertility, abundance, water, and vegetation. This figure was intriguing to Coomaraswamy and later scholars primarily because of its ambiguous moral demeanor and application. The yakṣa is associated with a variety of familiar mythological characters and symbols among the lower deities and demigods who inhabit the trees, rivers, oceans, rock mounds, and sacred spots that fill the cosmological landscape of India. After a few brief Vedic references, the body of associations with the yakṣa steadily increases in complexity and resonance. Through each of its facets—of trees, of water, of darkness—a distinct mythology is elaborated, forming labyrinthine connections to a staggering variety of iconographic applications and religious and cultural depictions.

I intend to place this symbolic and mythological data within a framework of inquiry that will permit the posing of new questions and concerns. Specifically, I propose to explore how large cultural symbols and expressions such as the yakṣa encompass and articulate wide fluctuations in application, intent, formulation, and stylization. In pursuit of these ideas, I will examine the factors, contexts, and contingencies that have shaped the metamorphosis of the yakṣa as a symbol.

One question that I will try to address in this book relates specifically to the yakṣa's status as demon: To what extent is it necessary or even possible to resolve ethical, rational, emotional, and aesthetic paradoxes in order to develop and sustain a consistent notion of the demonic? Or put otherwise, at what stage or level of formulation of categories of the demonic do such considerations of paradox become relevant or compelling? As we shall see, despite my focus on the demonism of the yakṣa, this aspect by no means dominates the historical representations of the figure. The yakṣa is both beneficent and demonic, but in his metamorphosis from one ethical mode to another, there is valuable evidence for extending and reformulating our conception of the demonic and its categories.

In employing the figure of the yakṣa, I will examine the ways in which this question of the demonic is answered in Hindu versus Buddhist contexts and, in the process, examine more general issues of the employment of rationality, justification, and classification in the proliferation of normative religious symbols and myths. I will be particularly concerned with the interpenetration that continually produces a new rationality and integration, a new solidity and substance out of the old ground of opposition and paradox.

The Problematic Function of Demons in Indian Ethical Paradigms

In general, the attributes that are almost always equated with evil in Indian ethical paradigms are: (1) the defilement of caste and ritual purity and (2) the delusoriness that prevents humans from perceiving *dharma* ("truth," "reality", the religious order). Of the two attributes, it is really the former that is the more absolute, since the notion of what is *dharmic* is relative and delusion or māyā has both positive and negative aspects. The perpetration of deceit and disguise may have the hidden motive of testing the strength, courage, or understanding of the protagonist.[3] Insofar as demons function as defilers or polluters, they are more despised than in their role as deluders. In considering the three "stages" of power in Indian religious history elaborated by Wendy O'Flaherty, the Vedic or sacrificial stage, the ascetic stage, and the devotional or *bhakti* stage[4], we may see that the concept of the demonic is central to each in a different fashion. It is within the second stage—of ascetical or insightful power—that the sin of illusion overshadows that of defilement and is raised to the pinnacle of evil. At this stage, demons represent that which obscures knowledge and spiritual attainment, and since true insight or gnosis realizes that all obstacles are illusory and temporary, demons are depotentiated, their powers evaporating with the growth of wisdom. In the more monistic (and ultimately humanistic) view that predominates in the philosophical texts, the Upaniṣads (700 B.C.) and in early Buddhist texts, *both* the demons and the gods are symbols of the manifold that obfuscates the one. For the Buddha, the struggle with the demon, Māra, is a battle with illusion, personified as its two primeval components, lust and death.

In the self-transcendence and empowerment of ascetic vision, "the distinction between the categories of gods, demons, and men"[5] is obliterated, and the pollution aspect of evil becomes all the more ethically necessary, for, as Mary Douglas has said, pollution beliefs "not only reinforce the cultural and social structure, but they can actively reduce ambiguity in the moral sphere."[6] Such religious notions as the transferral of merit and the power of the *peta*s (ghosts) take over the conveyancing of purity and pollution within Buddhism, in the wake of the abandonment of the caste taboos of Hinduism.

In addition to their changing but, overall, constant function as moral devices, it is clear to me that demons (and particularly yakṣas) also serve as vital psychological ballast in a perennially oscillating dialectic between internal as opposed to external responsibility for misfortune. In essence, the ongoing tension between the fundamentally dualistic worldview of Vedic tradition and the fundamentally monistic worldview of the ascetical traditions (including Buddhism and Jainism) has a psychological or therapeutic dimension: The early conception of the militant opposition between good and evil may be seen as a frightening precursor of an eternal repetition of frustrating, dissatisfying dualism. On the one hand, to conceive of the enemy as "out there" is to relinquish forever autonomy and control over one's fate. If one employs only aggression against or appeasement of the demonic powers, one is doomed to struggle. In the contemplative traditions of Indian religion, beginning with the period of the Upaniṣads, this inadequacy of the Vedic psychology is compensated for in the introspective paths that advocate the *transformation* rather than the destruction of demons. On the other hand, the demons are rarely obliterated, and the early mythology that deals with them never ceases as a tradition parallel to, and interwoven with, the more mystical texts and traditions, as is particularly seen in the case of the yakṣa mythology of early Buddhism. Even in the Vedāntic, Tantric, and yogic texts of medieval Hinduism, demons are a useful means for visualizing and conceptualizing the inner obstacles and terrors that the contemplative practitioner must overcome on his way to freedom. On the other end of the spectrum, excessive internalization of misfortune places too much pressure, emotional and moral, on the individual. In this sense, demons function as linchpins in the vital balance between pluralism and monism in the changing moral and religious economy.

My Approach to the Material

When Coomaraswamy first wrote about the yakṣa, the dominant tradition in Indological scholarship still entailed a bias against village or local religious expression and what early scholars considered to be a loosely woven fabric of archaic practices, characterized by violence, compulsion, and childish propitiation and magic. This approach, rooted as it was in Western theology, gave way in time to a scholarly discovery of the true extent of the influence of popular elements on the major religious traditions of India. In reviving Coomaraswamy's interest in the yakṣa, this work inevitably finds itself located in that earlier scholarly discovery. Among the first aspects of popular Hinduism to be studied seriously, the yakṣa (because of his pervasive representation in Indian sculpture) was seen by Coomaraswamy as a nexus of the "great" and "little" traditions of India. Accordingly, this project participates in the effort to harmonize these religious strata by bringing to the fore some of the classical questions of the Western disciplines of the philosophy of religion, ethics, and epistemology in order to apply them judiciously to aspects of the popular, the local, the colorful, the artistic, the theatrical, and the mythological.

I became fascinated by the yakṣa precisely because no historical or philosophical system seemed capable of accounting fully for his origins and for the extent to which the yakṣa-related mythology has permeated every aspect of Indian art, mythology, and legend. I felt, therefore, that, in the name of exhaustive and accurate research, I must be prepared to refer to aesthetic, historical, philosophical, epistemological, psychological, and anthropological data and theories. This did not seem excessive or inappropriate to me since many contemporary scholarly efforts to define myth now seem, if not to embrace all of these modes of explanation, at least not to rule them out completely.

I have divided my treatment of the yakṣa into six chapters: In the long first chapter, I will introduce general iconographic problems and issues. I will be searching particularly for the yakṣa's origins in the deep layering of mythology and symbolism that constitutes the phenomenology of the waters. Partaking of this fecund element, the yakṣa is connected with a spectrum of other animal and vegetal species and forms. These connections are manifest in both visual and narrative representations. As well as being part of the mythology of the waters, from which connection they derive their tendency to moral ambiguity, yakṣas and yakṣīs are members of a large family of less ambiguous, popular demons, with whom I will compare the yakṣa in the third part of the first chapter. The last section of the first chapter will be devoted to Kubera, the king of the yakṣas, who has a special status within the family of popular demons and demigods.

In the second chapter, my search for the origins of the yakṣa will focus on the earliest textual references in the Vedic literature. These early references will reveal close affiliations with other Vedic gods (particularly Varuṇa) whose careers have evolved along paths that are demonstrably similar to those exhibited in the transformations of the yakṣa.

The third chapter will explore one important theme that emerges from our analysis of the god Varuṇa in his relationship to the yakṣa—the "trial by water," a motif that is traced through three textual variants. This motif will serve to illustrate the ethical complexities and transformations of the yakṣa, which are the special focus of this book, and also demonstrate certain vital points of contrast between Hindu and Buddhist representations.

Chapter four will be concerned with the characteristic treatments of the yakṣa in Buddhist and Jain art and literature. As we shall see, the Jātaka tales particularly encode in mythological form important Buddhist cosmological and social ideals that have an impact on how the yakṣa (yakkha) is viewed within that tradition.

In chapter five, I will address the special role played by the yakṣī, as female, as goddess, and as demoness, in both Hindu and Buddhist representations.

To complete the spectrum of important yakṣa portrayals, in chapter six I will discuss Kālīdāsa's poetic rendering of a yakṣa in his dramatic poem, the Meghadūta. This aesthetic example will reveal yet another dimension of the yakṣa phenomenology. Having traced the yakṣa's progress from early equations with the absolute and the demiurge, to a powerful deity of the water, to a cannibalistic demon, we will finally encounter him as a lush symbol of eroticism and romantic love.

Chapter 1

THE YAKṢA AND THE WATERS

Introduction

Iconography and method

Ananda Coomaraswamy's investigations into the art, history, and culture of South Asia were in the forefront of a scholarly movement that began to look at some of the more popular aspects of Indian tradition and, in so doing, to open up a diversity of forms and issues to the kind of scrutiny that had previously been reserved for the massive intellectual domains of Indian philosophy and linguistics.

It is fitting that as a South Asian scholar Coomaraswamy (1877–1947) should have been an initiator of the movement toward an appreciation of the so-called popular culture of India, for the shift in scholarship that began around the end of the nineteenth century was accompanied by or, perhaps, engendered by the physical encounter of Western scholars with the geography, peoples, and art of the East. Indian scholarship in the West had been a purely textual tradition, such that many Sanskritists had never traveled to India at all. The legitimacy of this approach has never been completely discredited, and the extent to which the two domains of learned and popular traditions overlap and implicate one another will never be easily determined. At any rate, there is plenty of room to move in either domain with only casual reference to the other.

The physical encounter with Indian culture led to an awareness of the extent to which the use of sculptural forms and images has played an integral part in the religious life of the people. These images, consisting of the central cast of Indian religious characters, Śiva, Viṣṇu and his *avatāras*, the Goddess, and the Buddha, are an essential part of the great monuments of Indian art and architecture. The sculptures are displayed iconically either as the foci of worship or meditation or in the midst of a narrative scheme, illustrating important events in the life or mythology of the divine character. In addition to the major gods and goddesses, one is aware of the prevalence and importance of the minor, supporting cast of characters, like "extras" or shield bearers, anonymous forms, without whom the narrative fabric and visual continuity of the temple ornamentation would not flow. Within this visual stream of mythological characters and supernatural presences of all kinds, a familiar dramatis personae emerges that has a life of its own and that seems simultaneously to engage, on the one hand, our appreciation of the whimsical and playful and, on the other hand, the most serious of aesthetic and religious sensibilities. Heinrich Zimmer has commented on this paradoxical experience.

> The luxuriant display of religious sculpture so characteristic of the great temples of pilgrimage is therefore a readily legible pictorial script that conveys, through an elaborate, yet generally understood symbolism, not only the legends of popular cult, but simultaneously the profoundest teachings of Indian metaphysics.[1]

Certain images and motifs drawn from an iconography that precedes the explicit development of classical Hindu mythology are appropriated because of their suitability as easily reproduced and decorative forms. These forms, however, exceed their purely decorative function by acquiring and generating a symbolism that is capable of standing on its own, both aesthetically and theologically. This evolution of a symbol is facilitated by a decorative phenomenon that F. D. K. Bosch calls "morphological resemblance,"[2] in which visually similar elements of entirely different species or modes of being are translated into one another over time in a subtle process of perceiving and elaborating relationships between certain prevalent forms endemic to the self-expression of the culture.

The purpose of this chapter will be to trace the manifold connections and transformations that pertain to the iconography and mythology of the yakṣa. Lest it seem that the net that gathers these associated forms has been cast too widely, let me offer two assertions in defense of its inclusiveness. On the one hand, all of the iconographical elements that we will discuss are aspects of the mythology of water and cannot be understood on any level except in relation to that encompassing and profound medium and to one another. On the other hand, the visual transformation of images, inspired by "morphological resemblance," may be seen as a metaphor for the ethical and theological transformations that will be the special subject of this study.

Bosch focuses on the development of the motif of the *makara,* a crocodilelike aquatic creature whose use as a sculptural form spread throughout most of Asia.[3] The *makara* is one of a great variety of mythological hybrids and elaborations who have made their way into the vocabulary of Indian art and literature. Among these hybrids are to be found primordial and powerful symbols whose origins within the culture are steeped in mystery and yet whose popularity and usefulness within the art and culture are obvious. The yakṣa is one of these powerful figures, an image that has undergone change and reversal in three related discourses: the historical evolution of Indian religion and society, the morphological associations depicted in Indian art, and the development of literary stylization.

Yakṣa beginnings in Buddhism and Jainism

Yakṣas and yakṣīs fill the early Buddhist monuments of Sāñcī and Bhārhut, and the former serve as prototypes for the first iconic representations of the Buddha. Despite certain apparent conceptual contradictions between, on the one hand, the ascetic ideals and metaphors associated with the world-renouncing Buddha and his contemporary, Mahāvīra, the founder of Jainism, and, on the other hand, the life-supporting, sensual yakṣa, the use of such nature deities in Buddhist art represents a grounding of new religious ideas in current popular symbolism.

> At first sight these figures [trees and dryads] seem to be singularly out of place if regarded with the eyes of the Buddhist or Jaina monk. But by the time that a necessity had arisen for the erection of these great monuments, with their illustration of Buddhist legends and other material constituting a veritable *Biblia Pauperum,* Buddhism and Jainism had passed beyond the circle of monasticism and become popular religions with a cult. These figures of fertility spirits are present here because the people are here. Women, accustomed to invoke the blessings of a tree spirit, would approach the railing pillar images with similar expectations; these images like those of Nagas and Yaksas often set up on Buddhist and Jaina sites, may be compared to the altars of patron saints which a pious Catholic visits with prayers for material blessings.[4]

Yakṣas and their attendant iconography were employed in the aniconic stage of Buddhist art, in which certain symbols drawn from the life of the Buddha stood as shorthand stylizations representing the actual person of the Buddha, whose anthropomorphic depiction was forsworn. Early depictions of the yakṣa, such as the freestanding sculptures from Parkham (figure 1) and Mahārāshṭra (figure 2), saw him as a massive, full-bodied *devatā,* who would have borne the turban and umbrella of a royal prince or hero. These ancient, usually

Figure 1. Parkham Yakṣa

Figure 2. Yakṣa from Mahārāshṭra

damaged statues have been discovered standing in fields. Life size, they display maximum emphasis on the front side of the sculpture, with little or no attention to realistic modeling and detailing of all sides. Among the earliest sculptures of this type are two yakṣas from Patna, a yakṣī from Besnagar (figure 3), and the *caurī* or fly-whisk bearer (who may or may not be a yakṣī) from Didarganj (figure 4).

Figure 3. Yakṣī from Besnagar

Figure 4. *Caurī* Bearer from Didarganj

Because of the characteristic use of highly polished Chunar sandstone in the Patna and Didarganj sculptures, they are thought to have been carved during the Mauryan period (322–183 B.C.). These sculptures all exhibit, in addition to their massive physical extension, a "monumental" stiffness. This archaic quality of immobility persists in other, post-Mauryan (first century B.C.) freestanding statues as well, such as another yakṣī from the Besnagar area (figure 5). In this later period, the standing sculptures acquire a rounder, softer fleshiness, a foreshortening and thickening of the limbs, a greater prominence of belly (a characteristic that was to become intimately associated with the yakṣa iconography), and an element of more articulation in the rendering of draped garments. The compelling physical proportions and provocative nudity, signifying overt fecundity, of the Didarganj *caurī* bearer prefigure other voluptuous yakṣī sculptures, in particular the railing pillars from Bhuteśar in Mathurā (early second century A.D.), where similarly proportioned yakṣīs stand upon grotesque, dwarfish *vāhanas* (mounts), completely nude but for decorative girdles around their ample hips, necklaces, and anklets (figure 6).

It is the combination of the earthy and the regal in these early yakṣa images that, seemingly, provided a model for the religious ruler and reformer, Siddhārtha Gautama, whose own regnancy incorporated the realms of nature, society, and cosmos. Other symbols that stand in for the Buddha in notable depictions of his life include the parasol (to signify kingship), the empty throne (to signify his first meditation), the riderless horse (to signify his departure from his father's palace), the tree (to signify of course the *bodhi* tree under which he achieved enlightenment), and the footstool upon which the *buddhapāda* or footprint of the Buddha is visible. The use of this shorthand lexicon of images entailed a freedom of thematic association that permitted ever-widening circles of conceptual relationship, in which pre-Buddhist mythological figures such as the yakṣa became vital elements in the redrawn map of Buddhist mythology and narrative. Dietrich Seckel refers to an analogous process of symbolic dislocation and reassociation in his observations on the development of the Buddha image.

Figure 5. Yakṣī from Besnagar

> Thus a symbol that had its origin and proper place in one of the biographical scenes may acquire a broader significance and, isolated from the original narrative context, may be used anachronistically—or rather trans-historically—in contexts where it seems to be out of place; e.g., in a scene involving the new-born Sakyamuni where he is represented as the Enlightened One by the empty throne with the umbrella above and the footprints before it. Even in the early iconography with its overriding concern for "biographical" narration, a tendency is noticeable to liberate from the bond of time and space the Buddha and the symbols representing him and his actions; so the symbols become freely available and applicable in various contexts for new religious purposes.[5]

Because of the early reluctance to depict the human form of the Buddha, related, according to Seckel, to the "philosophically radical doctrine concerning his true Nirvāṇa essence, inconceivable, invisual form and human shape,"[6], a variety of related forms was permitted to adhere to the absent Buddha image. These forms were the first iconic figures to be fashioned in the development of Indian art and were created as subordinate figures in the retinue of the Buddha, surrounding some aniconic symbol of the Master himself. These figures included the "men, gods, demigods, and genii"[7] that supplemented the growing cast of characters in the depiction and embellishment of Buddhist legend. This cast is drawn from a pre-Buddhist compendium of popular images that includes an array of kindred demons and deities.

Certain elements of Buddhist and yakṣa-related iconography come to be linked in sculptural representations. For instance, on top of the north *toraṇa* at Sāñcī, one can see a triad consisting of the central symbol of the *dharmacakra* ("the wheel of *dharma,*" symbolizing the Buddha's first sermon at Benares) flanked by two (although one is now missing) yakṣas, carrying *caurīs*. Both flowers and *caurīs* are iconographic emblems associated with the yakṣa. The flower links the yakṣa with the domain of nature and fertility; the *caurī* is a symbol drawn from a vocabulary of social referents and has meaning particularly within the context of a political, courtly setting, in which a king is being attended by his servants. By implication, the use of these *caurī*-bearing yakṣas casts the Buddha in the role of a worldly monarch. The

---

Figure 6. Yakṣī from Mathurā

visual affinity among flower, *caurī,* and *dharmacakra* implies a symbolic relationship of the realms of nature, polity, and religion. When you add to these associations the iconographic reference of the *dharmacakra* to the solar *cakra* or disk of the sun, we can perceive the power of these symbols to enrich a religious tradition by constellating the myriad visual connections that have preceded it.

> The wheel (*cakra*) which later on becomes the mark of the Cakravartin, the discus of Viṣṇu, and the Buddhist Wheel of the Law, originally represented the Sun. The disk of gold placed behind the fire-altar to represent the Sun may well be the origin of the later *prabhā-maṇḍala* or *śiras-cakra* (nimbus). Radiance is predicated of almost all the Devas, is indeed one of the root meanings of the word, and most of them are connected in their origins with Sun and Fire. Just as the tree behind the empty altar or throne, representing the Buddha in the early art, remains in the later art when the throne is occupied, so the sun-disk behind the fire-altar may well have remained there when the deity was first made visible.[8]

In this way, imagery can facilitate the growth and transformation of concepts. Behind the use of this imagery, of course, is a historical context in which the ideas and movements that these visual images represent are in dialogical contact with one another.

Particularly interesting is the tendency of symbols to compress meaning, cutting radically across time and context through minute and subtle changes in the appearance of a formal element. In the case of Buddhist symbols, the *dharmacakra* comes to signify the teaching itself as well as the specific event of the setting in motion of that teaching. The Buddhist *stūpa* or stylized burial mound erected over, supposedly, some portion of the remains of the Buddha is, because of its association with his deceased body, a symbol of *saṁsāra* or the impermanence of life, while simultaneously the *stūpa* more strikingly symbolizes the immutable truth of the Buddha's teachings and the triumph of the Buddha over *saṁsāra*. The multivalency of this symbol might be compared to the Cross within Christianity, employed as a metaphor for both the crucifixion as well as the resurrection of Christ. Once a cultural metaphor has been empowered to move this freely between poles of meaning and varieties of experience, it has truly become liberated from its moorings in the historical context of its inception.[9]

Iconography and metaphor

It seems that religious metaphors acquire their fluency and multivalency because of the centrality of stark opposition and contrast in the formulation of sacred texts and artifacts (in contrasts between life and death, god and man, spirit and nature, etc.). The anthropologist Mary Douglas, however, in her criticism of Edmund Leach, suggests that the role of "mediation" is an inherent element of any mode of expression, whether it is a painting, a secular narrative, or a myth.

> Leach suggests that contrast, mediation, and resolution of opposites are characteristic of sacred texts. But this process, which he calls the encoding of religious mysteries, is essential in secular stories too. Composition of any kind starts with distinctive elements; it develops confusions and ambiguities, travesties and misperceptions, and goes on to sort out and recombine the initial possibilities.[10]

If we acknowledge that a symbol can paradoxically stand forth from the very substance of its creation, invigorated with a life and will that are unique to its formal limitations, then perhaps we can be allowed to speak of the life cycle of a symbol, like the life cycle of a star, another "individual" that we take for granted until it has gone out of existence. Because of its richness of meaning and breadth of application, I believe that the yakṣa is a fitting candidate for such a study of the life cycle of a symbol. It is possible to observe the process by which a fleeting, sketchy image acquires mass and distinction, becomes, in its prime, very important, then over time loses its vividness and individuality and, like a star, ultimately burns out, leaving an image that, nevertheless, remains visible (as an apparition) for succeeding eons. Even within this apparitional phase in the development of the metaphor, creative employment may be operative, often within the oeuvre of a particular writer or artist, in the same way that poets of our own century have utilized classical myths or sacred concepts to express and expand their own vocabulary of primary artistic metaphors (Rilke with the Angel, Yeats with Leda and the Swan, Cocteau with Orpheus). Later in the book, we will look more closely at the artist's utilization of yakṣa mythology in India in Kālīdāsa's poem, the *Meghadūta*.

Even when a symbol may have passed out of currency in the theological mainstream of a tradition, its "apparition" may be so reinfused with life through the media of poetic and artistic creation or celebration and devotion that it cannot be considered to be dead or inactive in any sense. Though we may cite numerous examples of this passing on from hand to hand of a symbol in the Western artistic context, it is in India that this practice acquires an importance and vitality unequaled in any other culture. In the varieties of Indian religious practice, we can see a relentless recycling of myths and images. Each new version produces its own root structure, which, like the shoots of a banyan tree, grow toward a new and welcoming plot of soil, growing from the outside in, in the way that artistic forms and images pursue a direction that is prescribed by the trajectory of their own formal capacities.[11]

In this chapter, I will examine in detail the network of symbols and relationships that comprises the mythological reaches and extent of the yakṣa's sway and meaning. This enterprise will have two basic facets: (1) an analysis of the symbols, metaphors, and iconography connected with the waters and (2) an inquiry into the relationships and similarities that the yakṣa sustains with other demons and demigods of the Indian pantheon, including the king of the yakṣas, Kubera. This is a project that has been done in the art-historical context by Coomaraswamy and, more recently, by Ram Nath Misra. Coomaraswamy truly paved the way for this kind of study, both with the extent of his research and linguistic competency and with his passion for speculative philosophy and cross-traditional comparisons. I am utterly indebted to his study of the yakṣa, as a means of opening to inquiry a vast amount of data and a trove of ideas that had been, prior to his scholarship, undisclosed. In my study, I will summarize much of what these two scholars have discovered and analyzed and use their insights to map out my own approach to the elucidation of the phenomenology of the yakṣa.

Mythological Background

Nature cosmology

In the earliest references, the sacrality of the yakṣa is expressed in terms of images drawn from nature. This ancient yakṣa may be seen to embody a nexus of natural principles and abstract metaphysical concepts, in other words, a nexus of the cosmic and acosmic. The mystery and fascination of this deity are rooted in its unique propensity to bridge the two religious dimensions and stand poised at a moment in the development of the philosophy and religion of India, which is perhaps analogous to a pre-Socratic Greece, when the philosophical inquiry into the nature of being incorporated both metaphysical and scientific explorations.

The yakṣa as a being that contains both cosmic and acosmic facets is featured in an important verse from the *Atharva Veda.*

> The Great Yakṣa, steeped in concentration on the surface of the water in the middle of the world, on him the various gods are fixed like branches around the trunk of a tree.[12]

This conjunction of the transcendent or acosmic waters of pure being with their manifestation in nature in the cosmic symbol of the tree is important for our investigation of the moral ambivalence and eventual demonism of the yakṣa. For it is precisely this spanning of, at one extreme, the highest and most abstract theism and, at the other extreme, telluric fertility worship, that both expands the yakṣa's symbolic valency and also vitiates its normative potential. We will adduce texts that equate the yakṣa with the impersonal (and asexual) absolute as well as texts that clearly define him as a genius loci, by turns ribald, lascivious, impudent, violent, and wholly of the earth. Like the cosmic waters with which he is connected, the yakṣa's iconography is intricately associated with a multiplicity of natural phenomena. To begin our analysis of this mysterious deity, we must place it in the medium in which all of these associations find their significance and coherence—in the potent, sacred waters. It is here that the yakṣa acquires its affinity with other symbols of fertility and creativity, such as trees, *nāga*s, and aquatic creatures such as the *makara.*

The Essence of the waters

Within the waters is a volatile, quickening agent or essence (*rasa*) that is to be found in the vegetal world in the form of the sap contained in trees and plants and in the animal world in the form of such substances as the venom secreted by the serpentine deities, the *nāga*s. This poison, which they harbor and control, is an aspect of the watery spectrum that encompasses the extremes of *amṛta* (the elixir of immortality) or *soma,* on the one hand, and venom, on the other hand. Venom may be seen to be a by-product, in fact, of the agitation of the vital essences contained in the generative waters during the mythic episode in which the gods and the demons churn the ocean for the *amṛta.*[13] In the course of their churning, the *kālakūṭa* poison is produced, after the milk, butter, wine, and various life-supporting and cosmological phenomena are engendered.[14] Coomaraswamy sums up the passage of procreative energy through the flow and circulation of the cosmic waters.

> . . . from the primeval waters arose the Plants, from Plants all other beings, in particular the gods, men, and cattle. *Rasa,* as an essence of the Waters, or as a sap in trees, is variously identified with *soma, amṛta,* semen, milk, rain, honey, mead (*madhu*) and liquor (*sura*); there is a cycle in which the vital energy passes from heaven through the waters, plants, cattle and other typically virile or productive animals, and man, thence ultimately returning to the waters. The clouds rain milk or *soma*; they are sometimes called cows, as is also Aditi, the goddess of abundance who is also a personification of the honey-whip of the Asvins, which may be the lightning. The myth of actual creation takes the form of origination of a tree from the navel of a Primal Male, who rests upon the Waters, and from whose navel the tree rises up; he is called a Yakṣa and was originally Varuṇa.[15]

Over and above the capacity of the waters to confer blessings, fertility, and abundance lies their propensity for containing sheer transformative energy. Water is a metamorphic medium that quickens life into being from latency, or compels living beings toward their demise. Apropos of this potential for both creation and destruction, Heinrich Zimmer speaks of the waters of illusion or *māyā,* citing in particular two myths about the holy seer, Nārada. In both myths, the seduction of *māyā* involves the unsuspecting seer in a complex series of dreamlike illusions about himself and his life that seem indubitably real and inescapably painful. In this sense, the waters contain the secrets of being and of *karma,* the inscrutable law of causality.

> When Nārada, the human disciple, asked to be taught this secret, the god did not disclose the answer by any verbal instruction or formula. Instead, he simply pointed to water, as the element of initiation.[16]

The creativeness and destructiveness of the primal waters may be seen as well in the fact that in the great conflagration or *pralaya* the god Viṣṇu, having withdrawn all of the moisture from all of the living things of the earth, thus causing a fire to spark from the friction of the dried up trees, puts out that fire with a continuous downpour of rain that drowns all beings, leaving only the endless expanse of undifferentiated water upon which he sleeps for thousands of *yuga*s as the unmanifest (*avyakta*) lord and creator.[17] The water and Viṣṇu are one life-producing substance; the waters of life are a concomitant to his creativity. The taming of the waters is essential for the creation of the world, and it is through the unleashing of the waters that god's creation is destroyed during the deluge. The taming and manipulation of the waters as a means of gaining power and mastery is a motif that is well-known in folk literature and world mythology. We will see its importance in the popular Buddhist literature where the power and sovereignty of the king is determined by his symbolic and actual mastery over the elements, particularly water in the form of rain.

The Demiurge in the waters

At some early stage of reflection on the nature of reality and being, the term "yakṣa" appears to represent a transitional description of the absolute, a phenomenon that would later be termed *brahman*. While the fully developed concept of *brahman* referred to pure being or the absolute that preceded the cosmic manifestation of life, the yakṣa encompassed both aspects of being, although moving steadily toward the cosmic.

> The Vedic Yaksha does not necessarily imply a personality to start with, and is more of a word-concept which was subsequently converted into a fully developed personage, invested with the attributes of spirit, form, nature and power.[18]

In many of the Hindu creation myths, the creator or demiurge is associated so closely with the new life that is being created that he is thought to be the fundamental germ or seed of life, out of which the array of created beings emerges. In one rendering of the *hiraṇyagarbha* ("golden egg") cosmology, the process of creation discloses sexual components when a primal male in the form of Prajāpati, Agni, or Brahmā breaks out of the golden egg that floats on the fecund potential of the feminine waters. The coming into existence of the egg is seen to be the result of the friction of the waves as they collide together. The egg arises from "the heat produced by the waters as they wanted to propagate themselves."[19]

> That egg floated about for a year and in that time a man, Prajāpati, the god of the primordial undivided world, came into being. He then broke the egg open but it had no foundation, and he floated about on that egg for another year after which he created the earth, the atmosphere, and the sky.[20]

Bosch speculates that the creation of the *hiraṇyagarbha* is the result of the commingling of the deities, Agni, the masculine golden god of fire, and Soma, the *rasa*-essence of the waters, providing, in this case, the feminine component of the creation odyssey.[21]

Another cycle of *hiraṇyagarbha* myths gives rise to a different conception of this primal creative act, in which there is no sexual element present.

> The waters are here identified with a sexless primeval being from whose navel, considered to be the germ of life Hiraṇyagarbha, rises the trunk of the cosmic tree, this trunk being both the axis of the universe and the prop of the firmament.[22]

It is this latter mode of cosmic creation that seems to relate more clearly to the problem of the yakṣa. As we have already seen, the yakṣa has been compared with a primeval cosmic tree in *AV* 10. 7. 38. In the implicit equation of the yakṣa with the impersonal absolute, *brahman,* the potency and latent fertility of the latter is emphasized at the expense of abstract connotations.

> Those acquainted with Brahman know that living being (*yakṣam ātmanvat*) which resides in this golden receptacle.[23]

This impersonality and lack of the creaturely, demonic aspect that came ultimately to be associated with the yakṣa is a prevalent aspect of the Vedic references.

Trees, water, and fertility

Among the important applications of tree symbolism in world mythology,[24] several classifications are particularly relevant to our discussion of the yakṣa, especially in the context of the previously cited *AV* quotation.[25] As a kind of "microcosm," trees may shelter stone altars dedicated to village fertility deities (often yakṣas); they may be utilized as an image or metaphor for the entire cosmos; or they may symbolize the absolute center of the world and support of the cosmos. The latter image is embodied in the Vedic ritual symbology in which the sacrificial post (*yūpa* or *stambha*) is an emblem of the tree as the axis of the universe. In another Vedic image of the god as a tree,

> Indra himself is said to be the *stambha* which holds apart the worlds. The gods live at the top of the pillar, while man and the ancestors abide at the lower regions. Communication takes place along this post or tree, for the sacrificial offering is tied to a pillar and thereby delivered upward to the gods, while the *yūpa* acts as a fecundator bringing the celestial waters to the earth.[26]

The equation of the potent, life-giving god with the fertile, phallic tree is most explicit in the symbolism of the Śiva *liṅgam* and in the rebirth as a tree of the god of love, Kāma, after he was burned up by Śiva.[27]

Just as the god Kāma serves as a metaphor for the stored fecundity of the tree, the iconographical image of the wishing tree (*kalpa vṛkṣa*) that is capable of fulfilling all human desires is a metaphor for the benefit of that fertility for human society. The wish-fulfilling capability of certain trees is seen particularly in regard to their fulfillment of desires for progeny. Coomaraswamy draws an example of this from the *Kadambari* of Bāṇa, where "Queen Vilasvatī, desiring a child, performs a variety of ceremonies, amongst which 'with sunwise turns, she worshipped the pippala and other trees to which honour was wont to be shown.' "[28]

In its latency, the creative power of the waters is conceptualized as a feminine element, holding within it the potential for life. When the waters, however, are embodied within a living thing, whether in animals, human semen, or the sap of plants and trees, very often that potency is conceived of as male. In regard to this, "an amulet of *udumbara* wood is called virile (vṛṣan)"[29] and "the virtue of the forest tree (*vanaspati*) *jaṅgiḍa* is called its virility (*vīrya*)."[30] The sexual ambiguity of the fluid element is best seen in the analogous ambiguity of *soma,* the Vedic plant and deity whose functional potency encompasses the dualities of male and female, as well as of fire and water.

> Soma as offering is female to the male Agni but—"So far as Soma himself is concerned, a liquid of the colour of gold as he is, constituting a drink which warms up and sets a flame in the heart, he is a male element like fire, with which he offers so many common features that we may call him liquid fire."[31]

It is also in the highly potent liquid, semen, that the dual nature of all liquids may be perceived and, ultimately, resolved into a single principle that, paradoxically, is its opposite, fire.[32]

This same fire or energy of procreation is thought to exist in both the animal and vegetal spheres. Preeminently vigorous and "male" in its profligacy is the Indian fig tree (*aśvattha*), which displays, in addition to the more female root system that serves to contain the productive essence of the tree, secondary roots that spread downward from the branches, becoming additional stems and trunks. This surplus of vigor may have something to do with the depiction of the tree in an ancient Indus Valley seal—as sprouting horns from its trunk.

Trees in Buddhist tradition

In many of the early Buddhist legends, drawn from such sources as the Jātakas, the *Dhammapādatthakathā*, the *Mahāvastu,* the *Dīpavaṁsa,* the *Divyāvadāna,* the *Aśokāvadāna,* and so forth, an important dialectic is set up between the morally and spiritually perfected Buddha and various nonhuman deities such as yakṣas (Pāli, yakkhas) and the serpent deities, the *nāga*s. On the one hand, the Buddha incorporates and presides over a pre-existent mythology of nature. In so doing, the new religion of Buddhism is able more readily to meet the needs of an unlettered laity. In reaching out to the populace, the symbolism, iconography, and appeal of Buddhism became ever more potent. On the other hand, the figure of the Buddha is posited as a transcendent hero, opposing the nonrational and pre-Buddhistic realms of both the natural and the supernatural, which include such figures as yakṣas, *rākṣasa*s, *nāga*s, and the ghoulish *piśāca*s. In these instances, he meets the demigods and minor deities on their own ground and outwits them at their own game of chicanery and mischief.

The tree has become a powerful iconographical symbol in Buddhist art, literature, and legend. Arboreal imagery plays a part in various stages of the Buddha's career. His birth is to have taken place in the Lumbini grove of *śāla* trees between the two towns of Kapilavatthu and Devadaha. His mother, Queen Māyā, pregnant with the *bodhisatta* (future Buddha), stops with her retinue to refresh herself in the beautiful grove, and feeling an urge to grasp the branch of a particularly auspicious-looking tree, she is quickly overcome by the onset of labor and is delivered there of the *bodhisatta*. The Buddha's enlightenment, of course, finally occurred beneath the Bodhi tree (probably a *pipal* or *aśvattha*), and in the early sculpture, the tree is one of the aniconic symbols of the Buddha himself. One Buddhist tradition identifies seven Bodhi trees, six of which are associated with the Buddhas of preceding millenia.[33] These trees are depicted in a range of friezes found on the surviving railings and *toraṇa*s of the *stūpa* of Bhārhut (184–72 B.C.). In all cases, the primary sacrality of the tree is recognized and incorporated into a number of Buddhist legends and Jātaka tales in which the divinity of the tree is either compared or contrasted with the Buddha himself.

In several of the Jātaka tales, the *bodhisatta* is portrayed as a *devatā* in order to deliver some important bit of moral teaching. For example, in the *Matakabhatta* Jātaka and the *Ayācitabhatta* Jātaka, the *bodhisatta* has taken the birth of a tree spirit (*rukkhadevatā*) and delivers a moral lesson against the taking of lives to make offerings to the tree god himself. This is a standard didactic mode to be found in the Jātaka tales, in which the Buddhist "message" is found in the moral instruction or conclusion that is tacked onto a fable or in the assumption by the *bodhisatta* of an unexpected role in the fable, namely, the form of a vicious animal or demigod who has renounced the violence of his nature and now practices *ahiṁsā* (nonkilling). Coomaraswamy makes the point that, though in many of the Jātaka tales yakkhas are also deities that live in trees, in those tales in which the *bodhisatta* is born as a tree spirit he is always referred to as a *devatā* and never as a yakkha, "the Buddhist tendency being to restrict the designation Yakkha to demons, although there are many places where Devatā and Yakkha are synonomous. . . ."[34]

The perception of these tree spirits and the value of worshipping them in the Jātaka tales shift, relevant to the moral precedence within Buddhism of *ahiṁsā* over animal sacrifice. As we shall see in chapter four, in the discussion of yakkha depictions within Buddhism, the yakkha is often used as a demonic device to illustrate the moral abomination of the slaughter and consumption of flesh. While the yakkha in the Jātaka tales represents, as Coomaraswamy has said, a more unambivalently demonic being, the tree spirits (*rukkhadevatās*) embody a more benign aspect of the fertility complex and as such are capable of being mouthpieces for the *bodhisatta*'s morally advanced teaching. In the *Palāsa* Jātaka (no. 307), the *bodhisatta* is again born as a *rukkhadevatā,* this time inhabiting a *palāsa* tree. Impressed with the devotion of a certain *brāhman* in bringing flowers and incense daily to the tree, the *bodhisatta* asks him why he exhibits such piety toward the tree. The *brāhman* replies that the tree has long been a natural habitation of spirits (*bhutānivasarupo*) and that he worshipped both the tree and any spirits who might inhabit it so that he might obtain treasure. The *bodhisatta* is pleased with the *devatā* worship and rewards the *brāhman* with the treasure he desires. On the other hand, in the *Dummedha* Jātaka (no. 50), the *bodhisatta* is a prince who is critical of the rampant worship of *devatā*s (*devatāmaṁgalika*), which he considers to be barbarous and irreligious (*adhamma*). In this example, the *bodhisatta* pretends to be a worshipper of the tree spirit as well and, in order to end the practice of slaughtering animals for offerings, tells his subjects that he has made a vow to the *devatā* to slay all who commit the five sins (*pancadussilakammani*), including the slaughter of animals, and so forth (*antavaddhimaṁsalohitādihi*). The only difference between the two episodes seems to be the practice in the latter case of animal sacrifice; the *devatā* worship itself is not condemned when it does not involve the reprehensible practice of taking lives.

The Buddhist assimilation of a complete range of natural symbols and metaphors is an important consideration in this book, and we will address it further in a later chapter. The employment of the yakkha within the Jātaka tales is relevant to the nature versus asceticism dialectic within Buddhism. The Pāli yakkha is a symbol of the dangers of undisciplined sensuality and unregenerate heathenish religious practices, living as he does on the fringes of towns and villages until his formal conversion to Buddhism assimilates him to a new, syncretic cosmology. For now, it is important to realize that the Buddha's enlightenment beneath the Bodhi tree was a vivid metaphor for his realization that transcendence must begin within the phenomenal context, using the support of nature, and yet must triumph over it. In this sense, the tree represents the harmonious alignment of the disciplined man with nature and his mature acceptance of himself within the fabric of the real world. This maturity is embodied in the Buddha's adoption of the "middle path" to *nirvāṇa,* avoiding the dual pitfalls of indulgence of the senses, on the one hand, and extreme denial of the senses, on the other.

The association of the Buddha with various sorts of trees in the early literature extends to the connection between the *aśoka* tree and King Aśoka, the great convert and patron of Buddhism who, in the third century B.C., erected *stūpa*s and created rock inscriptions and pillar edicts enjoining the practice of the Buddhist *dhamma* in the context of social justice and righteousness. This tree had the legendary reputation for not blooming until it was kicked or touched by a nubile female. The term for this motif, "*śālabhañjikā,*" refers literally to a female breaking the bough of a *śāl* tree but applies generally to this motif with respect to any tree. Seemingly quite early on, the term acquired a technical meaning that referred solely to sculptural representations of graceful girls (in some cases, yakṣīs or *apsaras*es) grasping the boughs of trees in characteristic dancelike poses with one knee bent and ankles crossed (the *ardha sama* position of the feet). The technical employment of the term is already known by Aśvaghoṣa's time (first century B.C.) in the following verse from his poetic treatment of the life of the Buddha, the *Buddhacarita.*

> Another [woman], leaning against the side of a round window, reposed with her slender body bent like a bow, shone with her pearls dangling like a *śālabhañjikā* statue in a *toraṇa.*[35]

The stylized motif of the young woman touching the tree is beautifully represented on railing pillars at Sāñcī, "not as a pillar-figure, sculptured in relief, but in the shape of a bracket, carved in the round, which supports the projecting ends of the lowermost architraves of the *toraṇa*s."[36] Examples of this motif have been found at Bhārhut (figure 7), where yakṣīs grasp branches; at Bodh Gāya, where a damaged sculpture of a yakṣī seems also to be cast in the traditional posture; and in railing pillars from Mathurā. The interaction of woman and tree is a "*dohada*" rite, a word that refers not only to the "longing of a pregnant woman," but also to the longing of the tree itself for its own blossoming and fruition, which is catalyzed by the human symbol of potential life in the Indian cultural context—the touch of a nubile maiden.

The lotus

In the iconographical association of water and fertility, the yakṣa often appears in conjunction with the lotus (figure 8 below). As far back as the Vedic sources and in subsequent cosmogonic myths, the germ of all life has been characterized, as Bosch has put it, in three different ways: "the grain or seed from which springs the tree of life; a being belong-

Figure 7. Bhārhut Yakṣī

Figure 8. Yakṣa on a medallion from a pillar base, Bharhut. Drawing by Peter Sutherland.

ing to the animal kingdom (a cosmic egg, a tortoise); and the navel [or mouth] of a deity. Frequently, a combination of these three motifs is to be found."[37] Indeed, it is the interplay and interchangeability of these motifs that are a source for the development of the decorative imagination, in which one form (a yakṣa, a lotus, or a *makara,* for instance) may metamorphose into a flowing continuum of other, loosely related forms.

Surely the lotus is the most refined and aesthetic metaphor for the fertile conjunction of water and plant. The beautiful lotus plant, arising from the mud and blooming on the surface of the water, has become the symbol par excellence for the transformative power of life. In the macrocosm, this transformation is seen in the ceaseless generation of form out of the primally unformed ground or "waters" of being. In the microcosm, that transformation has been homologized to the awakening of human consciousness out of the unreality (*māyā*) of conditioned existence (*saṁsāra*). Three traditions in particular have employed this symbol: the aesthetic tradition, both poetic and visual; Mahāyāna Buddhist philosophy and iconography; and classical and medieval Vaiṣṇava theology and iconography.

In the Vaiṣṇava theological context, Viṣṇu in his *avyakta* or unmanifest form is assimilated to the primal creator, characterized theistically in a number of ways (even, as we have seen in the Vedic and Brāhmaṇic references, as a *mahadyakṣa*). It is out of the great unmanifest body of the god, from his navel, that the lotus springs, containing either the demiurge Brahmā or the goddess Lakṣmī. The later theological conception of the lotus-born demiurge as a female, rather than as a male such as the yakṣa, Brahmā, Prajāpati, or Varuṇa (*ṚV* 1. 24. 7), is tied to the perception of the female principle as the *śakti* or energy of the inactive male principle.[38] Conceived in this way, the lotus is

> the most beautiful evidence offered to the eye of the self-engendering fertility of the bottom. Through its appearance, it gives proof of the life-supporting power of the all nourishing abyss. This is why the goddess Lotus (*kamalā, padmā*) is an appropriate consort or śakti of Viṣṇu—Viṣṇu being the cosmic water itself, the infinite ocean of that liquid life-substance out of which the differentiated phenomena and elements of the universe arise, and back into which they must again dissolve.[39]

In the Mahāyāna Buddhist wisdom literature (100 B.C.–A.D.600), the lotus or the personified lotus goddess is transformed from a goddess of fertility and good fortune to the subtle and refined queen of gnosis, "the highest representative of the world-transcending wakefulness, the most spiritual feminine symbol in all the iconographies of the East."[40] The ancient Indian metaphor for the world of form and primeval creativity becomes, in the *prajñāpāramitā* literature, a metaphor for pure transformation and transcendence of the world of form, pointing beyond *saṁsāra* to the unconditioned *nirvāṇa*.

Pots of plenty

Also associated with the yakṣa and found in the same context as the lotus-Lakṣmī iconography is that of the "full vessel" (*pūrṇa kalaśa, punna ghata,* and so forth), an iconographic motif that, in its containing and dispensing of the fecund waters of life, is also, along with the yakṣa, part of the complex of South Asian fertility symbols.

> The fact is significant that in many cases the lotus of the seat or pedestal, together with other lotus sprays and leaves, rises not directly from an implied lake, but from a "full vessel." It is well known that such a vessel (*punna-ghata,* etc.) with its lotus sprays, represents the waters, and is a symbol for prosperity and abundance; as such it occurs by itself in a well-known group of about eight auspicious symbols (*aṣṭamaṅgala*), as a finial, and as a decorative motif in the architecture of all periods.[41]

The earliest examples of this motif are found at Bhārhut and Sāñcī and somewhat later, as an iconographical element associated with certain deities. As the style develops, the simple water pot becomes a stylized, rounded vessel with a narrow, ornate neck encircled by decorative bands. The roundness of the jar becomes visually analogous to the exaggeratedly globular breasts of female fertility figures such as Lakṣmī and the many yakṣīs who adorn the temple facades, as well as to the fat bellies of yakṣas (see figure 9) and yakṣalike deities of good fortune and abundance such as Kubera (the king of the yakṣas) and Gaṇeśa (the elephant-headed deity). The tales of magical vessels that are recounted below are all connected to a basic conception of many of the gods and demigods as sources of supply and grace; various gods, in fact, possess vessels as part of their iconography: Varuṇa, as god of the sea, carries a water pot, and Kubera carries a magical device that dispenses an immortalizing and revitalizing elixir.

Another vessel image that has been assimilated to the larger motif of the *pūrṇa kalaśa* is the religious mendicant's begging bowl, which, through the medium of his holiness and transmutative power, may become a "grail vessel"[42] or bowl of inexhaustible supply, a motif that is well known to several traditions (New Testament and Arthurian legend, for example). The image of the vessel of plenty is treated in a few popular stories, most notably in the *Bhadraghata* Jātaka (no. 291) and in the much later (eleventh century A.D.) collection of stories by Somadeva, the *Kathāsaritsāgara* (*The Ocean of Story,* no. 75). In the Jātaka tale, the *bodhisatta,* reborn as Indra, king of the gods, grants a "wishing cup" (*sabbakamadadam kumbham*) to his dissolute son, with the warning that if he should break it he would lose all of his wealth. In drunken abandon, Indra's son smashes the cup, immediately becomes impoverished, and soon dies. The force of the message is similar in the *Kathāsaritsāgara* tale, where a poor woodcutter meets

Figure 9. Dwarf yakṣa from Pitalkhora, Aurangabad District, National Museum in Delhi (1st Century C.E.). Drawing by Peter Sutherland.

four splendidly attired yakṣas who take pity on him and give him the boon of possessing the inexhaustible pitcher, from which they feed themselves and satisfy their own needs; they also warn him to take care not to break it. Foolishly, in drunken celebration, he smashes the bowl, which is instantly magically mended and restored to its yakṣa owners, while the man is reduced to the poverty from which he has risen. The moral of both tales has to do with the impossibility of truly altering the fortunes of foolish men; no matter what sort of bounty they receive, they will ruin themselves from lack of self-control. The splendid yakṣas of the latter story refer, seemingly, to the early sculptural iconography of the yakṣa, where he is depicted as a lavish, princely figure who serves as a prototype for the early images of the *bodhisatta,* conceived as prince rather than mendicant.[43]

Coomaraswamy has emphasized the graillike nature of the bowl of plenty, particularly in reference to the South Indian Buddhist legend of *Manimekhalai,* the literary version of which dates from about the third century A.D. The sea-maiden, Manimekhalai (who is linked to a sea-goddess, Manimekhalā), possesses the magical begging bowl of the Buddha and, as it is prophesied, will feed and revive the whole world out of that inexhaustible bowl. Her grace will provide an abundance of water and plenty for the entire region and miracles will abound.

*Makara*s

In this web of artistic and mythological expression, we find images of the yakṣa in analogous relationships to both lotus *parvan*s (stem nodes) and the mythical aquatic animals, *makara*s. In numerous friezes (from Mathurā, Amarāvatī, and Sāñcī particularly), the figure of the yakṣa occurs as an image ejected from the jaws of a *makara* or from a lotus rhizome or connected to either through a stem growing out of its mouth.

The important and prevalent motif of the *makara,* an elaborated, fantastic crocodilelike creature whose head, with its curving, tendrillike snout, is one element in a complex series of ornamental devices. Although it is uncertain whether or not there is a precise zoological model for this fanciful creature, art historians have attempted, with limited success, to reconstruct the evolution of its form. They concur in attributing its evolved, highly wrought form to a pastiche of several aquatic animals—including perhaps the crocodile, the dolphin, the rhinoceros, the elephant, and the boar (semiaquatic in Indian mythology). As a decorative motif, it has been utilized and depicted in a wide variety of ways.[44]

The *makara* is of particular interest to us in our study of the ethical and aesthetic transformations of a mythological type. In it, we may observe how an aesthetic motif may undergo change in response to certain undefined pressures within the medium itself, pushing the style of its expression beyond the limitations of naturalistic representation, toward a purely ornamental significance.[45] Indian sculptors have traditionally seen a visual relationship between the lotus *parvan* and the head of the *makara*. The conjunction of the two images has amplified the symbolic valence of the two separate components.

> . . . so the Indian saw in the node of the lotus-plant with its jaw-like scale leaves a monster-head with gaping mouth or, to put it more accurately, in this vegetal formation he recognized the figure of the *makara*-monster with which art had made him familiar. Consequently, by adopting this figure, he provided art with a motif available whenever the need arose to represent the aquatic element in an adequately symbolic figure, the figure of a legendary aquatic monster.[46]

Bosch thinks that it is this fluidity or "instability" of the composite image of the vegetal lotus *parvan* and the animal *makara* that gives rise to or becomes a basis for the multiplication of symbolic images and ideas that is loosely associated with the entire complex of aquatic mythology. It seems that the process of association works dialectically, with images stimulating concepts, and concepts stimulating a new conjunction of images. The same process of extension of mythology and imagery through the amalgamation of naturally disparate images occurs in the formation of the *kīrttimukha* ("face of glory") (figure 10) or *siṁhamukha* ("lion-head"), a ferocious stylization that is developed most impressively as guardian sculptures surrounding Hindu temple arches. It has been speculated that the lion image was probably inspired by Hellenistic influence, yet underwent an indigenous process of stylization and transformation into a fanciful representation of a ferocious-headed being, symbolizing a more general notion of the demonic and destructive impulses embedded in the nature of material existence.

Figure 10. Beaten silver panel on the main door of the Bhimakali Temple in Sarahan, the old capital of Rampurbashahar state, H. P. Photograph by Peter Sutherland.

The *nāga*

Of utmost importance in our consideration of the images, symbols, and myths associated with the yakṣa is the figure of the *nāga,* a serpent deity of considerable complexity. The *nāga*'s connection with the rich mythology of the waters, the hidden treasures of the earth and sources of nature's abundance, the symbolization of evil, and the assimilation of popular mythologies by the literature and iconography of early Buddhism runs parallel in many ways to the yakṣa's mythological development.

> Nāgas are genii superior to man. They inhabit subaquatic paradises, dwelling at the bottom of rivers, lakes, and seas in resplendent palaces studded with gems and pearls. They are keepers of the life-energy that is stored in the earthly waters of springs, wells, and ponds. They are the guardians, also, of the riches of the deep sea—corals, shells, and pearls. They are supposed to carry a precious jewel in their heads. Serpent princesses, celebrated for their cleverness and charm, figure among the ancestresses of many a South Indian dynasty: a nāginī or nāga in the family tree gives one a background.[47]

As we shall see in the next chapter, both yakṣas and *nāga*s serve in the Epic literature in particular as fierce guardians of the waters and, by implication, of the abundance that lies beneath the earth.

While the yakṣa serves in many contexts to symbolize the explosive fecundity of the natural world, *nāga*s are strongly associated with eroticism as well as fertility. This symbolism is a manifestation of the nearly universal equation of serpents with sexuality, engendered principally by their phallic form, multiple progeny, unpredictable and insidious temperament reminiscent of the emotional behavior of the sexually jealous or obsessed (particularly women, as it is thought), and in the subterranean habitation of snakes that links them paradoxically with female sexuality and genitalia as well. This serpentine association with sex and lustfulness is reflected in a number of myths and stories that tell of the sexual treachery and licentiousness of the *nāga*s. These myths find parallels in the corpus of yakṣa myths where male and especially female demons of these two races are known to seduce and capture their unsuspecting human victims. We will say more about this in the context of our discussion of yakṣīs. For now, in regard to snakes, fertility, and popular cult, it is useful to mention the *nāgakal*s, the votive tablets with which South Indian village women worship snakes in order to have children,[48] and the popular Hindu festival, *nāgapañcamī*. The latter occurs in August, a time in which the monsoon is high and snakes have recently hatched from their eggs. The snakes are honored and propitiated all over India with offerings of milk and food, with the circulation of drawn and printed images of *nāga*s, and in some places, with the actual handling of snakes (in many cases, cobras).[49]

It is the tree that serves as a mediating symbol, anchoring both the yakṣa and the *nāga* in a far-reaching context of associations, including fertility, prosperity, and malevolence. As we have noted, in the Jātaka tales powerful deities are thought to inhabit trees. In recognition of their connection with the popular worship of trees and tree deities, once converted to Buddhism, the yakṣas are enthroned beneath trees. Snakes are found in trees and yet also inhabit the netherworld, beneath the ground (often in the moist dark spots at the roots of trees). The essential substance that links yakṣas, *nāga*s, and trees is water. The *nāga*'s connection with the waters stems, on the one hand, from the inhabitation by snakes of the moist underworld and, on the other hand, from the twisting forms of snakes that are homologous to winding rivers. The rivers contain the fertile waters that (like snakes) flee the destructive heat of the sun and go underground to withhold their fructifying waters.

While the yakṣa is often placed in the water either as a symbolic representative or extension of its creativity or as a fierce defender of his own watery domain, *nāga*s and trees are thought also to *contain* the life-supporting liquid they symbolize. The watery essence is manifest in trees, as sap and in *nāga*s as venom. The allopathic coalescence of the two liquids is seen particularly in the medieval Bengali myth linking the snake goddess, Manasā (who stores poison in her sightless eye, a poison that if turned on humans will kill instantly),[50] with the Sij tree, known to be an antidote to poison.[51] This association exploits the cultic tendency of propitiatory rites and images to become interchangeable with the destructive objects or personages they propitiate, so that the serpentine goddess, Manasā, paradoxically encompasses both destructive and compassionate qualities, on occasion bringing the victims of snakebite back to life.

The important relationship between the *nāga*'s venom and the most beneficial of substances, *amṛta* or *soma*, is a theme that underlies many of the myths about *nāga*s and is related to the transformative or alchemical attribute of water, the aspect with which we began our exploration of this network of symbols. The numinosity of both the yakṣa and the *nāga* is, in part, a function of their presiding over the power of transmutation that is contained in the waters. In the Yakṣapraśna episode of the *Mahābhārata,* which is analyzed in the next chapter, this power is exercised by the yakṣa, who is really the god Dharma in disguise. The *nāga* displays this power of transmutation by turning fluids (the underground waters and in some cases milk) into poison and by transforming poison into the sacred knowledge that is an antidote for deprivation and ignorance (as snake venom in small doses is an antidote for a snake bite).[52]

In the Epic cosmology, the earth and the waters are homologized as places that exist in the realm of the underworld and are the abode of hordes of semidemonic deities, such as yakṣas, *rākṣasas*, *piśācas*, and especially *nāgas*.

> The Nāgas live underground where Sunda goes to slay them (I, 210, 8) and the Nāgaloka described when Mātali seeks a son-in-law is entered by "descending into earth", avagahya bhumin (5, 98, 6; cf. praviveśa mahātalam, ib. 97, 21). But it must be remembered that "under earth" is water, a part of Varuṇa's domain. "The navel of the Nāgaloka is called Pātāla because water falls there sufficiently" (*pātāla* from *patanti alam*), and water-creatures called timis live there on the light of the moon in the water; also the Mare's Head and creatures slain by sunlight and demons of darkness (ib. 99. If.).[53]

This placement of the *nāga* deities in the *lokas* of the underworld occurs in Buddhist and Jain cosmologies as well. The tie with the underworld is perhaps the key factor in the curious interchangeability of serpent-*nāgas* with elephant deities also called *nāgas*. The equation or confusion of the two in numerous stories is thought to stem from the fact that both are water creatures, both have an under-the-earth role in the Indian cosmological picture (as *diggajas* or *dinnagas*, elephants are the caryatid-upholders of the world), and the snake's body resembles the elephant's trunk.[54]

Like Kubera, the king of the yakṣas, the *nāga* is also known to be a guardian of treasure, particularly precious gems. The harvesting of jewels, smelting of gold, and alchemy are all aspects of the underworld/underground knowledge, of and for which *nāgas* and yakṣas are conservators and guides. In his aspect of living deep within the earth, the serpent-*nāga,* a jealous possessor and occasional purveyor of gems, is often iconographically depicted with a jewel in his throat or on his hood.

In the Buddhist texts chronicling the spread of the new religion into new lands and territories, the conversion or vanquishing of hostile *nāgas* or yakṣas is a common element. In the *Mahāvaṁsa* and the *Dīpavaṁsa,* the Buddha rids an infested part of the island of Lanka (Śri Lanka) of its *nāga* inhabitants and establishes the Buddhist precepts as law.

> Hovering there in mid-air above the battlefield the Master, who drives away (spiritual) darkness, called forth dread darkness over the nāgas. Then comforting those who were distressed by terror he once again spread light abroad. When they saw the Blessed One they joyfully did reverence to the Master's feet. Then preached the Vanquisher to them the doctrine that begets concord, and both (nāgas) gladly gave up the throne to the Sage. When the Master, having alighted on the earth, had taken his place on a seat there, and had been refreshed with celestial food and drink by the nāga-kings, he, the Lord, established in the (three) refuges and in the moral precepts eighty koṭis of snake-spirits, dwellers in the ocean and on the mainland.[55]

In the *Dīpavaṁsa,* a similar routing takes place, but of yakkhas. Ironically, in the sorcery that the Buddha employs to banish the yakkhas from the island, he himself is compared to a yakkha, thus hinting at the complex and paradoxical relationship that the Buddha has with these representatives of autochthonous belief. His conquest describes an assimilation of images and legends of power and potency.

> There the hero stood, performing miracles by his (magical) power, like a Yakkha of high (magical) power and great (supernatural) faculties; gathering thick clouds, containing thousands of rain drops, he sent rain, cold winds, and darkness.[56]

An identical sort of conquest of the indigenous *nāga* inhabitants is encountered in the legend of the founding of Nepal, summarized by Lowell Bloss:

> It is said that once this land contained water in which dwelled numerous nāgas. Then Viṣṇu or Mañjuśrī (depending on whether one uses Hindu or Buddhist texts) makes a channel in the mountains, driving

> off all the water and all the nāgas except one. This last nāga made a pact with the god to guard the land's riches and thereby men were able to begin to populate this land.[57]

These legends point to the struggle between conquering tribes and autochthonous peoples whose lower status and depleted control of the area are reflected in their equation with nonhuman species, in this case snakes. We need only look at the history of imperialism, in which scores of aboriginal tribes and nations have been denigrated in similar ways, their resources plundered and their humanity denied, to accept the possibility that the designation "yakṣa" or "*nāga*" may have related to another imperialistic restructuring of a tribal society. The conversion of these native inhabitants of the conquered territories constitutes an important aspect of the legendary proliferation of Buddhism. Coomaraswamy translates a bit of the *Āṭānāṭiya Suttānta* where yakkhas are the demonic characterization of the irreligious, unbelieving, and unconverted (that is, non-Buddhists).

> They "haunt the lonely and remote recesses of the forest, where noise, where sound, hardly is, where breezes from the pastures blow, hidden from men, suitable for meditation. There do eminent Yakkhas dwell, who have no faith in the word of the Exalted One."[58]

In the historical development and geographical spread of Buddhism, both the yakṣa and the *nāga* come to occupy important positions in the multiplication of legends about the life and travels of the Buddha and in the iconographic attribution of certain characteristics to the Buddha himself and various of his disciples.[59] An important legend, linking the *nāga* positively with the Buddha, is that of the sheltering of the Buddha during a week of raging storms by the *nāga* Mucalinda (or Mucilinda), under whose eponymous tree the Buddha took refuge.[60] This motif is seen particularly on the *stūpa* of Amarāvatī, where the Buddha "sits upon Mucalinda, as if on a throne."[61] It is the Buddha's apparent mastery of the *nāga* here, along "with the symbols of the parasol, the stūpa, and Mount Meru, that suggests that at least on one level of symbolism Mucalinda and the Buddha is a symbol of the Buddha's rulership over the universe."[62] The use of such nature deities in Buddhist legend signifies the Buddha's assimilation of the heretofore polarized realms of nature, popular religiosity, art, and heroic legend and poetry. With respect to this phenomenon, we have the use of *nāga*s as protectors and guardians of sacred shrines and relics of the Buddha; even the Buddhist emperor Aśoka is reputed to have asked a *nāga* "for relics to fill his 84,000 stupas."[63] The Buddhist assimilation of the yakṣa and *nāga* cults reflects further the belief that the Buddha was born on earth to deliver all beings, regardless of species or moral attainment—"the creatures of the earth, of the heavens, and of the hells."[64]

The *nāga*s are perhaps never so demonically portrayed as their mythic counterparts, the yakṣas. This may be the case because of the marginal though significant connection of *nāga*s with the manifest world of nature as embodied in living animals (snakes). Though the yakṣas are also included in the symbology of nature, their connections with it are more obscure and metaphoric since they have no animal counterpart. The previously mentioned arboreal metaphor used to symbolize the relationship of the primordial *mahadyakṣa* to the various gods is echoed in the assimilation of the fall of Vṛtra, the Vedic serpent-demon and foe of Indra, "to the felling and cutting up of a tree."[65] These linked references underscore the fundamental association of yakṣa, *nāga,* and tree. The very image of the serpent hanging or sleeping in a tree echoes this coalescence of maleficence and beneficence through the intervening third symbol of the tree, which provides a metaphor large enough to unite them. We shall see more and more that contrarities and oppositions are often resolved within resonating intermediary symbols, and this is a factor that we must add to our growing analysis of how ethical ambiguities and transformations are comprised. Several layers of correlation exist uniting symbolic networks: a simple, often childish Rorschachlike sympathy between images or motifs (such as that seen in the association of *makara* and lotus *parvan*); the resolution of functionally opposed elements (such as sap and poison) in extensive cosmic essences (such as the waters); and complex historically developed associations that often encompass staggering contradictions (such as the above-mentioned link between elephant and snake, which is confused and contradicted by the paradoxical opposition of snake and elephant due to the latter's association with kings [Indra] who are snake killers.[66]

The magic fish

From the Vedic use of the yakṣa, as a numinous yet preeminently *alive* being, to its abbreviated employment in the later literature, there is a passage from its status as a symbol for a larger abstract concept to its tame usage within a more specific and functional system of metaphors. The symbolic life cycle of the yakṣa begins in the Vedic texts by expressing the ambiguity and mystery attending the inchoate divinity within the waters, a symbolism that is also found elsewhere in the legend of Manu and the fish. In the chronologically succeeding variants of this myth, we may chart a pattern of development similar to that of the yakṣa's in its sprawling but discernible evolution.

One of the most important illustrations of the manifold richness of the water cosmology, the story of Manu and the fish has cosmogonic, theological, and devotional applications and contains the Indian version of the legend of the archetypal Great Flood. In this story,[67] the first or exemplary man, Manu the son of Vivasvan (the sun), encounters, while performing his ablutions, a magic fish. The fish pleads with Manu, invoking its tiny size and vulnerability, to take it out of the ocean and care for it in a small vessel. Manu is touched by its plea and places it in a jar. The fish, flourishing so well in Manu's keeping, begins to grow rapidly, outgrowing by degrees its jar, a pond, and the Ganges River. Finally, the immense fish asks Manu to place him in the ocean, where he will now be safe. Manu complies and the fish reveals to him that the deluge that will destroy the world is at hand. Because of his protection of the defenseless but powerful fish, Manu has won salvation from the flood that is about to engulf the earth. The fish instructs Manu in how to construct and furnish a boat that will ride out the flood by being tied to the horn of the magical fish.

In the Brāhmaṇa and Epic versions of the story, the encounter with the fish is a rapprochement between the human domain and an unspecified otherness—as divinity, as animal, as nature, as the power and sacredness of the unknown. In this encounter, a balance is achieved between chance and predestination. The relationship is initiated for reasons that remain mysterious, but once formed, it is characterized by strict reciprocity. The salvation of the fish is exchanged for the salvation of Manu. In its simplicity of exchange, the agreement between Manu and the fish connotes the covenantal relationship between the natural, human, and sacred spheres. The basis for the cooperation is the extreme vulnerability of the fish, which stands as an anticipatory metaphor for the vulnerability of Manu himself and the human race that he represents. Manu's compassion toward the small fish and his tending of its apparently insignificant life are rewarded by the salvation of his own dispensable human life from the impending inundation of humanity by the power of divinity-as-nature.

The motif of the protection of the vulnerable is directly connected to the motif of the big becoming the little, which runs through Indian literature, particularly in the representations of the *avatāra*s of Viṣṇu. The connection to Viṣṇu becomes explicit in the Purāṇic treatments of the myth, in which the fish is revealed as one of his ten *avatāra*s, and Manu's service to the fish becomes the prototype of *bhakti*c devotion. This motif of the voluntary disguise and delimitation of the divine, as well as the motif of the testing of a human being by the disguised god, is an aspect of a comparable yakṣa myth (which I will recount in detail in the next chapter). In that episode from the *Mahābhārata,*[68] it is the god Dharma who assumes the diminished and demonic form of a watery denizen, a yakṣa, in order to test the virtue of his son Yudhiṣṭhira. In related variants of this yakṣa myth, we will see that, as in the cycle of Manu and the fish, there is a tendency in the development of the symbolism to diminish the inchoate power and mystery of the aquatic deity and to assimilate his power to a theologically more orthodox and specific source. In the Brāhmaṇa version of the Manu myth, the text stands unadorned in its three aspects: the fish, the flood, and Manu himself. The fish, which starts out tiny and grows to immensity, signifies the power of the divine, which, though enormous and capable of destruction, practices the self-circumscription by which the tenuous delimitation of the chaotic is sustained for the preservation of the phenomenal world.

In later variants, the allegorical nature of the myth is emphasized, especially in the *Bhāgavata Purāṇa* version. The fish is the navigator through the ocean of ignorance and dissolution. The last man is now the solitary devotee, adrift on the waves of the guru's compassion. All of the symbols become specified in the larger structure of the theological explication that, in the Indian genre, entails the piling up of symbols, connections, metaphors, and analogies, all of which serve to define the miraculous as a theological device, while reducing the more primal and distinct element of the mystery.

Although, as we have said, there is a distinct similarity in the symbolic progression of the two myths about the masquerading deity in the waters, there is an important difference to be noted: In the case of the fish, there is a kind of elevation of the status of the symbol as it becomes associated with a specific theological tradition, namely,

Vaiṣṇavism. In this sense, the symbol, by passing from a stage of generality or archetypicality to a stage of representing something more ideologically prescribed, is expanded by displaying its latent valency. Of course, in another sense the symbol begins to lose its evocative power by becoming exclusively linked with a specific tradition of thought and worship. In the case of the yakṣa, there is a somewhat different course of development in the symbol system. The yakṣa begins its life as a very general symbol for the sacred and for being itself; over time, it loses its association with the philosophical concept of the sacred and comes to stand for the mystery in nature that in turn comes to be viewed through the conflation of nature, mystery, and magic, as the demonic.[69] The divestment of the yakṣa of its grander hierophanous powers leaves it with a more limited range of meaning and expression, though in its continuing association with mystery it remains, even to this day, a resonant metaphor, capable of being employed in a variety of contexts and genres, retaining its potency as an amorphous symbol of sacrality in the lower reaches of the Indian hierarchy of sacred beings.

Local waters

Finally, it is essential to mention the religious symbolism and practice that are perhaps the apotheosis of the water imagery in all of its forms and expressions. I refer to the extensive myths and rituals associated with the sacred rivers of India; their inhabiting spirits (genii loci), such as yakṣas, yakṣīs, *nāgas*, *gandharvas*, and *apsarases*; and the religious complex of place, pilgrimage, and visualization that is encompassed by the Sanskrit/Hindu notion of *tīrtha,* a concept that came to be equated with the crossing or resting spots on a river where pilgrims can bathe and drink and that, in microcosm, symbolize the spiritual journey or path itself.

From the classical period onward, it is the Gaṅgā (Ganges) River that assumes the central focus of all river mythology and ritual.[70] The best example of the centrality of the symbolism of the river is to be found in the Epic tale of the descent of the Gaṅgā from heaven to earth through the protective hair of the great god, Śiva. In this myth, which is prominent in both the *Mahābhārata* and the *Rāmāyaṇa,*[71] the sixty thousand sons of the king, Sāgara ("Ocean"), sprung from the seeds of a gourd, follow the horse their father is to sacrifice in the royal *ásvamedha* ritual as it roams freely over the earth. The sons, numerous but not very bright, lose track of the horse, and threatened by their father, they comb the earth looking for it. Finally, having exhausted all other possibilities, they begin to dig beneath the earth (namely, the bottom of the ocean where the horse was last seen to enter), ruthlessly rending the earth (conceived of as a goddess) and killing masses of subterranean creatures, such as *nāga*s, yakṣas, and *rākṣasa*s. There, in the lower world (*rasātala*), they find the horse, but also enrage the meditating sage, Kapila (a possible multiform of Śiva or Viṣṇu, depending upon which epic one reads), who incinerates all of them with his fiery gaze. As it has been foretold, Sāgara's surviving son (born of another wife) is the progenitor of the great-great grandson, Bhagīratha, who is able to appease the souls of his sixty thousand forefathers who are still lying shriveled and unconsecrated in the hell-like lower world. In order to send their souls on to heaven, Bhagīratha must persuade the holy river, Gaṅgā, to descend to earth from heaven and lave, and thus purify their ashes. The goddess, Gaṅgā, is highly disposed toward the hero, Bhagīratha, but fears that the fall to earth will be too violent. Śiva is persuaded to shelter the goddess-river with his head and through his hair her waters are diverted into seven streams[72] before touching the earth. The ashes of the sixty thousand sons of Sāgara are duly bathed and liberated, and the restoration of the waters of the earth (stored in the ocean) is achieved.

In this myth, the reciprocity and interrelationship of the celestial and terrestrial waters (in cycles of rainfall and drought), represented by the heavenly Gaṅgā and the ocean (Sāgara), respectively, are established. On the simplest material level, the depletion of the earth's store of water is threatened. The myth of Sāgara, as ocean and king, represents the interdependence on earth of the sovereign and the supply of nature as symbolized by the waters within his land. The violation by his sons of the crust of the earth (*rasātala*) and the chthonic creatures who live in it and beneath it constitutes a violation of the divinity and power of the earth (also represented as a goddess) and its inhabitants. The king, who must function as a conduit of vital water and supply, linking the heavenly domain (through rituals and the generation of offspring) with the underground reservoirs of water and fertility (symbolized by the semidivine genii loci), cannot fulfill his royal responsibilities until reparation for his sons' crimes against the earth are made. The successful atonement constitutes a "plugging" of the hole in the earth beneath the ocean, through which the benefits of ritual appeasement had been leaking along with the life-producing waters. Ritual waters and irrigation waters are homologized and seen as interchangeable, the Gaṅgā being the apotheosis of the complex beneficence and sanctification of the waters in which sins are removed and from which life springs, a matrix for birth on earth and in heaven.

In the vertical symbolism and imagery of the Gaṅgā's relationship to the earth, we may infer a metaphor for the important relationship of the celestial, terrestrial, and subterranean world orders, a connection that may lie at the core of our investigation of the changing characterization within the Indian cosmos of the demonic and its representatives, particularly the yakṣa. As the conflict between the *deva*s and *asura*s is a central motif in the *Ṛg Vedic* corpus of myths, the encounter between the Epic heroes and the subterranean demons or demigods of the earth is an added focal point in the narrative of both the *Mahābhārata* and the *Rāmāyaṇa*. Constantly we will see that the dialectic between the disruption and support of *dharma* involves a confrontation with the yakṣa or his relatives, the *nāga* and *rākṣasa* among others, in which the balance of divine, human or social, and natural forces and personages is evaluated, challenged, and restructured. Interestingly, these heroic confrontations with the many characters of the underworld do not inevitably involve their (the latter's) demonization and polarization with respect to the human and divine. In many cases in later Hindu mythology, the ethical dualism embodied in the agnostic struggles between gods and demons in the Vedic myths is dropped, and the single yakṣa (or related figures) may stand forth from the masses of demons and emanate an aura of primordial divinity and numinosity.

To sketch in summary the vital points of connection in the iconography and symbolism of water, from which our central figure, the yakṣa, derives his significance: Water is the most basic symbol both of the absolute prior to form and of the generative principle in earthly form. It is a medium of creation as well as dissolution. This fundamental ambiguity assumes manifold expressions, one important example of which is the dual nature of the essence (*rasa*) of water, as the elixir of immortality (*soma* or *amṛta*) or as the venom found in the watery creatures, snakes.

The earliest (Vedic) reference to the yakṣa links him with other demiurgic deities such as Prajāpati, Agni, or Brahmā. In this connection, the yakṣa is homologized to a tree (another basic fertility symbol), just as the other demiurges may, in some myth variants, sprout trees (or lotuses) from their navels in their primordial acts of creation. The connection between yakṣas and trees is made explicit in early Buddhist decorative friezes, in the Jātaka literature where yakṣas are closely linked with tree spirits (*rukkhadevatās*), and in traditional Buddhist sculptural depictions of yakṣīs grasping boughs of trees. Iconographically, the yakṣa is also often conjoined with the motif of the *pūrṇa kalaśa* or "full vessel," a container of water and emblem of the inexhaustible supply of nature.

In the mythology and the iconography, the yakṣa is associated with other aquatic creatures, such as the *makara,* the *nāga,* and the magical fish of the Indian flood legend. Especially in the Hindu Epics and the Buddhist Jātakas, the yakṣa and nāga myths in many cases directly parallel one another,[73] both creatures encompassing complementary but opposite dimensions of fertility and destruction.

The Family of Demons

Introduction

In this section, I will mention briefly several other varieties of Indian demons who appear in the art and literature. It is necessary to complicate our portrait of the yakṣa with an acknowledgment of his brothers and cousins because of the generally hazy distinction made between the mythical demon races. Quite often, the designation "yakṣa" is used interchangeably with "*rākṣasa,*" "*piśāca,*" or "*gandharva.*" In the earliest citations of "yakṣa," the term referred to an ancient and powerful deity whose association with such elements as *māyā* and the dark and creative primal cosmos of water permitted his later evolution as a demon. The *asura*s, as the most ancient contingency of Vedic gods, included Varuṇa, Soma, and Agni before these latter went over to the ranks of the younger *deva*s. As the later demonic application of *asura* develops, a vital distinction is made between the high, heavenly, or cosmic demons, the *asura*s; and the low, earthly, existential demons, the *rākṣasa*s and the yakṣas. Despite their association with cosmic and natural phenomena, the *asura*s are linked with celestial rather than earthly elements and, in that distinction, are characterized as light in opposition to the dark demons and forces of the earth. We may see this in a *ṚV* hymn to Savitṛ, the god of the rising and setting sun.

> Let the merciful and helpful Asura, the good leader with golden hands, come toward us. Routing the demons [*rākṣasa*s] and sorcerors, the god to whom we sing has taken his place against the evening.[74]

In a cosmogonic myth from the Purāṇas, a clear distinction is made between the demon *asura*s and the lower demons, the yakṣas and *rākṣasa*s.

> After creating gods, demons, ancestors, and mankind, Brahmā became afflicted with hunger, and they began to eat his body, for they were Rākṣasas and Yakṣas. When Brahmā saw them he was displeased, and his hair fell out and became serpents. And when he saw the serpents he was angry, and the creatures born of his anger were the fierce, flesh-eating Piśācas. Thus Brahmā created cruel creatures and gentle creatures, dharma and adharma, truth and falsehood.[75]

The *asura*s are an elevated order of beings, an emanation of the first wave of Brahmā's creative impulses. The responsibility for the evil nature of the lower demons lies with their creator. Brahmā's own nature is thought to possess both a pure and an impure aspect, the latter of which is split off from the former as a shadow creator. Although in this version Brahmā is technically the creator of evil, a diffusion of responsibility clouds the fact. It is almost as though the hidden, dark impulses of the uncreated demons call forth Brahmā's own latent capacity for evil, and the products are monstrosities of shared unconscious detritus.

It is important to recognize the different orders of mythology that are woven into the Epic and Purāṇic narratives. In the cosmogonic legends, particular attention is given (naturally) to the ordering of the beings whose creation is being documented or rationalized. In other, "purer" narrative sections, where the tales of individual demons in their interactions with gods and men are being enumerated and embroidered, generic categories are blurred or glossed in ways that suit the myth rather than the preexistent hierarchies. Generally, however, the employment of individual *asura*s is less prevalent in the Epic narratives than the use of yakṣas and *rākṣasa*s, whose members turn up around every corner to challenge, torment, or (in rare cases) aid the heroes. As Edward Washburn Hopkins has pointed out, *asuras* in general do not enjoy the genealogical development that surrounds the characterizations of other demonic beings.

The narrative of the later mythology features well-developed, colorful individual characters whose particularities supersede the formal distinctions between the various demonic categories; and precise discrepancies between yakṣas, *rākṣasas*, *piśācas*, and others seem permanently obscured and fluid in accordance with the narrative thrust.

> The close connection between the various classes of evil demons and spiritual powers not exactly evil and yet not divine enough to be regarded as gods will often be a subject of special remark. This is sufficiently illustrated by the interchange of the same name among various groups. Thus in Mbh. the Rākṣasa Maṇimat is a friend of Kubera, and Maṇimat is also a name of a Yakṣa, of a Nāga; and of a king who is reborn as such after existing as Vṛtra, while Maṇimat designates a Daitya-town (in both epics Maṇimat is a mountain). It seems that certain characters stood out more as individuals than as fixed members of a group and that such individuals are sometimes considered as belonging to one and sometimes to another group.[76]

This confusion of the classes of demons has been noted by commentators on both Hindu and Buddhist texts and seems to be a distinct facet of the phenomenology of demons. This is how the demonic population in the *Jātakamāla* has been analyzed by one commentator:

> The different classes of goblins, Yakshas, and Rākshasas, Piśakas, are often confounded; in stanza 27 the general appellation is Rākshasas. In story IX, verse 66, yaksha and piśaka are used promiscuously, in the sense of "ogre." In the sixth story of the Pali Gataka (translated by Rhys Davids in his Birth Stories p. 180) the water-sprite is sometimes called rakkhaso, sometimes yakkho.[77]

The interchangeability of the demon races contributes to the ambiguity of ethical distinctions that proceeds from these mythologies, and the interbreeding of the races may be counted among the causal explanations for the irrationality and inconsistency of functional evil.

> . . . the interrelation of different groups is so close that marriage connections constantly occur between these different social, if spiritual, groups so that the offspring are, in terms of social life, half-

> breeds. No group, again, is wholly evil or wholly good. All that can be said is that each is prevailingly good or bad. The same in regard to appearance. Thus the following facts are applicable to individual or to limited groups of Rākṣasas, who are on the whole prevailingly evil. They help the gods; they fight against the gods. They are beautiful; they are hideous. They are weaker than the gods or Gandharvas; they overcome the gods with ease. They protect; they injure. They are different from Yakṣas; but they are so much like Yakṣas that the same terms are applied to both.[78]

As Van Buitenen has noted in his introduction to the Araṇya Parvan of his translation of the *Mahābhārata,* the interchangeable employment of the various demons and divinities often serves to reestablish a narrative thread that has been obscured or lost and may function in the phenomenon I will explore in Chapter 2, of the recapitulation or "rehearsal" of myths in the Epics, where one myth mirrors and expands, with a variant cast of characters, an earlier version.

> During the Pāṇḍavas' visit with him [Vṛṣaparvan], Draupadī once more sends Bhīma off in quest of saughandhika flowers. In his first encounter he got embroiled with Rākṣasas; in the present one with Yakṣas, which is indeed more appropriate, for Kubera, whose playground he violates, is the king of the Yakṣas, who are generally portrayed as genial leprechauns. One has the impression that the present story is a recast of the first one: it corrects the "mistake" of introducing Rākṣasas where Yakṣas ought to roam and play—although Kubera does have genealogical connections with Rākṣasas.[79]

In the *Mahābhārata,* the motif of bloody encounters between the Pāṇḍavas and armies of yakṣas and *rākṣasa*s is common. In particular, it is Bhīma, the strongest and most brutal of the Pāṇḍavas, who ruthlessly slaughters these demon races whenever he crosses their paths, an excess that earns the censure of his brother Yudhiṣṭhira. At Vana Parvan 152, despite the warnings of Hanuman, Bhīma infiltrates Kubera's province, which is guarded by *rākṣasa*s, seeking flowers for Draupadī. He plunges into the lake they guard, and they attack him. He defeats and kills them, drinks the waters (a violation that will acquire special meaning in our discussion of the "Yakṣapraśna"), and gathers lotuses. Later, in the Yakṣa Yuddha Parvan, Bhīma slaughters an enormous quantity of yakṣas and *rākṣasa*s for no reason other than to indulge his overweening anger and physical prowess.

Central to the Epic cosmology (and theology) is the displacement of responsibility for the control of demons from the realm of the gods to the realm of men. While the primeval struggle between *deva*s and *asura*s may rage in the heavens, the mythic morality of the Epics stresses the opposition of men and demons (particularly *rākṣasa*s). As the viceregents of the earth, it is particularly the function of the *kṣatriya* heroes to vanquish the demonic hordes and affirm the social and generic boundaries separating the human world from all other levels of being. This theme is clearly underscored in "The Slaying of Jātasura,"[80] where the *rākṣasa,* Jātasura, abducts Yudhiṣṭhira, Draupadī, and the twins, Nākula and Sahadeva. To trick them, the *rākṣasa* has assumed the guise of the brāhman, but having achieved his purpose, he resumes his demonic form, and the outraged Yudhiṣṭhira addresses him:

> Your righteousness is disintegrating, fool, and you don't see it. The humans, the animals, the Gandharvas, the Rākṣasas, the birds, and the cattle all live off men, and so do you. Your world prospers by the prosperity of ours. The deities grieve along with the grieving world, but they flourish when worshipped with oblations and ancestor offerings. We are the herdsmen and protectors of the kingdom, Rākṣasa. If the kingdom is unprotected, how can there be good fortune, how can there be happiness? A Rākṣasa must never be disrespectful toward a sinless king and we have never committed the slightest offence, man-eater.[81]

This transference of the cosmological and ethical locus from heaven to earth and the concomitant elevation of the human-demonic agon to the focus of cosmic ordering imply a paternalistic respect on the part of the human executors for the other species and members of the multileveled cosmos. The ability to assume disguises and other forms (particularly animal forms) is a characteristic that demons share with gods, but rarely with men, except insofar as humans have experienced nonhuman forms in previous lifetimes or inherit them in future lifetimes as the result of misdeeds. This point is perhaps one subtle factor that, in this *bhakti*c period of Indian religious development, with its emphasis on human emotions and capabilities, reinforces the implied moral superiority of men over gods as well as demons. Without the employment of amoral powers of illusion (*māyā*), the human realm of dominion and mastery is dependent upon ethical righteousness as the empowering principle.

Ram Nath Misra has elaborated the ways in which the yakṣa is similar to other divinities, both of the celestial half of the spectrum, which includes *gandharvas* and *apsarases*, and of the lower realm of *rākṣasas*, *piśācas*, and *guhyakas*, the class of demigods who, like the yakṣas, attend Kubera, especially in his guise of lord of concealment and treasure ("*guhyaka*" having to do with that which is "concealed" or "hidden").

Similar to the *gandharvas* (as Misra points out), the yakṣas like fragrance, carry off people (especially women), are often found near or in connection with water, are receptacles of secrets, fond of music, and possessed of beauty.[82] Like the *apsarases*, yakṣas are (again) connected with water and trees; they like dancing, singing, and playing musical instruments; they are fond of dice games and "bestow luck at play"; they are (only sometimes in the case of yakṣas) beautiful; and they have been known to enjoy sexual adventures with humans. Yakṣas share numerous characteristics with *rākṣasas*: There is a strong familial connection, in that Kubera, the king of the yakṣas, and Rāvaṇa, the great leader of the *rākṣasas*, are brothers, both sons of the ancient *ṛṣi*, Pulastya; both races are known to have monstrous and occasionally beastly forms; and both engage in many forms of demonic mischief, including murder, rape, theft, and cannibalism.[83] Although *piśācas* seem always to be encountered in a purely demonic or evil form (a characteristic that they do not have in common with yakṣas), they share with yakṣas (in their lowest form) the penchant for eating human flesh.[84] It is perhaps the shape-shifting power of the yakṣa that facilitates the movement between aspects that are "fierce and friendly, raudra maitraś ca,"[85] of which the fierce are, in some cases, assimilated to the *piśāca* nature.

Yakṣas and *rākṣasas*

In the Vedic literature, *rākṣasas* are clearly delineated as a group of purely evil beings, in which characterization they are grouped along with another similar class of demons, the *yātus* or *yātudhānas*. Both groups are known particularly for their aggressive impiety and animosity to prayer and sacrifice. Perhaps as human enemies of Āryan ritual, they are known to disrupt or withhold offerings for the sacrifice.

One Epic text that expounds an etymological origin for the terms "yakṣa" and "*rākṣasa*" does coalesce the two orders of beings, connecting both to the primal waters for the protection of which they have been created by Prajāpati.

At one time, Prajāpati created the element water as a source of the waters. In order to protect them, he made the creatures. Those creatures, trapped and fearing hunger and thirst, meekly approached their maker, saying, "What shall we do?" But Prajāpati, smiling, said to all the creatures, "Sons of Manu, protect [the waters] diligently." Some of those miserable creatures said, "Rakṣāmi," ("We will protect.") and others said, "Yakṣāmi." ("We will sacrifice.") Then the creator of the beings said "Let those who have said, 'Rakṣāmi' be Rākṣasas and those who have said 'Yakṣāmi," be Yakṣas."[86]

Rather than clarifying the distinctions between the two groups, this text serves to underscore their similarity. If there is a relevant ethical contrast to be made, we are not made aware of it. The primacy of hunger and consumption as the catalyst for the continuation of life is well known in Indian cosmology,[87] but in its raw, unreflected form, it becomes the source of danger (in life) and parody (in literature). In yet another Epic cosmogonical paradigm, the *rākṣasas* are known as *nairṛtas*, the symbolic offspring of Adharma, who was born from "the creatures who, hungry for food, began devouring each other," and Nirṛti, a goddess of death and destruction.[88] The actual birth of the *rākṣasa,* however, is, as previously mentioned, a spontaneous generation from Pulastya, one of the six "will-born" sons of Brahmā,[89] as are their cousins, the yakṣas.

In the Purāṇas, both yakṣas and *rākṣasas* have been employed as vehicles for the exploration of the theme of ethical ambiguity, with respect to the traditional Hindu opposition of *sanātana* (eternal) *dharma* and *sva* (individual) *dharma.* The development of religious scruples in a demon protagonist gives rise to a fundamental clash between the two levels of *dharma.* Two parallel myths, one about a yakṣa and the other featuring a *rākṣasa,* illustrate the conflict between the two dimensions of *dharma.* In both cases, the god Śiva,[90] whose own complex persona encompasses extremes of ascetical purity and antinomian excesses of violence and sexuality, grants the boons to the demons that bring them into conflict with their inherited demon's *dharma.*

There was a majestic yakṣa known as Harikeśa, son of Pūrṇabhadra, who was devout and righteous. Ever since his birth, he was unsurpassed in his devotion to Śiva. He did obeisance to him; he was utterly dependent on him; he thought of nothing else—sitting, sleeping, walking, standing, following, eating, drinking—he thought only of Rudra.

> His father, Pūrṇabhadra, said to his very proper son, "I do not recognize you as my son. You are ill-born, a mistake. Your conduct is not correct for the families of yakṣas. You are a Guhyaka and by nature, hard-hearted and an eater of flesh. Brahmā has not ordained us to follow the life you pursue. One ought not to abandon his own order and follow the life of another. You should, therefore, forsake your human feelings and pursue the course of your family, otherwise I should think that you have been born of men. I am a typical yakṣa who also performs various works pertaining to my class of beings, so mark my ways". . . . On being thus addressed by his father, he left his home and relations and went to Kāśi, where he devoted himself to rigid asceticism. His eyelids did not fall; he curbed his passions and stood motionless like a dried up piece of wood or a piece of stone. By continuing his austerities like that for one thousand divine years, he was surrounded by ant-hills on all sides and white ants and insects began to feast on him. After sometime, all the flesh and blood were consumed, and that devotee of Śiva's bones began to shine like a white shell.[91]

The yakṣa's austerities are noticed by the Great God, who grants him a boon:

> "Yakṣa, you will be exempt from all diseases and completely free of old age and death. You will be the lord of the Gaṇas, the giver of wealth, worshipped by all. You will also be invincible, a refuge for many and the most skilled in yoga. You will be a giver of food and a Kṣetrapāla for the worlds. . . ."[92]

In the *Vāmana Purāṇa*, Śiva's demonic devotee is a *rākṣasa* whose piety puts him at odds with the vocation and destiny of his kind. This text also contains a description of one way in which the differences between the groupings of beings has been conceived.

> There was a great Rākṣasa named Sukeśin, who received from Śiva the boon that he could not be conquered or slain. He lived according to dharma, and one day he asked a hermitage full of sages to teach him about dharma. They began by describing the particular dharmas of gods (to perform sacrifice, know the Vedas, and so forth), Daityas (fighting, politics, aggression, devotion to Śiva), Yakṣas (study of the Vedas, worship of Śiva, egoism, aggression), Rākṣasas, (raping other men's wives, coveting others' wealth, worshipping Śiva), and Piśācas (eating flesh, lack of discrimination, ignorance, impurity,

falsehood). Then they went on to explain dharma in general, including the tenfold dharma for all classes, such as noninjury. They concluded: "No one should abandon the dharma ordained for his own class and stage of life; he would anger the sun god. Let no one abandon his svadharma, nor turn against his own family, for the sun would become angry with him."[93]

Sukeśin rebelliously refuses to ignore the call to understand and practice eternal truth.

Sukeśin invited all the demons in his city to an assembly and taught them the primary and ancient dharma—noninjury, truth, and so forth (i.e., absolute dharma). All the demons began to practice his dharma, and their brilliant luster paralyzed the sun, moon, and stars; night was like day; the night-blooming lotuses did not bloom, thinking that it was still day; owls came out and crows killed them. People thought that the city of the demons was the moon, and that it had overcome the sun. Then the glorious sun thought that the entire universe had been swallowed up by the Rākṣasas, and he learned that they were all devoted to dharma, worshipping gods and Brāhmins. Therefore the sun, who destroys Rākṣasas, began to think about their annihilation. Finally he realized the weak point of the Rākṣasas; they had fallen from their svadharma, a lapse which destroyed all their (absolute) dharma. Then, overpowered by anger, the sun cast upon the city of the Rākṣasas rays that destroy enemies. The city dropped from the sky like a planet that has exhausted its merit. When Sukeśin saw the city falling he said, "Honor to Śiva!" and all the devotees of Śiva began to cry, and when Śiva learned that the sun had hurled down the city of the demons he cast his glance at the sun, and the sun fell from the sky like a stone. The gods propitiated Śiva and put the sun back in his chariot, and they took Sukeśin to dwell in heaven.[94]

In his excessive piety and self-reflection, the demon, Sukeśin, has run afoul of orthodoxy, which, as we can see, is at least as much a social as it is a theological issue. Evil is conceived as an eternal otherness or "outside" of that which is the self-defined "inside" of orthodox religiosity. From the socially dangerous perspective of absolute *dharma* or truth, even demons or untouchables or foreigners may question the authority of *brāhman*s and the cosmos that their texts and concepts regulate, in which the sun, symbol of rationality, conservatism, and "mainstream" morality, reigns supreme.

Harikeśa's and Sukeśin's devotion to the god Śiva in particular is not irrelevant. Śiva, of course, is the apotheosis of destruction, danger, and death and, as such, is the lord of demons. His cohorts and supporters are a band of ghoulish undesirables. In the lexicon of *bhakti* theology, however, his sponsorship of these miscreants does not purify their behavior; rather, they find sanctification in him as they are. Over all, however, the unconventional but still orthodox god Śiva exerts the most powerful control and has the final say. We can see clearly here that the category of the demonic must not be collapsed, not merely because the opposition of good and evil is a basic ordering principle in the cosmos, but also because *brāhman*s are threatened by the truth claims of non-*brāhmans*. This loose employment of the term "demon" to indicate deviancy is seen as well in Upaniṣadic texts where redefinitions of terms are a common aspect of the more philosophical and logical appreciation of moral categories.[95]

Another text describes the transfer of Śiva's dangerous, gloomy insanity, brought on by the immolation of his wife, Satī, to the yakṣa, Pāncālika (or Pāncāla). It seems that Śiva's troupe of demons functions to understand and withstand the erratic and often violent moods of their lord and master.

> Smitten by the arrows "Insanity" (*unmada*) and "Torment" (*śān-tapāna*) Śiva noticed Yakṣa Pāncālika, the son of Kubera, and transferred to Pāncālika his insanity, torment, and yawning (*vijṛmbhaṇa*), for he knew Pāncālika to be capable of bearing these afflictions (*Vm P* 6. 44–49). Pāncālika took them over and Śiva bestowed a boon on Pāncālika that "whoever will see you at any time in the month of Caitra, touch or worship you with devotion, be he an old man, a child, a young man, or a woman, shall go mad. O Yakṣa, they shall sing, dance, sport and play on their instruments with zeal." Even as they speak mirthfully in front of Pāncālika, they will have magic powers.[96]

In this text, it seems, the stolid earthiness of the yakṣa allows him to bear Śiva's torment, and yet as a *devatā,* his association with the many aspects of *māyā,* including madness and art, is capable of transmuting the funereal heaviness of Śiva's mourning.[97]

The ethical ambiguity of yakṣas and *rākṣasa*s is raised by Hopkins in a slightly different context when considering the conflation of the complementary oppositions or dual functions of "injuring" and "guarding," both subsumed by the characterization and etymology of "*rākṣasa.*"

> Red eyes and dark bodies characterize the Yakṣas who guard Kubera; the Rākṣasas are always red-eyed and those guarding Kubera are like fiery smoke in color. Here the function of the Rākṣasa is to guard. Whether, in India, the injurer became the guardian, or the "guardian" (of treasure) became the injurer, is still debated (rakṣ means injure and guard); but the application and growth of the words would favor the first interpretation. Rākṣas (Rākṣasa) was at first one of the many harmful spirits, injurer of those opposing it, the Rākṣas is also protector of what it values, so that rakṣin, etc., became words exclusively indicating protector; yet the demon-group, when once formed as injurious, seldom passes over into the opposed conception.[98]

Kubera, as the god of treasure, is surrounded and defended by those fierce guardians who resist plunderers and invaders and in that sense are analogous to the Vedic "demons" (or tribes), the *paṇi*s, who guarded and withheld their cows from the plundering Āryan cattle rustlers.

*Piśāca*s

Lower on the scale of beings than the *rākṣasa*s are the entirely demonic *piśāca*s, flesh eaters or desirers of flesh. They share this carnal appetite with yakṣas[99] and *rākṣasas*, but unlike them, they seem never to veer from their hideous preoccupations and have no benevolent side to their natures.[100] Along with the *rākṣasa*s of the Epics, these monsters guard Kubera's mountain, protecting the treasures stored there and fending off all intruders. They are often mentioned in texts that enumerate the varieties of beings in the world, usually at the end. . . . "rākṣasas and piśācas. . . ." And in some, they are ascribed specific forms of wrongdoing commensurate with their low level of existence: "eating flesh, lack of discrimination, ignorance, impurity, falsehood," as opposed to the *rākṣasas*' "raping other men's wives, coveting others' wealth, etc."[101]

*Gandharva*s

Another important mythical deity closely linked with the yakṣa is the *gandharva,* who is mentioned in the *Ṛg Veda,* prominent in the Brāhmaṇas and Epics, and often represented in early paintings and reliefs. While the *piśāca* is tied to the yakṣa through their shared alimentary obsessions and infractions, the *gandharva* is associated with the sexual side of the demonic spectrum and partakes liberally of the aquatic, fertility symbolism.[102]

The complex of characteristics that the *gandharva* embodies (nature, fertility, beauty, sex, and water) is summed up in the *Mahābhārata* episode, 1. 158. 4–14, in which the king of the *gandharvas*, Citraratha, has come upon the Pāṇḍavas who have invaded his part of the forest.

> There in the secret, pleasurable water of the Ganges, the jealous Gandharva king arrived to revel in the water along with his playful wives. He heard the sounds of the Pāṇḍavas as they approached the river and, gripped by that noise, he flew into a mighty rage. And when he saw the troublesome Pāṇḍavas there with their wife, he drew his bow and uttered this frightful speech: "At the time of the dangerous, reddening dusk, at the beginning of the night, except for 80 seconds, that moment has been given to the Yakṣas, Gandharvas, and Rākṣasas to roam wherever they please. The remainder is determined by tradition as belonging to human beings. If they rebelliously wander in these woods, we, along with the Rākṣasas, capture those foolish men. For, the educated brāhmanical seers reproach all men for going to the water at night, even if they are powerful kings. Stay where you are and don't come near me. Standing at the holy Ganges, how can you not recognize me? Know that I am the Gandharva, Aṅgāraparṇa, who has faith in his own strength. I am proud and jealous, Kubera's close friend. This is my wood and it is called Aṅgāraparṇa. It is lovely—both near the Ganges and the Baka, where I live. Neither corpses, nor deer, nor gods, nor humans are to set foot here; then, how do you dare to wander in?"

No respector of the *gandharva*'s claims of territory and status, Arjuna looses the *agneya* missile and burns up his chariot. The *gandharva*'s wife pleads with Yudhiṣṭhira to save his life, and Arjuna relents. In return, the *gandharva* bestows the magic upon Arjuna for which his species is famous.[103] In the person of the *gandharva,* the baser elements of the demonic are transmuted into an aesthetic equivalent: Pure sexuality and lust become beauty and enjoyment; raw illusion becomes protective magic and artistry.

Particularly in the sculpture, the sexual playfulness of the *gandharva* is seen to be shared with his mythic partner, the *apsaras,* nymph of the celestial waters and attendant upon King Soma. Both are known to bestow their prodigious sexual talents from time to time upon human consorts, who are often driven mad with rampant desire. In the sculpture, *gandharvas* and *apsarases* are closely related to the benevolent yakṣas and yakṣīs, though the *gandharvas* have been "kicked upstairs," as it were, and their graceful attributes have been imputed to their celestial rather than terrestrial origins.

> To sum up, Gandharvas and Apsarases appear to have been at first genii of vegetation and fertility, connected with Varuṇa and Soma, and when later they are reduced to the status of attendants on Indra, they are replaced, functionally, by the Yakṣas and Yakṣīs. Yakṣas and Yakṣīs are identical with Gandharvas and Apsarases as originally conceived, and perhaps this is a point on which considerable emphasis should be laid, as partially explaining some of the numerous other links which seem to connect the Yakṣas, including King Kubera, with Varuṇa.[104]

Kinnāras or *kiṁpuruṣas*

To complete the list of closely related mythic deities, mention must be made of *kinnāras* or *kiṁpuruṣas* (literally, "what sort of men?"), creatures with the bodies of humans and the heads of horses. They are casually referred to in mythical narratives where they are usually numbered among the colorful retinue of the yakṣa-god, Kubera. The females of these races function as sirens and seductresses, like the yakṣīs in the Jātaka tales.

Kubera

Introduction

Earlier in this chapter, in the section on Mythological Background, we explored the ways in which the ancient complex of fertility and water symbols and associations establishes a basis for the moral ambiguity of the yakṣa. Then, in the section on the Family of Demons, we briefly reviewed the assortment of more purely terrestrial demons (with the exception of the *gandharva,* who is celestial and, like the yakṣa, not thoroughly demonic). In this section, we will discuss the king of the yakṣas, Kubera, (figure 11), who is connected with fertility, but of a more distinctly terrestrial, rather than aquatic variety.[105] Kubera is a figure of cultic attention in India and throughout other parts of Asia,

Figure 11. Kubera from Pabhosa, Allahabad District. Drawing by Peter Sutherland.

primarily because he is the guardian deity of wealth and treasure. In the latter connection, he has many epithets: Dhanapati, Dhanādhipa, Nidhipa, Vittapāla, and Vitteśa. Historically, he has minor associations with *piśācas*[106] and more extensive connections with the *rākṣasas* in the Epics.

Kubera was known in the *Śatapatha Brāhmaṇa*[107] as the lord of thieves and criminals. In another example of the generalization (and often, in the process, reversal) of the attributes of deities, Kubera becomes a patron of merchants and a respectable world guardian (*lokapāla*), in connection with which he is mentioned in *Manu.*[108] Kubera, his name possibly stemming from *kumb,* "to conceal," has a number of aliases: Kuvera (a later Sanskrit word that Cunningham derives from *ku,* "earth" and *vīra,* "hero"); Vaiśravaṇa ("son of Viśravas" [Pāli, Vessavana], with the contradictory derivation from "Visana," which is Kubera's kingdom [*Sutta Nipāta* commentary 1. 369]); and in Japan, Bushamon.[109] Among his attendants, along with yakṣas, are *guhyakas*, from "*guhya,*" the "hidden," "concealed," or "secret." In his connection with Kubera, the yakṣa once again articulates the notion of ethical ambivalence and supplies a useful syncretic symbol for Kubera's association with evil and wrongdoing as well as his representation of the earth and the treasures concealed within it.

Perhaps the most interesting myths surrounding the cult of Kubera are those that have to do with his genealogical links with the *rākṣasas* through his half-brother, Rāvaṇa. The story of this connection is expounded in both Epics. The *Mahābhārata* version[110] summarizes the story of the two brothers and their diverging paths: The god Prajāpati has a son, Pulastya, who sires Vaiśravaṇa (Kubera) on a cow. Vaiśravaṇa forsakes his father and joins his illustrious grandfather who gives him the boons of immortality, the lordship of wealth and riches, the friendship of Īśāna (Śiva), a son, Nalakūbara, the vice-regency of one quarter, and the capital seat, Laṅkā, where he is attended by hosts of *rākṣasas*. In anger at Kubera's desertion, his father creates a new son, the hermit Viśravas, out of one half of himself. Trying to placate his father, Kubera sends him three *rākṣasa* servant women, Puṣpotkaṭā, Rākā, and Mālinī, who set about to please their new master with their prowess at singing and dancing. As boons, he gives them sons. Puṣpotkatā gives birth to Kumbhakarṇa and Rāvaṇa; Mālinī bears the pious Vibhīṣaṇa; and Rākā gives birth to the twins, Khara and Śūrpaṇakhā. Because of their hatred and jealousy of Vaiśravaṇa-

Kubera, these *rākṣasa* sons of Pulastya undertake awesome feats of asceticism for a thousand years, culminating in Rāvaṇa's burned offering of one of his ten heads. The severity of their discipline pleases their grandfather, Prajāpati, who restores Rāvaṇa's missing head and grants them the powerful boons of their choice, with the exception of the boon of immortality. Once Rāvaṇa receives his boon—the power to be invincible at the hands of *gandharva*s, gods, *asura*s, *nāga*s, *kinnāra*s, and *bhūta*s (but significantly, not yakṣas or men), he proceeds to wage war on Kubera and captures his kingdom and his celestial chariot.[111] In leaving Laṅkā with a retinue of yakṣas, *gandharva*s, *kiṁpuruṣa*s, and *rākṣasa*s, Kubera flings a mighty curse at his half-brother, predicting that Rāvaṇa will never ride the plundered chariot.[112] The righteous brother, Vibhīṣaṇa, follows his brother, Kubera, to his new seat on Gandhamādana (a mountain to the east of Meru), for which he is granted the marshalship of the armies of the yakṣas and *rākṣasa*s. In Kubera's stead, Rāvaṇa is consecrated king of Laṅkā.

In terms of our discussion, the conflict and separation of Pulastya's two sons underscore a central difference between the yakṣas and *rākṣasa*s, of which Kubera and Rāvaṇa are both (respectively) apotheoses. The yakṣa temperament, which Kubera ably represents, is a combination of cunning (as seen in his self-interested abandonment and ultimate appeasement of his father) and a more benevolent earthiness, seen particularly in his iconographic feature of potbelliedness, a common Asian motif, expressing good luck and abundance. Within the context of the *Mahābhārata,* the rivalry between the half-brothers, Vaiśravaṇa and Rāvaṇa, is homologous to the growing rivalry between the half-brothers of the central tale, Yudhiṣṭhira and Duryodhana. In terms of the *Rāmāyaṇa,* the theme of fraternal rivalry is also focal, and Rāma's defeat of Rāvaṇa serves symbolically to punish both Rāvaṇa's aggression toward his older brother and the aggressive unseating of Rāma from the throne by his stepmother on behalf of her son, Rāma's younger half-brother.

In association with his fertility and good fortune aspect, Kubera's wife is called "Bhadrā," "Lucky," and also "Ṛddhi," "Success." In the Buddhist legends, Kubera is equated with Pāñcika, whose wife is Nandā, Abhirati, or Hārīti (Bahuputrikā), another symbol of abundance (as we will see in a succeeding chapter) in her having given birth to thousands of sons. Also, in these texts, Kubera is sometimes worshipped as Maṇibhadra (sometimes considered a yakṣa chief separate from Kubera and sometimes equated with him), who protected travelers and traders, saved people from epidemics, and, in Benares, saved people from floods.[113] His brother is Pūrṇabhadra (father of Harikeśa) or Punnabhadda (Pāli), whose followers "are mentioned along with those of Vāsudeva and Bāladeva, whose cult is as old as Pāṇini."[114] Kubera's iconography verges only slightly on the unethical in his joviality being linked with drunkenness. In some sources (the Jain *Yaśastilaka* for one), Kubera is depicted as a drunkard, iconographically signified by his holding a "nectar vessel."[115]

Again, the strong link with images of fertility and earthly supply confers a changeable persona upon our yakṣa figure, in this case, Kubera. The operative factor in the ethical characterization of these sexual beings seems to be whether or not their sexuality can be sublimated to domestic fertility. In the case of the *rākṣasa*s and particularly Rāvaṇa, their strident erotic impulses cannot be tamed. Rāvaṇa ravages his female captives for pleasure, not in order to make *rākṣasa* babies, and what is worse, these women (who are mostly *rākṣasīs*) enjoy their lustful, undomesticated lover. In the figure of Kubera, fertility becomes a safe issue. Through his protective guardianship and his distribution of the secret resources of the earth, he has become a paternal, manipulatable figure. His wild half-brother, however, lacks the *lokapāla* responsibilities that would utilize his ferocity for good.

Kubera and the *lokapāla*s

Along with fertility and abundance, the other central aspect of Kubera's character and dimension of his kingship is his status as one of the four *lokapāla*s ("world guardians") or eight *dikpāla*s ("guardians of the directions"). In this respect as well, he embodies yakṣalike characteristics. The yakṣa's penchant for guarding and testing (an aspect that will be fully explored in the next chapter) is raised to a cosmological level in Kubera, the world guardian.

In the four-part version of the classification system, Indra, Yama, Varuṇa, and Kubera preside over the east, south, west, and north, respectively. In the eight-directional version, Agni, Vāyu, Soma, and Sūrya rule, respectively, over the southeast, the northwest, the northeast, and the southwest. Numerous configurations of these directional guardians exist, varying with the texts that describe them.[116] Heinrich Zimmer attributes the origin of the four *lokapāla*s to an ancient pre-

Āryan Indian cosmological system in which "they have their domains in the four slopes of the quadrangular central mountain of the universe, Mount Sumeru, which rises from the mid-point of the surface of the earth (somewhat to the north of the Himālayan ranges) as the vertical axis of the egg-shaped cosmos."[117] The slopes of Mount Meru are "peopled by divine beings, among whom are the yakṣas, nāgas, gnomes, and gandharvas, while on the quadrangular summit stand the palatial mansions of the great gods, the 'deathless ones' (amara). This summit is known, therefore, as Amarāvatī, 'The Town Immortal,' and it is the capital of Indra, the king of the Hindu pantheon."[118]

Whatever the origin of the mythology of the four kings or guardians of the four directions, it was evidently not Vedic. The scholar and art historian L. A. Waddell, in his history of Buddhist cult and art, finds no mention of them in the earliest literature, although the *Gṛhya Sūtras*[119] mention a house-building ritual that involves offerings (*bali*) to the *lokapālas*.[120] As with all of the important symbols of Indian cosmology, the Buddhists employed the mythology of Sumeru (Mount Meru) and Amarāvatī as well in their own cosmological system, which was represented on and around the early *stūpas*, where "the kings of the quarters, the so-called 'Protectors of the World' (*lokapālas*), stand guard precisely as in Hindu sanctuaries."[121]

The Buddhists list the world rulers or "vice-regents" as Virudhāka (Pāli Virulhaka) (south), who rules over the *gandharvas* (Pāli *gandhabbas*); Dhṛtarāśtra (Pāli Dhatarattha) (east), who rules over the Kumbhāṇḍas (a grotesque group of demons with testicles in the shape of a *kumbha* or pitcher); Vaiśravaṇa (Pāli Vessavana=Kubera) (north), the lord of the yakṣas; and Virupakṣa (Pāli Virupakka) (west), the leader of the *nāgas*.[122] The *lokapālas* figure actively in all of the events of the Buddha's life, as mentioned particularly in the *Nidānakathā:* as bearers of the infant Buddha's palanquin, as bearers of his horse, Kanthaka, during the Great Renunciation, and as among the first converts to Buddhism.[123]

Sculpturally, these figures have come into their own as the favored door guardians in various Buddhist temples and shrines outside India, a function that persists in decorative remnants in Hindu temples as well.

> Their statues or frescoes confront the visitor to every temple in Tibet, China, Japan, as well as in most temples in Southern Buddhism. One of their numbers, *Bishamon* [=*Bushamon*] (*Vaiśravaṇa*), the king of

> the Yaksha genii, is an especially favourite subject with Japanese artists; and in later times I find their figures have survived in India as frequent doorway motives in decorative art; for the chief function of these guardians in Buddhism, as well as in Brahmanism, was to protect buildings from the four directions.[124]

The *lokapāla*s have as their animal mounts or *vāhana*s elephants (or *diggaja*s, "elephants of the directions"), though Kubera is also uniquely described as "*nāravāhana,*" "one whose mount is a man." This epithet refers to Kubera's often being carried about by or pulled in his chariot by (the anthropomorphic) yakṣas. In the later mythology, these elephants themselves, minus their riders, become the *lokapāla*s. In all of its manifestations, the role of the *lokapāla*s may be compared in certain crucial aspects to the guardian role occupied by yakṣas. On a cosmic level, the four (or eight) deities of the directions are protectors of territory and sacred spaces, just as their yakṣa counterparts are on the terrestrial level.

One mythological strain connects Kubera and his retinue with Śiva, who presides in splendor over the pleasures and beauties of Kubera's neighborhood on Mount Meru. Śiva's very presence, it seems, creates a paradisical setting wherever he goes, despite the strange and scruffy company he is known to keep.

> There was once a peak of Mount Meru, reknowned throughout the three worlds and called "The Illuminator." Descended from the sun and ornamented with all the jewels, it was immeasurable and invincible. There, on the slope of the mountain which glitters with gold and minerals, the God held forth while reclining. At his side, the daughter of the Mountain King, Pārvatī, remained constantly seated. At that time, the great-souled gods, the strong Vasus; as well as the best of physicians, the Aśvins; along with King Vaiśravaṇa, the powerful lord of the Yakṣas who has his residence on noble Kailāsa, surrounded by the Guhyakas with the best of the divine sages, Aṅgiras, at their head; and the Gandharva, Viśvāsu; Nārada; and Pārvata; and the gathered multitudes of Apsarases—they all came together. A mild, sweet wind blew, carrying various pure scents. The great trees have blossoms which bear fruit throughout every season. At that time, the Vidyādharas, Siddhas, and ascetics attended the Great God, the Lord of the Animals. And the Ghosts, Rākṣasas, and the powerful Piśācas, taking many forms and holding all sorts of weapons, stood there like fires, serving the god and rejoicing. And

> the lord Nandin stood there with the consent of the God, holding the fiery trident which blazed with its own energy. The Ganges, the Best of Rivers, born of all the sacred waters, in bodily form served the God. Thus, the Lord, the Great God, was worshipped by the holy sages and by the gods of extreme good fortune.[125]

This worship of the major gods by the minor gods, of course, is not unusual; a valuable narrative purpose is served. The gods and their exploits are placed, like precious jewels in a setting, each contained by a world or *loka* that is a cosmos unto itself. In the case of Śiva in particular, the precise location of that world is often left obscure. It may exist in the exalted reaches of the divine dimension, or it may be close at hand, within the possibility of human encounter and perception. The representable elements of the Indian mythological cosmos are familiar, interchangeable motifs and characters who are arranged to represent, as we have seen, either hellish or heavenly worlds. In the world of *bhakti,* for the devotee, the physical universe holds the possibility of complete transformation according to the grace of the adored deity. In these narrative texts, the *lokapāla*s serve, like the yakṣas and *rākṣasa*s, as framing devices, whose wrath and power, now subservient to the great hero or god (in this case Śiva), enhance the god's own circumference of power.

Chapter 2

THE YAKṢA IN HINDUISM

Vedic Sources

In this chapter, we shall begin to see even more clearly how the fusion of characteristics that permitted the broad expression and metaphysical ambivalence of the early yakṣa soon split into two categories of benevolent and malevolent qualities, the latter being the increasingly dominant aspect of the yakṣa nature. We will begin by examining the small body of Vedic references that may be adduced as "original" citations of the elusive figure of the yakṣa. These references are "original" only in the sense that they are the earliest texts available to us. Unlike the major Vedic gods, most of whom are tied to some specific elemental phenomenon, the yakṣa seems to be linked to a parallel Vedic tradition in which speculations about the origin of the universe are entertained in relation to various elemental principles and demiurgic personalities, particularly Prajāpati. In these early citations, the term "yakṣa" seems a shadowy metaphor for being itself. And in its inclusiveness, it straddles the important Indian philosophical categories of *vyakta* and *avyakta* ("manifest and unmanifest" or "immanent and transcendent").

An array of etymological attributions have been adduced by Ram Nath Misra to explain the mysterious term "yakṣa," encompassing such notions as "to honor" (from ✓*pra-yaks*); "to move quickly" or "to reveal" or "be revealed" (Vedic ✓*yakṣ*); a derivation of ✓*yaj,* "to sacrifice" (put forward by the commentators Sāyana and Mādhava); or connected with the Iranian word "*yaxs,*" with the sense of "appearing." In the later, more popular and mythic etymologies of the Epics and Purāṇas, other, more colorful explanations are put forth. In the Rāmāyana (7. 104. 12–13), the etymology of both yakṣas and *rākṣasas* is given: "In Brahmā's creation of the waters and creatures to guard it, some cried out *rakṣāmah* ('let us guard') and so they became the *rākṣasas* and others cried out *yakṣāmah* [Misra says ('let us gobble') [?], probably 'let us worship'] and they became the yakṣas."[1]

In all of the Vedic references to the yakṣa, a pervasive aura of mystery adheres to the concept. As a metaphor for mystery and wonderment about the origins of the universe, the yakṣa becomes linked to the deepening strain of philosophical speculation about the single essence or sole creator of the cosmos, standing apart from and above the gods,[2] or identified with one of the gods. It is the quality of mysteriousness that also contributes to the growing sense of fear and dark malevolence that comes to be associated with the yakṣa. His obscurity is assimilated to another aspect of the unknown or the primal mystery, its dangerous or abysmal potential for obfuscating the luminous elements of creation that are related to the sacrifice.

In some cases, the word "yakṣa" appears to be used adjectivally, in the sense of "mysterious" or "secret." In any case, there are examples in which it is not possible to determine whether the term is used as a noun that pertains to some type or order of beings or in the descriptive, generally adjectival sense. For instance, in the following citation, previous translators have interpreted the term in both ways, often hedging the translations to accommodate any possibility. For ṚV 4. 3. 13, *mā kasya yakṣam sadamiddhuro gā* ("Do not go to the mystery [or "snare" = yakṣa] of the dishonest man"), Coomaraswamy leaves the "yakṣa" untranslated as if it were an animal or creature ("Do not [O Agni] consort with the Yakṣa of any smooth swindler . . ."), and Geldner translates it as "secrecy" or "mystery" ("*Geh nicht zu der Heimlichkeit irgend eines Unehrlichen* . . ."). In *ṚV* 10. 88. 13, addressed to Agni Vaiśvānara, it is equally difficult to assign status to "yakṣa"—as either proper noun or abstract concept: *yakṣasyādhyakṣam taviṣam vṛhantam,* describing Agni as "the powerful, high overseer of the mystery" (or "of the yakṣa"—in the sense of "lord of the yakṣas"). Another verse, *ṚV* 8. 61. 5, addressed to the composite deity, Mitra-Varuṇa, is again ambiguous in the preceding respect: *amura viśva vṛṣṇavima vam na yasu citram dadṛśo na yakṣam*, translated by Arthur Macdonell as: "O wise mighty ones, all these (praises) are for you two, in which no marvel is seen nor *mystery* [italics mine]"[3] but Coomaraswamy construes "yakṣam" as "invisible" in contrast to "*citram*" as "visible."[4] I myself would alter the latter translation to stress "form" as opposed to "formlessness" ("yakṣam").

Many more references may be found in the somewhat later verses of the *Atharva Veda* (900 B.C.). These references (which follow) indicate that a strong direction in the development of the image of the yakṣa has emerged—toward a clearer personification and deification. In these verses, the yakṣa is seen to be a "great being" or "living," "animating being," or "great spirit," situated at the center of the world, the heart of creation. The sense of the concept is then pushed in the direction of an embodiment of the life force itself, and yet I have come to the conclusion that in the *Atharva Ved*ic verses, the concept still remains situated ambivalently between the impersonal absolute (brahman) and the theistic absolutes and creator gods (primarily Viṣṇu and Brahmā/Prajāpati).

In some verses, the yakṣa seems creaturely, animallike, and in others, like a god. As we will see, the conjunction of the bestial and the celestial is a common motif in Hindu and other religious traditions, yet Indian mythology and thought, in attempting to accommodate this fusion, which is, to the Indian imagination, an uneasy consortship, generate various complications and epicyclical explanations. The alliance with the wildness of beasts is most plain in *AV* 11. 2. 24:

> For you, beasts of the woods and creatures such as deer, *haṁsa* birds, eagles, and other small birds were placed in the forest.
>
> Oh Lord of Beasts (*paśupate*), the divine waters increase your being (or "spirit" or "life" = "yakṣam"), flowing into the waters within you.

The equation with absolute being that these verses imply strongly suggests an identification with the later Upaniṣadic absolute, brahman, and yet all of the references are tinged with a sense of the animate, immanent possibility of the great spirit or creative absolute. The yakṣa does not seem like an impersonal principle but rather like a breathing, animate being. Still, paradoxically, his (or its) being, though immanent, is hidden—at the center of the universe, perceptible only to those who have achieved some subtle understanding.

> The wise know the sacred as that living being (yakṣam *ātmanvat*) in the golden vessel which has three spokes and three supports.[5]
>
> Oh seers, she is Virāj [a kind of queen or creatrix] in the highest heaven, in the aid and service of whom the spirit (yakṣam) moves.[6]
>
> He lives far away with plenty; he is sent far away with little. The great Yakṣa of the world, to him his subjects, unbidden, bring tribute.[7]

The preceding verses hint at the mystery and ambiguity that are associated with the character of the yakṣa. He is powerful and yet he dwells far away, perhaps not by his own choosing; he is worshipped and yet perhaps he is feared as well. The yakṣa is linked in this context as well with the search for the one absolute principle of being, sought from among the multiplicity of gods and sacred phenomena.

> Who is the cow? Who is the one seer (*ṛṣi*)? What is the law and what are the prayers? What on earth is the one single spirit (yakṣam) and which of the many seasons is the one right time?[8]

In this case, the sense of "yakṣa" is more generic: spirit as "spirithood" rather than a specific sense of the absolute, whether theistic or nontheistic. The yakṣa-spirit is the starting point for a more detailed and exhaustive inquiry into the nature of that which is one and undifferentiated or, simply, that which is the sacred power or deity in charge of everything, the perimeter beyond which no delving can go, the cause into which all other notions of causality must dissolve.

The literature of the Brāhmaṇas continues this "generic" interpretation of "yakṣas," in some cases equating it with *brahman,* particularly as the deity or principle that generates his/its own being as well as the world.

> By means of *tapas* I became the original yakṣa.[9]

> Brahmā was this in the beginning, just the one, self-sustaining. He thought, "I am the Great Yakṣa who is the one and only. Oh, let me make from myself a second deity who is my equal.[10]

More and more, the use of the term "yakṣa" implied an intermediate stage in the process of metaphysical inquiry into the nature of absolute reality, a line of thinking that emerged in the *Ṛg Veda* but came into its own in the Upaniṣadic literature (700 B.C.). In the Upaniṣads, the absolute came to be given the name that once and for all adhered—*brahman*. The full emergence of the concept *brahman* represented a philosophical certainty about something that, in its nascent conceptualization, could only be discussed as a great presence or spirit or being, and it is in this context that once again the term "yakṣam" (the abstract, neuter form) was employed.

> He who knows that great first-born being (yakṣam) as the true *brahman,* conquers these worlds. That which is conquered ceases to

exist for him who knows the great first-born being as the true *brahman.*[11]

The application of the yakṣa as an appositional concept describing (in its amorphousness) the ultimacy, pervasiveness, and hiddenness of *brahman* is seen particularly in the allegorical section of the *Kena Upaniṣad* 3. 1–12 and 4. 1–4, in which the Vedic gods attempt to determine the nature of the impersonal power that is beyond their own knowledge and sway.

Brahman vanquished the gods and the gods were downcast by that victory of Brahman's. They thought, "Ours is the victory, ours is the greatness."

Brahman knew this and appeared to them. They did not know what yakṣam ("spirit" or "being"?) this was.

They said to Agni, "Oh, Jāta-veda, find out what yakṣam this is." "Alright," he said.

He ran up to it and it said to him, "Who are you?" "I am Agni," he replied. "I am Jāta-veda."

"What power is in you?" it asked. "I can burn up everything whatsoever that is on the earth," Agni answered.

It put down a blade of grass in front of him and said, "Burn this." Agni rushed upon it with all of his speed, but he was not able to burn it. He returned from that place and said, "I have not been able to discover what this yakṣam is."

Then they said to Vāyu (the wind god), "Vāyu, find out what sort of yakṣam this is." "Alright," he said.

He ran up to it and it said to him, "Who are you?" Vāyu replied, "I am Vāyu, I am Matariśva."

It asked him, "What power is there in you?" "I can carry away anything whatsoever on earth."

It put a blade of grass before him and said, "Carry this off." He rushed upon it with all of his speed but he was not able to carry if off. He returned from there and said, "I have not been able to find out who this yakṣam is."

Then they said to Indra, "Maghavan, find out what sort of yakṣam this is." "Alright," he said. He rushed up to it but it hid from him.

> In the sky, he came upon a lady, the exceedingly beautiful Umā, daughter of Himavat, and said to her, "What is this yakṣam?"
>
> She replied, "This is brahman. In the victory of brahman you will delight." Only then did he (Indra) understand that it was brahman.
>
> Because of this, these gods, Agni, Vāyu, and Indra, are better than other gods; for they touched it the closest. They were the first to know that it was brahman.
>
> Therefore, Indra is better than other gods for he touched brahman most closely. He was the first to know that it was brahman.

The charm of this episode lies in its transparent, conciliatory deference to the Vedic gods, who attempt to understand the ineffable with the crude knowledge and powers available to the elemental deities. The Vedic notion of power and gnosis, derived from the straightforward manipulation of elemental phenomena through ritual, is comically inadequate to comprehend the elusive spirit (advanced in the Upaniṣads as the superseding hierophany), which is all-pervasive, encompassing the three worlds of the cosmos, heaven, aether (*antarikṣa*), and the earth. It is perhaps in this period, in the course of the denomination of the absolute, that the concept of the "yakṣa," a nebulous term, now subsumed by the potent metaphysical understanding of the Upaniṣadic *brahman,* becomes diminished and circumscribed.

In a late section of the already late *Maitri Upaniṣad,* "yakṣa" is mentioned twice, in both cases during the course of a long meditative enumeration of the kinds of beings and phenomena, sacred and earthly, that are encompassed by the true self, the *ātman.* At *Maitri Up* 7. 6, the yakṣa is mentioned in company with various celestial phenomena, animals, men, and *rākṣasas*: "*śani-rāhu-keturāga-rakṣo-yakṣa-nāra-vihaga-śārabhebhada.*" In another passage, the yakṣa is incorporated into a fascinating historical glimpse of a world of heretics and spiritual charlatans, against which the king is being warned by his mentor, an advocate of some opposing school of philosophy or priestly sect.

> Now then, Oh King, these are the afflictions of knowledge. This, indeed, is the source, of the net of illusion, that one of the heavenly associates with the unheavenly. Though it is said that there are gardens before them, they cling to the shrubs below. Now, there are others who are always blissful, always living abroad, always begging, forever subsisting by means of manual labor. There are others

> who are beggars in town, performing sacrifices for outcastes, disciples of *śūdra*s, and, though *śūdra*s, are learned in the *śāstra*s. There are those who are rogues, who wear matted locks, who are dancers, mercenaries, mendicants, actors, and those who have fallen low in the service of the king. And there are others who, for money, say "We can pacify all the spirits, such as the yakṣas, *rākṣasa*s, *bhūta*s, *gaṇa*s, *piśāca*s, and snakes." And there are those who wear skulls and serpent earrings for fashion and others who foolishly want to obstruct in matters of sacred knowledge with the conjuring and jugglery of parables and logic. One should not associate with these people. These demons are obviously thieves and not worthy of heaven, and so they say:
>
> > The world, bewildered by false examples and rogues who discourse on the no-self, does not have knowledge, since they must be saved by the knowers of the Vedas.[12]

The yakṣa is clearly seen here to be among the ranks of the lower orders of demonic creatures and, by implication, is grouped with all sorts of popular, cultic, and therefore antignostic religious proponents and practitioners. The fall from "yakṣa" as a great, wondrous, and numinous "Spirit" to a magical "spirit" of the masses and the underworld is perhaps analogous to the difference between "Spirit" in the Western sense of the "Holy Spirit," the spirit of God or the universe, and magical "spirit," as fairy, sprite, or evil "spirit."[13] In both cases, the vital distinction lies in the characterization of one as a unified, ubiquitous, but undifferentiated presence or power of being or God, and the other as lacking unity with a greater, spiritualized power, being merely a particularized embodiment of something mysterious, unknown, irrational, dark, or otherworldly.

The *Gṛhya Sūtra*s depict an image of the yakṣa that is fully transformed into a demigod and popular earthly deity, lumped indiscriminately with *asura*s, *gandharva*s, *pitṛ*s, and *rākṣasa*s (and often equated with them).[14] In many cases, however, the invocation of yakṣas and other beings (*bhutāni*")[15] occurs in a new context: It now seems that such beings are worshipped—in familiar and prevalent rituals in which they are beseeched for various favors and boons. The *Mānava Gṛhya Sūtra,* 2. 14. 29–30, recounts a *pūjā* in which a whole array of Tantric-style demons are called forth to please the devotee, among them a character called "*bako*yakṣah" ("crane-yakṣa"), along with Vaiśravaṇa (Kubera), who begins to come into some prominence in the Buddhist Jātaka tales and comes fully to the fore in the post-Vedic Hindu literature, where he is invoked in the marriage ritual.[16]

Varuṇa

It may be useful for our inquiry to imagine that, during this early Vedic stage of the yakṣa's career, the simple, unified concept that was called "yakṣa," a concept which altered and diminished during later periods of religious and literary history, was already threatened by latent ruptures. If we look closely at the symbolism and mythology of the Vedas, we can specify several important areas of ambiguity that may have given rise to the morphological transformation and splitting into dual functions of the yakṣa deity, which was well established by the period of the Gṛhya Sūtras. Many of these manifest and latent dualities, which were such an inherent part of the Vedic scheme of sacrifice and symbolism, were undoubtedly active constituents of the transformation and decline of other Vedic gods, particularly Varuṇa. In his close association with the waters and their attendant symbolism, his characteristic employment of *māyā* or illusion, and his fall from the stature of a great god to that of a demigod, Varuṇa's career follows a course that is analogous to the yakṣa's trajectory of decline and demonization. The link between the two deities is made more explicit in later texts, which we will analyze in the next chapter.

The composite divinities, Mitra-Varuṇa, closely linked to the Avestan gods, Mithra and Ahura Mazda, were important deities of the *Ṛg Veda.* Mitra, an obscure figure, was eventually subsumed by the more dominant Varuṇa. As a solar god, Varuṇa was characterized as a world monarch, responsible for maintaining the moral law of the universe (*ṛta*) in all of its three dimensions: (1) the physical order of nature and the cosmos; (2) the proper performance of the sacrifice; and (3) the moral law of society. It is in the complex mingling of the three Vedic notions of *ṛta* that the challenge to the cohesion of the deity, Varuṇa, resides. It is along such stressed seams of theological and mythological construction that these multifaceted gods may become weakened and fragmented. *Ṛg Ved*ic hymns such as 5. 85 celebrate the multiple domains and powers of Varuṇa, in creating and measuring out the cosmos, controlling the fructifying waters, punishing sinners, and employing magic (māyā) as a means of exerting control in all of those domains.

The crux of Varuṇa's complexity and decline as an important Indian god rests with his dual influence over two elements and his highly ambivalent inclusion of the utter extremes of, on the one hand, the highest moral judgment and righteousness and, on the other hand, aspects of secrecy, darkness, and deception. Like the yakṣa, Varuṇa began his career as an exemplar of universal notions and in association with the highest Vedic gods. Ultimately, however, those lofty beginnings were overshadowed by elements of the underworld that his elusive persona also contained.

In the just and measured regulation of the life-supporting waters, Varuṇa particularly acquired his reputation as arbiter of cosmic righteousness. His punishing, judgmental side is thought to be responsible both for the constriction or "binding" of humans in the bonds (*pāśa*) of sin and for the withholding or "binding" of the waters. In this sense, he has been assimilated to the primordial Vedic *asura,* Vṛtra, the supreme serpentine power imprisoning the waters that the heroic god Indra was to release.[17] These fetters or *pāśa*s of Varuṇa are part of the symbolism and iconography of what Mircea Eliade calls the "Terrible Sovereign," a deity who is contrasted with both the "Sovereign Lawgiver" and the warrior god.[18] On both cosmic and human planes, Varuṇa's propensity for binding is an aspect of the remote, celestial deity whose displeasure with sinners is expressed through a fearful ensnarement of life itself, bringing on, supposedly (again through his control of the waters, or liquids in general), the disease dropsy or edema (an excess of water in the tissues) and death.

Varuṇa's fearful aspect grew beyond his other characteristics principally, I think, for two reasons: First, his celestial supremacy is linked with both solar and lunar symbolism. (Varuṇa's name is cognate with the Greek *ouranos,* the word for "sky" or "heaven" [and the proper name of the sky father of Zeus, whose binding of his sons is punished by the rebel Zeus, by castration].) Varuṇa, as king of the daytime sky, is (along with his fraternal complement, Mitra) the eye of the sun, boldly disclosing the apparent and inescapable order of the cosmos through reason, symmetry, and the temporal consistency of the seasons. As god of the night sky, Varuṇa is associated with those bodies that shine in the darkness, the stars and the moon. It is primarily in this association with the moon in its capacity to move the terrestrial waters that Varuṇa comes to be linked so closely with the aquatic realm. Whereas, the daylight order produces a sense of harmony and clarity, the ordering principle of the night is associated with the stars, the "thousand eyes" of Varuṇa, thought to be the "spies" (*spāśa*) of the secretive and angry judge whose punitive weapons are the subtle "magic" of tortured conscience, disease, and sudden death. These devices of the dark, nighttime side of Varuṇa are aspects of his *māyā,* a term that means, like the English word "craft," both "skillfulness" and "art" as well as "deceit" and "wile." The etymological link[19] is provided by the Sanskrit root √*mā,* "to measure" or "divide." The term is employed in the rational sense of creation through delimitation, making something plain or distinct, but also in the artistic sense of creating something that was not there before. We will see that the transformative and transforming capacity of Varuṇa is strongly associated with a similar function of the yakṣa; in both cases, the employment of *māyā* or the shroudedness of form and personality is an important facet—of the "demotion" of Varuṇa to an elemental deity and of the yakṣa to a demon.

The second factor that has contributed to the conception of the solar Varuṇa as a dark and malignant force is a familiar phenomenon in the history of religions that seems to be partly responsible for a number of puzzling ambiguities in the characters and theologies of several deities (found particularly in the Indian pantheon). This phenomenon, which we might term "guilt by association," involves the identification and interchangeability of a sin or wrongdoing with its nemesis. The dark and fearsome aspect of the nemesis or judge becomes equated with that which is judged, and the deliverance from sin or wrongdoing is also (in a confusion of cause for effect) a deliverance from the punishment of sin. Paul Ricoeur has discussed this phenomenon in the context of the "defilement" level of sin, a stage of ethical conceptualization in which evil and misfortune have not been dissociated, in which "the ethical order of doing ill has not been distinguished from the cosmo-biological order of fearing ill: suffering, sickness, death, failure."[20] This "ethical terror" is the primordial connection of "vengeance with defilement."

> Vengeance causes suffering. And thus, through the intermediary of retribution, the whole physical order is taken up into the ethical order; the evil of suffering is linked synthetically with the evil of fault.[21]

The dissociative generalization of evil that conflates the ethical and the emotional, the wrongdoing with the retributive suffering, is constellated in early Indian thought by the notion of *ṛta* or "world order," with its three interchangeable dimensions of law and transgression, which Varuṇa controls. The free association of ideas and images obtains again in the philological switch of cause for effect engendered by the similarity of the words to describe evil, "*pāpa,*" and the "snare" or punishment for evil, "*pāśa.*" From this reversal and confusion, we may extrapolate a conceptual nexus that can be posited as the elusive factor in creative transformations and reversals of metaphysical, ethical, and artistic forms: A theology of fault becomes a theology of terror; an ethos of responsibility becomes an ethos of avoidance; an aesthetic of light and clarity becomes an aesthetic of shadow and cruelty.

F. B. J. Kuiper attributes the transformation of Varuṇa from universal overseer of righteousness to the limited guardian of the waters to a much larger reordering of the cosmos. The Vedic cosmos was restructured and delimited from its original totality of being and nonbeing, symbolized by the primal waters, and reduced to a bifurcated universe of chaos and order or *asat* and *sat.*

> . . . before Indra's demiurgic act Varuṇa and the Asuras were the gods of the primordial world which consisted of the waters. After the emergence of the earth floating on the waters and the subsequent creation of the organized world, the waters (*āpah, salila, samudra*) were thought of as being under the earth, as its foundation (*pratiṣṭḥa*), as well as surrounding it. Varuṇa's association with the waters, therefore, is due to the fact that the *primeval* waters along with their lord Varuṇa, have been incorporated in the cosmos as part of the nether world. Hence it is that Varuṇa is said to dwell amidst his seven sisters and that these seven rivers, when they flow from the central mountain over the earth, are said to emerge (from the *samudra* in the nether world) through Varuṇa's throat as through a hollow reed.[22]

The developing cleft in Varuṇa's characterization is related to the distinction of the "big" waters of inclusion, encompassing both being and nonbeing, from the "little" waters of the ordered, bipolar universe, demarcated by means of the creative act of splitting apart the earth and sky.

By the time of the Epic literature, Varuṇa's identification with the lower world and the subterranean waters is complete. He is known as the king or demigod of the waters and recognized as one of the four world guardians (*lokapālas*) along with Yama, Indra, and Kubera.

Previously, he had been identified with the waters in the sense of controlling them (by obstructing or releasing them), but in this later era, he comes to be a metaphor for water itself. His *loka* or domain is a watery netherworld, a refuge for slain demons[23] and various *asuras*.[24] His world is equated with the *nāgaloka,* and he himself is compared (even in the *Atharva Veda*) with a serpent.[25]

By the time of the Epics, Varuṇa has been firmly ensconced in his watery domain, given a nominal and propitiatory sovereignty over a questionable, vaguely threatening, and loosely demarcated zone of the cosmos. Like the other *lokapāla*s, he seems to stand guard over regions to which no one wants to go but from which everyone has hopes of receiving some bounty at some time. These *lokapāla*s, along with the various *kṣetrapāla*s or local guardian deities of villages and towns, function as barriers or doors "swinging both ways." While keeping unsavory elements of the disordered and demonic cosmos out of the "daytime," socially ordered, and stratified world, they also provide a sanctuary or safe harbor for those demonic outcasts.[26] They serve as officials in both worlds; hence their dubious status as symbols of eschatological ultimacy and kings of dissolute kingdoms. Of course, behind this lies the understanding that allows that evil and demons can never be totally destroyed, but must be kept at bay, especially since in many cases they are guardians of the necessary "evils" of unpredictable nature and potentially polluting sexuality. Skirmishes between the representatives of good and evil must be confined to the appropriately "militarized" zones—border areas where the two worlds collide, where territorial claims are not fully registered and the delimitation of order from chaos is an ongoing feat of demographic classification.

The career of Yama, the god of death, follows a similar trajectory to that of Varuṇa. The fearful propitiation of the latter, most prevalent in the Brāhmaṇas, was already known in the *Ṛg Veda,* where the punishing aspect of Varuṇa's rulership of law and righteousness is styled as a "curse" and is assimilated to the growing mythology of Yama, who was considered to be the first mortal to have passed over to that feared and respected kingdom over which he subsequently reigned.[27] The cosmic realism embedded in the Vedic notion of Varuṇa's and Yama's functions as impartial metaphors for necessary and revered aspects of the ordering and balancing of life and death becomes imbued with a subjective theology of terror. As guarantors of harmony, they precisely measured out "portions" of life and the justice of death that insures "space" for the living and the righteous.[28] Over time, however, these impartial judges began to be seen as avenging demons, exacting their due and dragging humans kicking and screaming into a frightful, demonized otherworld that had lost the early comfort of a welcoming abode of all of one's *pitṛ*s ("fathers") who had passed before one to death.

> Hieratical conceptions connected with the sacrificial worship of the fire were transposed to the cremation of the corpse. Heaven became the place where the deceased ancestors revelled with the gods. With the development of a more explicit theology with implicit ethical notions by the Vedic theologians the image of Yama became connected with death and judgement. The ruler over the dead became the lord of Death to whom the dead had to render account of their deeds.[29]

In post-Vedic descriptions of the world of Yama (and Varuṇa), underground imagery has been substituted for the heavenly, "upper-world" imagery of the Vedas. The association of the underworld with demons and unquiet spirits of the dead was a crucial factor in the transformation into dangerous and defiling ghosts or demons of many figures associated with the numinous and otherworldly (such as the yakṣa).

The "demotion" of Varuṇa is obviously complete by the time of the Brāhmaṇas, where he is described as "bald" and "bucktoothed," with "yellow eyes."[30] In the *Viṣṇudharmottara Purāṇa,* Varuṇa's iconography has become replete with water symbols and signatures such as seven *haṁsa*s (geese), representing the seven seas, and a *makara* for his *vāhana.* His evil aspect too has been reduced from the terrifying to the puckish, as we see him here with a potbelly (like a yakṣa and particularly like Kubera), carrying a conch shell and jewel vessel, representing the dark but abundant land of the deep.

In the Epic period, kingly symbolism was more strongly linked with Yama and also with Varuṇa (thus restoring to a small extent the royal imagery of the Vedic persona of the latter). In many cases, the two figures, Yama and Varuṇa, become conflated into one deity, Dharmarāja, or simply "Dharma," the absolutely impartial judge, reigning supreme over the kingdom of the dead. This image of kingship becomes a model in the *Mahābhārata* for the impartial, ethical perfection of the earthly ruler, who, like Varuṇa, is responsible for control of the three dimensions of *ṛta:* in his management of the generous supply of nature (particularly in the form of rain), his righteous maintenance of the social order and punishment of wrongdoers, and his patronage of sacrifice through the support of *brāhmans* and ritual celebrations.

> The ideal king who functions as a righteous judge is compared with Yama in Mbh 12. 68. 45:
>
> > When he (the king) inflicts stern punishments to all who have acted against the law (*dharma*) and when he recompenses the righteous, then he is called Yama.
>
> Yama as the impartial judge who binds the human beings by his sentence is also called King of the law (Dharmarāja) because he maintains the law by his judgement. In this respect he takes in the Epic period an important function over from Varuṇa who in the ancient texts is closely connected with the *ṛta,* the cosmological and moral order of the universe. The noose (*pāśa*) with which Varuṇa once bound the sinners becomes in the Epic texts an attribute which is characteristic of Yama.[31]

The splitting, recombining, and sharing of aspects by Yama and Varuṇa, as well as other deities of the "second string" Hindu pantheon, may relate to dual interpretations of the chthonic realm that they come to represent. In some contexts, this category of the chthonic is expressed as one large domain of the underworld, and in other contexts, it is separated into two distinct classifications, split along an important line of demarcation distinguishing the "good" underworld from the "bad." It is this dialectic of inclusive versus exclusive categories within a complex structure that is operative in the mythology and theology of the god Śiva as well. He also partakes of the contradictory symbolism of the dark, the otherworldly, the earth, and death. In the Indian *mythos,* it may, in fact, be just this capacity to constellate many complementary and contradictory aspects that characterizes these enduring gods. The acknowledged tendency of such transcendent and complex deities to split into the many functions and aspects that they encompass is compensated for, on the one hand, by the multiplicity of myths that accrue to their personalities, each set in a corpus expressing (often) radically diverse qualities and, on the other hand, by the useful proliferation of innumerable demigods who can, with their own iconographies and mythologies, fill in for the major god or expand his province of power into a particular geographical region or theological debate (which is not to imply the necessary chronological priority of great over little and universal over local).

In this chapter I have tried to establish a historical and textual basis for understanding the yakṣa's transformation from beneficence to maleficence. We have noted that the Vedic references to the yakṣa describe a deity who encompassed both manifest and unmanifest, immanent and transcendent dimensions. Because of the yakṣa's* affinity with a particular natural element (water), this synthesis, though compelling, proved to be difficult to sustain. The pattern of rupture between these uneasily conjoined domains is illustrated by the career of the Vedic god Varuṇa, whose close association with the waters and their attendant symbolism, characteristic employment of *māyā,* and fall from the stature of a great god to that of a demigod are comparable to aspects of the yakṣa's career. One cycle of texts, which we will fully explore in the next chapter, specifically treats the theme of the uneasy but important conjunction of the yakṣa as a local divinity of the water with the universal god of righteousness Dharma (who is equated, as we have seen, with Varuṇa and Yama).

*Unlike the later Hindu great gods, Viṣṇu and Śiva, who do encompass both dimensions.

Chapter 3

TRIAL BY WATER IN HINDU AND BUDDHIST TEXTS

Introduction

In this chapter, I will explore a group of (four) myths that embodies the network of associations that I have been building. In these myths, drawn from the *Mahābhārata* and the Jātakas, there is a clear fusion of references to the yakṣa, Varuṇa, Yama, Dharmarāja, *ṛta,* and water. All of them disclose a fundamental aspect of kingship, the "initiatory ordeal,"[1] in which the worldly ruler must be tested by a chthonic ruler, represented in two variants by yakṣas, in one by a *nāga,* and in the other by the god Varuṇa himself. In all of the variants, the testing of the ruler or hero by the watery guardian is effected by means of *māyā,* which, as we have indicated, is a primary attribute of yakṣas, *nāga*s, and Varuṇa. All of these texts entertain the problem of how the power of illusion and deception that the guardians of the water possess can be used to test the cleverness and righteousness of the king or hero. In all four stories, the demonic character presides over a fertile, mysterious, and treacherous watery domain. In each case, the hero must confront the deity at the frontier of his aquatic kingdom and win back beloved relatives who have been abducted and concealed.

In considering these myths together, I seem to be violating the ordering principle of treating Buddhist and Jain yakṣa references separately (in Chapter 4). In this case, however, the comparison of the Epic and Jātaka variants is not only justified but essential. This will be demonstrated in the course of interpreting the myth cycle. That the Jātaka story of the *bodhisatta* and the yakkha is based on a source from which the Yakṣapraśna episode of the *Mahābhārata* is also drawn is, I think, obvious from the blatant similarities. The different applications of the common tale of the yakṣa in the water, in the Hindu as opposed to the Buddhist context, bespeak a fundamentally different synthesis made by the two traditions, of local and more universal religious modalities.

The symbolic universe that these myths share is formed of overlapping images and themes: of the element of water, ruled over by the god Varuṇa; of local bodies of water, controlled by fierce despots, yakṣas and *nāgas*, who must be appeased if their kingdom is trespassed upon; of naughty gods and beneficent demons; of trickery, concealment, and abduction; of the testing of bravery and righteousness; of the disclosure of the rightful ruler, hero, or king; of the relationship of the chaotic, the unknown, the primitive, and the bestial to the rational, the just, the civilized, and the ideal.

Two of the texts, *Mbh* 3. 178. 29–45 and *Mbh* 3. 295. 1–25, are exact parallels, being an example of the "rehearsal" structural motif that often occurs in the Epics. In this particular narrative motif, a story may be the precursor of another that is identical in structure and meaning, but less intense and less important, due to the use of minor characters.[2] In the first tale I will discuss, the demonic being encountered is a *nāga;* in the second, it is a yakṣa. And though the format of the two myths is the same, as we will see, the yakṣa is in fact a high personage and the encounter with him is the turning point in the whole narrative, firmly establishing Yudhiṣṭhira as the ruler of the earth and lord of *dharma*. Both are examples of the essential testing of the king, a motif that is a central aspect of the body of yakṣa myths and legends.

The testing *nāga*

The Pāṇḍavas have been wandering through the mountains and forests for twelve years and are now living on Mount Yāmuna. It is there that Bhīma, while roaming about the idyllic woods, is seized by a hungry snake who keeps him immobile within his massive coils. Amazed by the strength of a serpent who is capable of subduing the fierce Bhīmasena, heretofore unvanquished by "*dānavas*," "*piśācas*," or "*rākṣasas*," Bhīma questions the *nāga* about its origins, not believing it to be an ordinary snake. Like so many demonic characters in the classical Indian narratives, it has assumed its form due to a curse. In this case, the accursed one was formerly a king whose great sin was the kicking of a *brāhman*, for which he was punished by being afflicted by his present lowly and malevolent form. Meanwhile, Yudhiṣṭhira, worried and searching for his bother, comes upon the unique sight of Bhīma captured by the serpent-foe. Yudhiṣṭhira is equally incredulous about the true nature of the amazing beast, and to him, the snake pours out the story of his fall and also says that he will release Bhīma if Yudhiṣṭhira is able to answer the questions he will put to him. The snake asks Yudhiṣṭhira, "Who is a *brāhman* and what does he know?" Yudhiṣṭhira replies that one knows a *brāhman* by his virtuous conduct; the snake counters that this implies that birth and caste are irrelevant, and surely this can't be correct. Yudhiṣṭhira holds to his argument and convinces the *nāga,* quoting Manu Svayambhuva: "Continuation of caste has to do with what has been accomplished. If no conduct can be observed, it is assumed that there is an overwhelming confusion [mixing] of castes, Oh Indra of snakes."[3] The snake goes on to lecture Yudhiṣṭhira about the constituents of consciousness, and the king, overwhelmed by the serpent's knowledge, questions him still further about the course of events that has put him where he is:

> How could blindness take possession of you while dwelling in heaven, omniscient and capable of supernatural feats? I don't understand this.
>
> The snake answered:
>
> No matter how wise or strong he may be, success causes a man to go astray. My thought is that no one who is intent on pleasure is capable of understanding.
>
> The madness and delusion of power seized me, Yudhiṣṭhira, and having fallen, I am now restored to consciousness and will now enlighten you.
>
> You did what was necessary for me, Oh King. By my talking with you, the curse is now completely expended.
>
> I used to travel about in heaven in a celestial chariot. I was so drunk with power that I was completely oblivious of everyone else.
>
> The inhabitants of the three worlds, *brāhman* seers, gods, *gandharvas*, yakṣas, *rākṣasas*, *kinnāras*, all paid taxes to me.
>
> On whatever creature my eye might chance to fall, I would take away his glory. Such was the power of my glance.
>
> A thousand *brāhman* seers carried my palanquin and it was this wicked behavior that caused me to fall from glory.

> For right there, while carrying me, the wise *brāhman* Agastya was touched by my foot. And then, an unseen angry person called out, "Perish, you snake!"
>
> Whereupon, my ornaments fell away and I was expelled from that grand chariot. As I was falling, I realized that I had become a snake, suspended upside down.
>
> I begged him, "Let there be an end to this curse quickly. You are able, *bhagavan,* to pardon me of this act which was the result of my ignorance."
>
> So, being merciful, he said to me as I fell, "Yudhiṣṭhira, the king of *dharma,* will free you from the curse.
>
> Lord of men, when the fruits of aggressiveness, wrath, and pride have withered away, then you will gain the fruit of purity."
>
> I was amazed then, having seen the power of that which was born of austerity [meaning the *brāhman*'s understanding] and so I have questioned you about *brāhman* and *brāhman*hood.
>
> Truth, the practice of self-restraint, yoga, non-violence, and eternal charity are always the factors which are fulfilling for human beings, not birth or family.
>
> Your long-armed brother, Bhīma, is free, King. Good luck to you, great ruler. I will now return to heaven."
>
> With these words, King Nahuṣa abandoned his snake's body and assumed his divine form as he went back to heaven.[4]

The testing yakṣa

The central motif in the preceding episode of the examination of the king's knowledge of *dharma,* in particular his correct assessment of caste values (the incorrect treatment of which was the cause of Nahuṣa's downfall), is echoed and expanded in the following version of these related myths. This piece is found at the end of the Vana Parvan and concerns the magical demise of four of the Pāṇḍava brothers as the result of the drinking of enchanted water. Having been approached by a distraught *brāhman* whose implements for the performance of the *agnihotra* sacrifice have been spirited away on the antlers of a deer, the five Pāṇḍava brothers go deep into the forest in search of the *brāhman*'s fire sticks and churning staff. They follow the deer but are unable to kill it, and finally it mysteriously disappears. The Pāṇḍavas, stricken by hunger, thirst, and exhaustion, stop in the forest. Nākula climbs a tree to search for some source of water or for trees that might be growing near water. He sees a spot that is surrounded by trees, and he hears the sound of cranes. Yudhiṣṭhira requests that he go and bring water back for the rest. Nākula finds a beautiful lake and eagerly prepares to drink. A voice from the sky, however, forbids him to drink of this water until he has first answered a series of questions. Nākula disregards the voice, drinks the water, and drops dead on the spot. When Nākula has been missed, Yudhiṣṭhira charges his half-brother, Sahadeva (Nākula's full-brother), to go in search of him and the water. The same thing, however, befalls him, and Yudhiṣṭhira charges Arjuna and Bhīma separately with the same mission, and both of them die in turn of the cursed water. Finally, Yudhiṣṭhira alone goes in search of his four brothers and comes to the lake, where he sees all of them lying dead. He begins to lament and wonder at the bloodless demise of these, the strongest of heroes.

> Yudhiṣṭhira thought:
>
> "How could this water be contaminated by poison when, though they appear to be dead, there is no visible change in their bodies? Their color seems normal to me.
>
> Each one of these was like a mighty stream. Who, except Yama who is the end of time when one's appointed time has come, could be a match for these brave men?"
>
> Overwhelmed by this turn of events, he immersed himself and, while plunging into the water, he heard these words from the sky, spoken by a yakṣa:
>
> "I am a crane who eats Śaivala fish. I have taken these four to the region of death; you will become the fifth, Oh King, if you don't answer my questions. Do not act rashly; all of this property is already mine. When you have answered my questions, Oh Son of Kuntī, then drink and take as much water as you like."
>
> Yudhiṣṭhira answered:
>
> "Are you the most excellent of the Rudras, or the Vasus, or the Maruts? I ask you what kind of a god you are. No bird did this.
>
> Who has been able to fell the four mighty mountains (the Himavat, the Pariyātrā, the Vindhya, and the Malaya)?

This is an exceedingly great feat which you have done, Oh Mightiest of the Mighty. You have slain even these great archers, my family.

Neither gods, nor *gandharvas*, nor *asuras*, nor *rākṣasas* could subdue them in the heat of battle, but you have done it.

I do not know what your business is nor do I know what you want.

The great curiosity and fear which have overtaken me have made my heart unsteady and my head feverish. Who are you, I ask, and why do you dwell here?"

The yakṣa spoke:

"I am a yakṣa, if you please. I am not a water fowl. I have detained and killed all of your brothers."

When he heard this painful speech with its harsh words, the king trembled while standing before the yakṣa who spoke it.

This yakṣa had an enormous body like the elephant Virupakṣa who holds up the surface of the earth. As bright as the sun, as high as a mountain, he was disquieting and overwhelming.

Yudhiṣṭhira, the descendant of Bhārata, saw him standing there. After the yakṣa had established his boundary, he made a loud rumbling sound like a threatening rain cloud.

The yakṣa said to the son of Kuntī who was grieved because of his brothers:

"Oh King, I repeatedly warned these brothers of yours. These boys wanted to take my water away and so I had to kill them. King, if they wanted to live, they should not have drunk this water.

Oh Pārtha, do not act rashly; this water already belongs to me. First answer my questions, Son of Kuntī, and then drink and take as much as you like."

Yudhiṣṭhira answered:

"Yakṣa, I do not want what is already yours. True men always despise covetousness.

Therefore, I will answer your questions; go ahead and ask."[5]

The questions with which the yakṣa tests Yudhiṣṭhira constitute a thorough examination of the religious, social, and moral precepts that must be held and exercised by a wise ruler and pragmatic man. These riddles, the tone of which is homilistic rather than metaphysical, are about *brāhmans*, virtue, sacrifice, cosmology, and agriculture. Yudhiṣṭhira is able to answer all of the yakṣa's questions without hesitation, and when he is satisfied with Yudhiṣṭhira's moral perfection, he bids the king choose one of his brothers to be brought back to life. Without a pause, Yudhiṣṭhira chooses his half-brother, Nākula. The yakṣa is amazed that he would choose him over his own two "uterine" brothers.

> "Men say that Bhīmasena is dear to you. Then, for what reason do you want your half-brother to live?
>
> Forsaking Arjuna, whom all of the Pāṇḍavas honor for his strong arm, why do you want Nākula to be revived?"
>
> Yudhiṣṭhira said:
>
> "He who destroys *dharma* is destroyed; he who protects *dharma* is protected. I will not forsake *dharma,* and having destroyed it, have it destroy us.
>
> Compassion is considered to be the best *dharma* and the highest truth. I will endeavor to practice compassion. Yakṣa, let Nākula live.
>
> Let men know that I, the king, am always disposed to *dharma*. I will not veer from my duties. Yakṣa, let Nākula live.
>
> My father had two wives, Kuntī and Mādrī. Let them both have sons. That is my wish.
>
> As Kuntī, so Mādrī; there is no difference between them to me. I want equality for both mothers. Yakṣa, let Nākula live."
>
> The yakṣa said:
>
> "Since devotion to compassion is higher to you than profit or pleasure, therefore, let all of your brother live, Oh Bull among Men."
>
> Then, because of those words of the yakṣa, the Pāṇḍavas got up and in a moment their hunger and thirst disappeared.
>
> Yudhiṣṭhira said:
>
> "I ask you who stands tirelessly on one leg in the tank, what god are you? You don't seem to me to be a yakṣa.
>
> Are you the foremost of the Vasus or the chief of the Rudras? Or are you the best of the Maruts or the lord of the three directions himself, the wielder of the thunderbolt?

> Are you our friend, sir, or perhaps our father?"
>
> The yakṣa answered:
>
> "Child, I am *your* father, Dharma, possessed of power and gentleness. Oh Bull of the Bhāratas, know that I came here with a desire to see you.
>
> Fame, truth, self-restraint, purity, honesty, modesty, steadiness, charity, asceticism, chastity; these are my body.
>
> Non-violence, impartiality, peacefulness, purity, and detachment are the doors leading to me. Know that you are my beloved son.
>
> I am Dharma, if you please. I have come here to test you.
>
> I am pleased with your compassion. I will give you a boon, Oh Sinless One."[6]

The yakṣa in this text is connected to Varuṇa, in that he encompasses and exemplifies both the natural and the moral senses of order (*ṛta*). In his role of protector of the natural order, the yakṣa presides fiercely over the specific forest locale and the water that nurtures and empowers it. He protects that place in the person of one of his own creatures; he is the beast in the water, the crane swooping over the lake. In the guise of local, forest deity, however, he is bound by his own fetters, so to speak. The outer limits of the natural order lie dangerously close to bestiality and abrogation of the order established in the centers of human society. The ultimate harmony of these divergent senses of order must be maintained by the king who is responsible for the protection of the entire earth in its need for the blessings and bounty of nature and for the active presence of social justice. The balance of these two basic concerns is precarious, and as this text indicates, cannot be maintained in a simple fifty-fifty fashion. At the outermost limit of the social order, the righteous ruler must bring back with him from his test two things: a modicum of the bestial empowerment of the waters of truth and the deity who protects them, and a rededication to the ultimate triumph of justice and impartiality over that which is purely local, natural, and bound by ties of blood alone. It is this capacity for the assertion of royal impartiality and compassion that is being tested in Yudhiṣṭhira by the yakṣa. He is questioned on every conceivable aspect of *dharma*, and finally he is given the ultimate test of his ability to rule fairly: Can he put aside his stronger affinities for his full blood-brothers to honor a moral principle that would first grant life to those who are less closely related? It is a dilemma that is close to the very heart of the *kṣatriya*'s predicament. He must respect and fight for the concerns that have been dictated by his familial affiliations, and yet in order to be the ruler of a people, these concerns must be transmuted into a broader category of ethical commitments.

The *Bodhisatta* and the yakkha

In the Jātaka version of the myth, we can recognize the familiar Indian theme that is so central to the *Rāmāyaṇa* in particular: The second wife of the king makes an insidious and unjust demand that the right of succession pass over the legitimate heir, the eldest son, and devolve upon her own son, the youngest heir of the king.

The *Devadhamma Jātaka* version relates the story of a king who has two sons by a first wife: Prince Mahiṅsāsa, who is the *bodhisatta,*[7] and the younger, Moon Prince. Their mother dies and the king remarries. The second wife gives birth to a delightful boy, the Sun Prince. The king, in the excess of his joy at the third son's birth, promises his wife a boon. She doesn't claim the boon immediately but waits until her son is grown and then asks that the king grant this youngest son the rule of the entire kingdom. Out of love for and fairness to his other two sons, the king refuses his wife's request. He realizes, though, that this wife will probably continue to plot against the other boys, and so he sends them into the forest to remain until he is dead, at which time they are to come back to rule over their rightful kingdom. The younger son hears of this plan and runs away to join his exiled brothers in the forest. At a certain point in their forest exile, they stop for a rest and the *bodhisatta* sends the Sun Prince to a nearby pond for water for their use. The pond is ruled by a demonic being called variously, "yakkha" (yakṣa), "*rakkhasa*" (*rākṣasa*), and "*dakarakkha*" (*udakarakṣa?*). The pond has been given over to the yakkha by Vessavana (Vaiśravaṇa or Kubera), the king of the *vidyadhāra*s,[8] who has permitted the yakkha to detain and ultimately to devour anyone who enters the water and cannot properly answer the question of what true divinity (*devadhamma*) is. When the Sun Prince approaches the water, he is immediately seized by the yakkha and asked this question. He answers by saying that the sun, the moon, and the gods are truly divine. He has not answered correctly, and the yakkha takes him down into a cave where he is bound. After a while, the *bodhisatta* sends his full brother, the Moon Prince, to look for the other brother and to bring back water. He too meets the same fate and answers the yakkha's question with "the far-spreading sky." This too is incorrect, and the Moon Prince is also seized. The *bodhisatta* finally goes in search of his brothers. He, unlike the others, realizes immediately that the pond must be haunted by a supernatural being, and he does not go into the water. The yakkha, taking the form of a woodsman,[9] tries to persuade the Prince-*bodhisatta* to enter the water and refresh himself (as the limits of the yakkha's demonic power extend only to those who actually enter the water), but the *bodhisatta* is aware of the woodsman's real identity and accuses him of taking his two brothers. The *bodhisatta* says that he will answer the question about *devadhamma* but cannot do so until he has been bathed and refreshed with food, water, and unguents. The yakkha is persuaded to do all of this and finally sits at the *bodhisatta*'s feet to hear him recite this verse:

> With shame and fear for sin,
> with minds settled in the good *dhamma*,
> these are the righteous men in the world
> who are to be called the truly divine.[10]

Immediately, the yakkha is repentant and offers to return one of the brothers, leaving it to the *bodhisatta* to decide which one. The *bodhisatta* chooses his half-brother, the Sun Prince. The yakkha says:

> "Teacher, you know all about the true divinity, yet you don't practice it."
>
> "In what way?"
>
> "Having abandoned the elder, you send me for the younger; you do not practice the honor that is due those of greater age."
>
> "Yakkha, I know what true divinity is and I also practice it. It is on account of the boy that we entered the forest. For his sake, his mother asked our father for the kingdom. However, our father did not give him the boon and ordered us to go into the forest for our own protection. The young prince did not stay in the palace, but came along with us. If I were to say that some yakkha had eaten him in the forest, nobody would believe it. It is for this reason that I have sent you for him."[11]

The yakkha is moved and brings forth both of the boys. The *bodhisatta* tells the demon that he (the yakkha) has taken his present form because of evil deeds in a previous lifetime and that he should put aside wrongdoing forever. The yakkha readily agrees to this and is converted to Buddhism on the spot. Prince Mahiṁsāsa perceives, by means of a conjunction of the stars, that his father has died, and he prepares to return to his kingdom.

> So, he took the yakkha and went to receive his kingdom. He gave the Moon Price the office of viceroy and the Sun Prince the command of the army, and he made a home for the yakkha in a pleasant spot and took care that he received the best garlands and best flowers and best food. Thus, he ruled the kingdom with righteousness until he passed away according to his deeds.[12]

In this variant of the yakṣa-king tale, the moral complexities have been greatly simplified, or perhaps obscured. The yakkha's connections to the vitality of nature have been ignored until the very last section of the story, when he is taken back to the kingdom and installed in a *caitya*. This installation of the yakkha is commonly considered to constitute an active assimilation on the part of the figure of the Buddha (and the institution of Buddhism) of the indispensable dimension of the wilderness, the unexplored, the profusion of nature, and particularly, the bounty associated with the waters in the form of plentiful rainfall. All of these factors and the powers that they confer upon the patron of the converted or tamed yakkha are symbolized by the *caitya* or throne that the king erects.[13]

The element of the story that transforms the potential moral ambiguity of the yakṣa legend is the figure of the *bodhisatta* himself, in whom moral perfection is presupposed. When he converts the yakkha, the myth crosses over into the category of moral fable, which is, of course, what the Jātaka tales essentially are. The yakkha *was* demonic prior to his conversion, and afterward, he is good and beneficial to the kingdom. The logos principle that illuminates the Jātaka narrative is fixed in the very being of the *bodhisatta*. As we can see, his actual teaching lacks the explanatory appeal that Yudhiṣṭhira's responses possess. Beyond this, of course, the larger frame of each tale is the teaching of Śākyamuni Buddha for whom these stories are parables, illustrating to the *saṃgha* (the Buddhist monastic community) often very tangentially related points of ethical concern. A vestige of the frightening unknown—the moral and cultural wilderness that is to some extent the setting of the *Mahābhārata* variant—is present in the *bodhisatta*-prince's treatment of his brothers when he charges them to go out into the forest to search for water. Though he tells the yakkha that the Sun Prince's welfare is his primary concern, the fact is that he has sent him (even before his blood brother) into danger. Of course, the sending of the brothers, one after another, is a well-known folk motif that serves the narrative purpose of building steadily toward the resolution that only the hero can finally effect. Still, in the latter two variants, the psychologically suspicious sibling complications add an important emotional dimension to the working out of the ethical implications. In the second *Mahābhārata* tale, Yudhiṣṭhira's remorseful pain carries a hint of the guilt that must certainly be an aspect of the tale of fraternal justice. This facet has been passed over completely in the Jātaka version, which makes the *bodhisatta*'s inexplicable behavior seem all the more questionable.

Varuṇa as yakṣa

In the third *Mahābhārata* text, the final one to be considered in this cycle, we move slightly away from the structure we have been exploring. In the other two myths, the fierceness and bestiality of the yakṣa fit more closely the universal paradigm of the heroic encounter with the magical beast, the dragon, or the genie—the supreme test of the bravery, humanity, and self-confidence of the noble hero. In the following text, the guardian of the waters is not a yakṣa per se, but the god Varuṇa himself. The issues involved here are not fraternal rivalries and justice toward one's charges, but rather, the very old issue of legitimate sexual claims and ownership, encompassing the classical Indian delineation of the types of marriage, ranging from abduction and ravishment to the traditional, familially sanctioned variety. These two major themes are certainly not unrelated, as the example again of the *Rāmāyaṇa* proves, in which both themes are inextricably connected and vitally important. The following text extols the resourcefulness and bravery of the *brāhman,* Utathya, who was able to stand up to the misadventures of the god Varuṇa.

> The wind god said to Arjuna: Listen, king, to the story of Utathya who was born in the race and family of Aṅgiras.

Bhadrā, who was the daughter of Soma, was thought to be unrivalled in beauty. Some considered Utathya to be a suitable husband for her.

And that illustrious and fortunate girl undertook severe austerities so that she might marry the lucky Utathya.

Then, having sacrificed, her father gave the glorious maiden to Utathya. And the bridegroom, who offered all sorts of sumptuous presents, took her for his wife.

But it just so happened that Lord Varuṇa had desired her for a long time. And coming to their forest retreat, he seized her as she was bathing in the Yamunā river.

And having carried her off, the Lord of the Waters took her to his own abode, the magical mansions of 6100 rays of light [lightning].

These many mansions filled with heavenly Apsarases and splendid objects of enjoyment can not be surpassed in the pleasure they afford.

There, inside, Oh King, the Lord of the Waters dallied with her. Then, Utathya became aware of his wife's abduction.

After he heard the whole story from Nārada, Utathya spoke to him "Go to Varuṇa and speak harshly to him for me, saying, 'Why have you stolen my wife?'

Tell him, 'You are a *lokapāla* [world protector] not a *vilopaka* [ravisher]. Soma gave me my wife, but now you've carried her off.' "

Nārada addressed the Lord of the Waters with this command: "Release Utathya's wife," and Varuṇa answered him: "This beauty is my wife now; I cannot bear to let her go."

When he heard this, Nārada went back to Utathya and said, "Never before have I been treated like that.

Oh Great Seer, he grabbed me by the throat and threw me out. He is not going to give your wife back. Take any course of action you please."

When he heard Nārada's speech, the descendant of Aṅgiras was furious. So, that extraordinary ascetic used his energy and, having settled the waters, he drank them.

When Utathya had drunk all of the waters, the Lord of the Waters was irritated and became abusive to those around him. But even so, he still did not release her.

> Then, the furious Utathya, the best of *brāhmans*, spoke to the earth: "Please show me the place where the 6100 rays of light are." Then the ocean crept back, creating a desert, and that excellent *brāhman* spoke to the river of his region.
>
> "Go secretly, timid Sarasvatī, to the desert. Oh fair one, leave this region bereft of virtue."
>
> When that region was completely destroyed, the Protector of the Waters was brought to his knees and he gave Utathya's wife back to him and went back to his own abode.
>
> And when Utathya got her back, he became content and released Varuṇa from this all-pervasive misery.
>
> Then when that possessor of *dharma,* Utathya, with his extraordinary energy, took back his wife, he said to Varuṇa, "Listen to what I have to say, Oh Lord of Men.
>
> Oh Lord of the Waters, I have accomplished this with my *tapa*s and made you yelp with pain." Having said this, he took his wife to his own abode.
>
> Thus, Oh King, was Utathya, the best of *brāhmans*. So I have answered you. Now you tell me, is there a *kṣatriya* who is better then Utathya?[14]

Knowing what we do about Varuṇa and his guardianship of universal justice, this text seems extremely ironic. In fact, it may be a myth about irony. Varuṇa here displays all of his attributes, only turned inside out or utilized in the service of mischief rather than good. All of the qualities we associate with him are present: his control of the waters, his binding propensities, his lordliness, his stealth and use of illusion, his omniscience. The only attribute that is missing is the important integrating faculty—of preserving the moral order. In the matter of morality, justice, and *dharma,* Varuṇa has not lived up to his early reputation.

The closer we look at this myth, the more apparent it is that, in a sense, it is a parody of the format and sensibilities displayed in the other *Mahābhārata* texts. The yakṣa who tested Yudhiṣṭhira is a local deity who grew beyond his demigod limitations to become a great and wise deity, the patron of *dharma*. Varuṇa, who has disgraced Utathya and violated his wife, is a guardian of justice who has slipped from his high estate and is dangerously close to becoming a garden variety yakṣa again. The testing of the king is underscored ironically in the myth about Varuṇa and Utathya. The message is clear: The king is very vulnerable indeed; even Varuṇa, a universal divine monarch, can backslide and lapse into lustfulness and swaggering, warrior bravado. Comparisons to Indra come immediately to mind and seem particularly pertinent to the picture of the voluptuary king that we have seen in this text. Indra, the Vedic king of the gods, rules with lusty abandon and often with despotic disregard for the established rules of moral and sexual conduct. His kingliness is attributed to his physical power, his wanton cunning, and his heroic bravery and prowess, not to his wisdom or sense of justice. The Vedic models of Indra and Varuṇa, in fact, represent two notions of kingliness that are subject to constant reevaluation and recombination in the myriad myths about kings and kingly behavior found in Indian literature. It is just this process of analysis and reevaluation that can be observed in our examination of these four particular texts.

There are two opposing, but equally dangerous extremes to which a king may revert. On the one hand, he may lose, or not have developed yet, a strong sense of impartial justice, in which case he will be in danger of acting out of familial biases and/or passionate and unlawful desires. With the power of his office, he may fall to bestiality, brutality, and despotism. On the other hand, he may become cold, aloof, and removed from the basic needs and concerns of his people. Lost in affairs of state, he will be unable to fulfill his function as guardian of nature and guarantor of material providence.

Trial by water continued: moral conclusions

In all four myths, we can see that the demonic guardian of the waters (yakṣa, *nāga,* or Varuṇa) is a frightening and powerful figure, the extent of whose fearfulness and power is perceived by the human hero in each tale to be limited and possible to traverse by means of clear thinking, clever retorts, and righteous behavior. In each case, the watery domain that is overseen by the attending deity seems impassable and far-reaching because of the dark concealment of its inner recesses. In each case, however, the watery world is tamed and deprived of its imprisoning power; the captivating deity releases his prisoners in the face of the superior cunning and understanding of the hero. The kingdom of water is found not to be endless and binding; its power is circumscribed and localized. Although in the final variant Varuṇa is lord of all of the waters, the universal sovereign of the watery kingdom in its full extent, even he is tamed by the chastising power of asceticism (*tapas*), which is highly developed in Utathya.

This brings us back again to the two notions of kingship, exemplified in the Vedic cosmology by Varuṇa and Indra and in our texts by Yudhiṣṭhira and Varuṇa. The two notions correspond to two aspects of power that are inherent qualities of the monarch's effectiveness: knowledge (or justice) and force (or aggression). It is precisely this effective knowledge that is being tested in the king in three of our texts and in the *brāhman* Utathya in the final example. The split in the classical image of the king occurs along this particular cleft between aggression and justice, two qualities that are subsumed by the larger classification of "*kṣatriya.*" As we can see in the Varuṇa-Utathya episode, the knowledge-justice aspect has split off from the kingliness of Varuṇa and has been assimilated to a *brāhman*ical attribute that is posited in Utathya. In the yakṣa-Yudhiṣṭhira episode, we can see even more clearly how the splitting and reintegration along the opposition in kingship occur. In this case, the opposition is camouflaged by *māyā:* The yakṣa *was* local and demonic, but presto, now he is universal and totally ethical. The contradiction is subsumed by the abstraction, "water," a medium that contains both local and universal, destructive and beneficent properties.

The union of the elemental and the moral is obviously fundamental and yet extremely difficult to sustain as is demonstrated in the characters of both the king/hero and the yakṣa/demon in all four variants. Varuṇa, despite his elaborated symbolism and more elusive and complex theological application, is, *au fond,* a Vedic nature deity who is doomed to relinquish his universal rulership when the element he is linked with is stripped of its universal associations. It is a complex mythological and religious problem, in which the deity is empowered precisely because of his association with a primary element and yet is also limited in his power by that association; the most powerful gods in the pantheon are not tied to or hampered by any particular element or function.

What is particularly fascinating in the comparison of these texts is the way in which the theme of the moral instigation of the yakṣa deity has been differently employed. In the first text, the *nāga* serves primarily as catalyst and negative moral example, providing an instance of what may happen to the king who misuses his power. The bestial potential of the *kṣatriya* is "acted out" by the king Nahuṣa, who becomes a serpent because of his "venomous" behavior. In the second *Mahābhārata* text, the yakṣa, in his association with Varuṇa as a manifested principle of moral and natural order, is a standard against which the truthfulness of the king is being measured. The magical propensities of the yakṣa are integral to both his destructive and creative activities: After he has brought the brothers back to life and revealed his true identity as Dharma (a variant name for Varuṇa), he tells them that he took the form of the deer who initially stole the *brāhman*'s sacrificial implements. He, in fact, has magically instigated the whole series of events that have led to his own self-revelation and the revelation of Yudhiṣṭḥira as the authentic son of Dharma and deserved king. The moral ambiguity of the text is clarified and "saved" by the ultimate insight that this yakṣa is, in fact, no ordinary yakṣa. As a lower divinity or *devatā,* the yakṣa is problematical. His magic consists of more than the ability to enchant and enslave (which is what it is confined to in the *Devadhamma Jātaka* and in the *Mahābhārata* myth about Varuṇa and Utathya); this yakṣa is truly omniscient and his manipulations of reality are justified by his ultimate connection with a higher order of divinity and morality. He is the very personification of an ordering principle that encompasses both the moral and natural dimensions. This is an important conjunction that is inherent in the very meaning of *dharma* and made more explicit in its association with Yama, the personification of death. This difficult opposition in the yakṣa—of the creative and the demonic—is reified by his link with Dharma. The mixture of fear and affection that is felt for the yakṣa is made, over all, acceptable by means of the deity/principle, Dharma, who also embodies this conjunction of the beneficent and the cruel, and yet, over all, is obviously a positive deity. Moreover, it is fitting that Dharma should be Yudhiṣṭḥira's father/patron. The king must administer justice within the context of the complexities of social justice where the acknowledged norms still inflict pain upon certain members of society. This state of affairs is characterized in Yudhiṣṭḥira's decision to revive his half-brother, Nākula, rather than either of his two full brothers. The moral and natural orders are in conflict here, and yet the final message is clear: If one remains steadfastly true to the moral order, the recalcitrant natural order will also fall in line; even the dead may awaken.

This priority of the moral over the natural is also conveyed in the

Devadhamma Jātaka, in which the powerful demonic yakṣa is converted to the Buddhist Dharma. What is significantly different in the Buddhist version is that the magical and the *dharm*ic cannot be conjoined in any being other than the *bodhisatta,* who is capable of reading events in the placement of the stars and of outwitting the evil magician, the yakkha. There can be nothing sacred or genuinely moral about a being who has not been formally converted to the Dharma (as the body of Buddhist doctrine). Wisdom and sorcery cannot coexist in a single personage as they do in the preceding text. When the yakkha is converted by the *bodhisatta,* he is tamed and brought back to civilization and installed in a symbolic wilderness of his own. The natural order exists within the larger and more powerful dimension of social justice and political efficacy. In this text, the device of the yakkha's testing is employed more as a narrative tool than as a significant philosophical motif. In fact, the yakkha does not test the *bodhisatta* at all; it is precisely the other way around (as, in fact, it is with Varuṇa and Utathya). The *bodhisatta* is the absolute against which all standards of justice and knowledge are to be gauged. The yakkha relinquishes his claim, established by magical means, and surrenders them to the *bodhisatta,* who manipulates the yakkha into bringing the princes back, rather than convincing him with his brilliance and erudition as Yudhiṣṭhira does.

The examination of these basically similar texts reveals a web of significance that underlies the individual examples in the cycle. The importance of the comparative approach has been brought to light especially by a reading of Lowell Bloss's article, "The Buddha and the Nāga: A Study in Buddhist Folk Religiosity," which examines only the Buddhist context of the mythical figure.

> A more detailed analysis of these myths reveals that the chaotic or ambiguous side of the nāga and the yakṣa was accentuated by the Buddhists in order to illustrate the Buddha's compassionate activity and superior power. There is a hint in each of these myths that the nāga in human form or the yakṣas of a certain territory were at one time fulfilling their function of supplying the correct amount of rain or children to a specific region.[15]

This seems to me to be a slight misperception, in light of a thorough reading of the *Mahābhārata* texts. While it is true that in the *Devadhamma Jātaka* the negative side of the yakṣa is exclusively depicted until his final conversion to Buddhism, the impact of this emphasis is more extensive even than Bloss's thesis would indicate. It is not simply that the numerous local folk deities did not receive their proper due in the Buddhist reworking of elements of folk religiosity, but also that the reduction of the yakṣa and *nāga* represented a more basic cosmological and metaphysical shift—even further in the direction of the bowdlerization of myths containing fundamental moral and cosmological paradoxes. These paradoxes were problematic in the Hindu context as well as in the Buddhist and, of course, there were other agendas to be addressed by the Hindu rationalizations of ancient notions. But in the *Mahābhārata* variants at any rate, the rationalization of the mysterious, shifting nature of the divinity remains partially, but significantly, unresolved; and it is precisely in this inability or reluctance to resolve the deity into a tame, ethically unambiguous pet, that the persistent power of the moral example and the Epic narrative resides.

Since all of the important Indian gods have necessarily complex, many-faceted natures, it is not the fusion of contradictions alone that is responsible for the "demonization" of Varuṇa. In fact, there has been much discussion about how such gods as Śiva are, in many cases, indistinct from demons. It is, however, as we have seen, the uniquely ill-fated combination of stern moral retaliativeness, equation with a particular terrestrial element, employment of unseemly stealth and magic, the compromising association with death, and the moral ambiguity of the king in his dual roles of warrior and sage-father that are responsible for the fall of Varuṇa from the moral heights of the Vedic pantheon to the depths of the Epic *rasātala* or subterranean underworld.

The increasingly difficult encompassment of the three dimensions of *ṛta* (natural, social, and sacrificial) with which Varuṇa (a king among the Vedic gods) was linked is analogous to the problematic reign over those three domains by the earthly sovereign. The analogy was exemplified in this chapter by the interpretive treatment of four related myths, all of which establish a legitimacy for the guardian of the earthly order, which must be wrested from the divine, but morally ambiguous, guardian of the waters, of which the preeminent example is, we suggest, the yakṣa.

Chapter 4

THE YAKṢA IN BUDDHIST AND JAIN REPRESENTATIONS AND THOUGHT

Buddhist Cosmology and Myth

As we are beginning to see, the range of conceptions of the yakṣa and, by implication, the demonic can and should be analyzed synchronically *and* diachronically. Whereas within each particular period and tradition certain concepts, concerns, and expectations inform the changing and often contradictory image that we can trace, the phenomenon of "yakṣa" (Pāli "yakkha") is also changing and acquiring mythological accretions historically. While the diachronic analysis has revealed the internal structural transformations in the life cycle of the yakṣa as a symbol, I shall now concentrate on examining the contextual relations of the yakṣa within a relatively self-contained corpus of texts, namely, the Buddhist Jātakas. I feel that it is useful for a historian of religions to examine the specific cultural context with its cosmology, ethos, and metaphysics, of which the singular religious phenomenon is but a part or a reflection. In the case of the yakṣa, this entails (for our purposes) a brief examination of several important cosmological and metaphysical notions that have been vital in the shaping of the mythology of the yakṣa (yakkha) in the Buddhist as opposed to the Hindu contexts. The mythology of the yakṣa is part of a much larger corpus of ideas and images that serves in the growing and changing self-definition of a people. The exigencies of cultural self-image are informed by historical occurrences, ideological commitments, social stratification, and patterns of ritual.

This mythology, as we have seen, is embedded in a larger symbolism and iconography of water as the medium of creation and bounty. In the Buddhist context, this water symbolism is still employed to refer to that which is fecund and productive in nature and can be conferred upon the social realm. This view of nature (which is essentially shared by the ancient and classical Hindus) is widely expressed in the sculptural friezes and adornments that are found on *toraṇa*s, temples, and in fragments at Sāñcī, Bhārhut, Mathurā, Kārlī, Amarāvatī, and Ajanta. It is in these lush sculptural representations that we find the most benign characterizations, within the Buddhist sphere, of yakkhas, yakkhīs, *nāga*s, and other nature deities. There are, of course, examples of benevolent yakkhas in Buddhist literature as well. These examples express generally three functions of the yakkha: the bestowing of wealth, of progeny, or of protection.[1]

By way of illustrating the especially beneficent representation of the yakkha, we might focus briefly on the depictions of yakkhas and yakkhīs at Bhārhut (second to first century B.C.). Serving as guardian deities, friezes of both adorn the railing pillars. The yakkhas are depicted as stately, turbaned princes and the yakkhīs as voluptuous young females in the classic bent-knee pose, grasping fly whisks or tree branches. In the guise of protectors, they suggest their ancient guardianship of precious metals and jewels, hidden deep in the earth, and their function as household tutelary deities.[2] Among the figures found at Bhārhut are listed: Kuvera yakkha ("Kupiro yakkho" in the dialect local to Bhārhut), the king of the yakkhas and *lokapāla* or guardian of the northern quarter; Virudhāka yakkha, the king of the Kumbhāṇḍas (demons with "testicles shaped like pitchers") and guardian of the southern quarter; Gaṁgīta yakkha, an unidentified yakkha thought by some to be the king of the *gandharva*s and guardian of the east; Supavasa yakkha; Suciloma yakkha; Ajakalaka yakkha; Sudasana yakkhī; Canda yakkhī; and Batanmara yakkhī. Also depicted as deities that are obviously interchangeable with the yakkhīs and yakkhas are the female *devatā*s Mahakoka, Culakoka, and Sirima, and the *nāga* king Cakavaka (also anthropomorphically depicted, but with a turban of snake hoods). Each of these figures stands astride a *vāhana,* which further identifies its sphere of power as primarily terrestrial or aquatic.[3] None of these friezes displays a demonic characterization, though other, probably later, depictions have emphasized fierce aspects of some of these yakṣas—Suciloma, for instance, whose name means "needle-haired."[4]

The forms and images that we can see at these monuments seem to emerge from a source that is deep and common to the iconographical traditions of Buddhism, Jainism, and Hinduism. The contrast between the predominately benign representations of yakkhas and yakkhīs found in the early Buddhist monuments and the predominately fierce literary depictions found in the Jātaka tales suggests, I think, two factors: On the one hand, the genre of ancient, mostly pre-Buddhist, folk tales that constitute the Jātaka collection is a compendium, chiefly, of frightening demon stories and animal stories. The demonic potential of these morally ambiguous deities is stressed in the Jātakas in order to satisfy the constraints of the folk genre, which exploits the frightening, suspenseful, and ghoulish. On the other hand, there are certain contextual, cosmological points that have a bearing upon the more pointedly demonic portrayal of the yakkha and of the *nāga* in the Pāli literature.

For instance, the waters with their rich allusive and fertile potential, going back to Vedic as well as aboriginal sources, in the Pāli Buddhist framework, have lost their cosmogonic and ritual references. In the *Patika* and *Aggana Suttas* of the *Dīgha Nikāya,* we find the Buddhist cosmogonic myth describing the origins of both cosmos and society. This Buddhist view of cosmology differs significantly from the Vedic view. The latter variously posits the origins of the cosmos as *either* emergent out of the self-reflective will and desire of a demiurge (Prajāpati, Brahmā, Mṛtyu, the yakṣa, etc.), floating on the primal waters that predate all form, *or* with the sacrifice of a primal man (*puruṣa* in the "Puruṣa Sūkta," ṚV, 10. 90), an act undertaken by the gods for the foundation of the physical and social worlds. This sharply contrasts with the fundamentally dualistic and antievolutionary view of the Buddhist texts. In these texts, a myth that is complementary to the more important (from the Buddhist point of view) doctrines of psychophysical causation ("codependant origination" [*paṭiccasamuppāda*]) is offered to explain the origin of the macrocosm of material form and social organization. According to this myth, the primal waters exist from the beginning, dark and obscuring, but coeval with original beings of pure radiance and consciousness. These two dimensions exist in absolute separation from one another until a "fall" occurs. Then an inexplicable coagulation of the waters occurs for the "enjoyment" of those beings, producing solid earth, which is of a delightful consistency, odor, and taste. Before long, one of those beings becomes "restless" (*lola*) and tastes the earth. He finds it pleasing and develops a "thirst" (*tṛṣṇa*) for it, whereupon other beings follow his lead and fall upon the earth greedily. Because of their consumption of the material food, their "luminosity" disappears, thus initiating the emergence of the heavenly bodies. From this follows, logically and ineluctably, time, the seasons, and all manner of other separations and distinctions, both physical and psychological: The growing coarseness of the bodies of the once pure beings produces concepts of physical differences among human bodies, which then gives rise to notions of beauty, ugliness, pride, and envy. Out of this fall into embodiment arises sexuality, food production, covetousness, theft, clans, government, social classes, and *brāhman*ical privilege.[5]

The Buddhist Cosmos and the Demonic

The dualism inherent in the Buddhist cosmological myth has an impact, I think, on the ways in which the yakkha is depicted in Buddhist texts. First of all, the fundamental conjunction of animate and inanimate life, of *tapa*s (or asceticism) and desire (which is a part of the Vedic and Upaniṣadic myths about the emergence of the cosmos out of the will of the creator-god who desires another being to keep him company), contributes to a more complex and multifaceted portrait of the yakṣa. The perceived baseness of matter and the "fall" into life of the Buddhist myth do not lend themselves to the paradoxically "*dharm*ic" portrayals of demonic beings, of the sort we explored in the previous chapter. The precisely complementary images of light (in the form of beings of pure consciousness) and dark (in the form of the obscuring and heavy waters) seem to serve as loose metaphors for the classic encounter of *bodhisatta* and yakkha in the Jātaka tales: The *bodhisatta* embodies the principle of light, illuminated by the superiority of his enlightened consciousness and purified by the excellence of his moral conduct; the yakkha in most of the major examples embodies the coarseness and impurity to which that watery fundament gave rise. The quality of cannibalism that is often attributed to the yakkha (as well as the *nāga* and *rakkhasa*) is a metaphor expressing the understanding that the inherent nature of the impermanent material world (*saṁsāra*) is based on a process of consumption. Whereas in the *Bṛhadāraṇyaka Upaniṣad* the same insight into the literally all-consuming nature of everything that comes into being is sanctified as sacrifice with its attendant philosophy and rituals, this sacrificial view of life is reinterpreted in the Buddhist texts and confined to a moral conception: the donation of food and alms to the poor, particularly religious mendicants and Buddhist monks (*śramaṇa*s and *bhikkhus*). In Vedic cosmology, the imposition of order and causality is a sacred manifestation, and the primary impulse to will that order in creation and to recollect it in sacred verse is fundamentally good. In Buddhist cosmology, creation is a negative phenomenon that is offset only by a second creation, that is, by a withdrawal of that basically pure and unfettered consciousness from the filth and bondage of material and social existence. In Buddhist mythological texts, the second creation or reversal of the *saṁsāric* trajectory is symbolized by the conversion of the demonic being to Buddhism. By implication, the self of the yakkha or demon is literally cast aside through his commitment to the moral ideology of Buddhism.

Transformation and Conversion

In their emphasis on conversion, the Jātakas in fact follow a paradigm of transformation that is established in the foundation myth of Buddhism: the conversion and metamorphosis of the prince, Siddhārtha Gautama, from a life of sybaritic decay within the confines of the delusory world of Vedic *dharma* and royal privilege in his father's palace, to a life of austerity and clarity through freedom from sensual pleasures and sexual passions. The seeming dualism of the Buddhist metaphysical views is offset by the unifying notion of the interdependence and connection of all beings in their shared affliction by the three poisons—hatred (*dveṣa*), lust (*lobha*), and delusion (*moha*)—and their fundamental need for enlightenment no matter what their status or caste. The principle that connects and releases the myriad categories of beings is *dhamma* (*dharma*) itself—as "reality" (i.e., the rules governing *saṁsāra*) and as "truth"—in the form of the Buddhist doctrine that offers a way out of the bondage of *saṁsāra*.

The opposition to the bestiality, cruelty, and cannibalism of the yakkha is the logic and rationality of the *dhamma,* as expressed by the *bodhisatta* in each of the tales. In the context of the morality fables of the Jātakas, where the virtues of truth and nonviolence (*ahiṃsā*) are enjoined and embodied by the *bodhisatta,* the conversion of the demonic being, whether yakkha, *rakkhasa,* or *nāga,* is effected by means of argumentation, proof, intelligence, and insight into the true cause of the yakkha's state of being, his moral disease that has produced his low birth as a demon. The triumph of the *bodhisatta* over the yakkha takes the form of either outwitting or appeasement; in the latter, the element of rationality is also present since the pacification is usually made after the demon has been outsmarted and thwarted in his evil plans.

The Hindu sense of the eternal, ritualized conflict between the "good guys" and "bad guys" is in the Buddhist tales significantly amended by means of the notion of conversion, which permanently alters the behavior, if not the nature, of the yakkha. The ongoing agonistic strife that pits *deva*s against *asura*s in the *brāhman*ical literature is replaced in the popular Buddhist literature with the philosophical contention between *bodhisatta* and yakkha; the *bodhisatta* employs the weapons of sophistry and righteousness rather than the tools of physical destruction. His triumph over the demon represents an impersonal victory over the enemies of *dhamma* in all of their forms, whether creatures of the night that incapacitate the moral and rational faculties through fear; proponents of animal sacrifice, metaphorically depicted as cannibals; or aboriginal opponents of the political invasion of Buddhism. In all cases, we can see that, following the Vedic notion, evil as embodied in these demonic populations constitutes social deviance as much as moral abomination. The Buddha, though characterized by his moral superiority in all of the fables, asserts this superiority in ways that facilitate the establishment of institutional Buddhism. The demons are put down and won over, but left intact, not, as in the Hindu myths, to rise again and rechallenge the gods, but to testify—to the wisdom and compassion of the Buddhist *dhamma*.

The Fluid, Physical, and Moral Forms of the Demons

In part, it is the ability of yakkhas and *rakkhasa*s to assume a variety of forms that permits their employment as metaphors for the moral state of humans and human communities. The *nāga*s especially, with their composite forms, are useful in expressing the notions (inherent to Buddhist thought) of the interconnectedness of all life forms and the transformations wrought upon human nature through moral commitment and neglect. In the *Bhūridatta Jātaka* (no. 543), a complex tale involving parallel kingdoms of human and *nāga* royal families and their commingling of blood in two separate generations of contact, the *bodhisatta* is born the son of a human princess and a *nāga* king. His life in the *nāga* kingdom, with its sensuality and material splendor, is comparable to the legendary life of Śākyamuni Buddha, who, though ensconced in the pleasurable life of the court, still conceived of a longing for the purified life of spiritual mendicancy. In the Jātaka story, the *bodhisatta*, a *nāga* named Bhūridatta, visits the kingdom of the gods along with a retinue of *nāga* worthies. While in the company of the celestial deities, where he develops an interest in philosophy, he becomes impatient with his *nāga* form with its snakelike body and undertakes a fast to lose this form entirely and enter the world of the gods. The *nāga* form, though not conducive to the attainment of spiritual prowess, does not utterly prevent it, and we see that the birth of the desire for something higher may occur even in the lower realms of the demigods. In all species, there is some special quality that may be developed and utilized toward the attainment of wisdom and religious purity if it is powered by extraordinary discipline and insight. That insight which resides within the *bodhisatta* is capable of cutting through the illusory sheath of form, whether the form is his own or another's.

In Buddhist legend and later cosmology, the Buddha, from the pinnacle of the cosmos, reigns triumphant over all beings, including the Vedic gods who defer to his knowledge and transcendence of human limitations. In the *Ayakūṭa Jātaka,* the subservience both of gods (in the person of Indra [Sakka]) and of yakkhas is achieved through the moral transcendence of the *bodhisatta* over the whole system of sacrifice that benefits both classes of beings equally. In this tale, the *bodhisatta* is shielded by Indra from a yakkha[6] who threatens to split his head with an axe. His moral and spiritual superiority compel the cooperation of the heavens to protect him from the unseen but powerful demons who are angered and repelled by his righteousness, expressed in an edict forbidding animal sacrifice to the *devatā*s.

> If Maghavan-Indra, king of the gods, lord of
> Sujani, protects me,
> let the Piśācas circle all around.
> The Rakkhasīs' brats cannot terrify.
>
> Let the Kumbhāṇḍas and all the Piśāca sirens wail;
> these tormentors are not equal to the battle.[7]

All of the classes of beings who seek to thwart the teachings of the *bodhisatta* in the many Jātaka tales in which demons are invoked by way of allegorical illustration and instruction are situated within a multilayered universe, determined and quantified by the unifying principle of *dhamma*. The fact of religious conversion and its attendant moral transformation is the hinge upon which the complex unity of being and beings swings. This important focus contributes to a somewhat contradictory analysis of the hierarchy of incarnate creatures. From one point of view, within the Buddhist scheme, the classifications of the many beings are more fluid than they may be in the Hindu scheme or even within other traditions, such as the medieval Christian Great Chain of Being. From another point of view, the genealogical separations are more rigidly defined. All beings are united and consubstantial insofar as they exist within the encompassing framework of *saṁsāra*. All are affected by it and, through the twelve links of causation, are created by it. However, the identification of the common obstacle, *saṁsāra,* and the way out of the causal nexus entail a decisive rational movement and moral commitment, the propensity for which is contained in all beings to some extent, just as the entrapment in *saṁsāra* is a precondition for existence and impedes all living beings to one degree or another. The degree of implication in the causal network is a function of certain irrevocable birth-related factors, such as species, gender, and class. Still, however, it is a fundamental axiom of Buddhist philosophy and psychology that the possibility of enlightenment (or *bodhicitta* as it is understood in later texts) lies nascent within the consciousness of all beings. In lower orders of life, this possibility is faint; in higher orders, it is stronger; and in humans, it exists as the special gift that this order of birth confers. The Jātaka tales, in fact, employ, however tangentially, this concept when they relate the events that have occurred in the previous animal birth of the *bodhisatta,* always demonstrating that the protracted development of wisdom that culminates in the enlightenment of Śākyamuni Buddha had germinal forms. In each case, the species of the *bodhisatta* does not prevent the manifestation of his superior intellect and compassion. By his example, he demonstrates that there are, indeed, good animals and bad animals, good demons and wicked demons, intelligent humans and ignorant humans. The poison that contaminates our lives and wills is never so virulent as to take away our hope for cure, though it may be great enough to kill our bodies and impel us to new births.

Humans, Gods, and Demons

The Buddhist stories and myths that so frequently explore the delineation, transformation, and combination of species and categories of beings reflect the problematic, shifting relationship between gods, humans, and demons that continued to be expressed in the evolution of

Indian mythology vis-à-vis theology.[8] The Buddhist cosmological notion of the centrality of the human state of birth and sphere of action to the attainment of *nibbana* (*nirvāṇa*) has to do with an important reinterpretation of pleasure and the rewards of heaven. In the Vedic scheme, the attainment of the world of the gods represents the highest spiritual reward, but in the revisioning of Buddhist thought, certain dangers and obstacles still persist in the heavenly sphere and may cause the eventual "demotion" of even the gods to states far below the human. (In this sense, archaic Buddhism has a view of the centrality of human experience and achievement that is analogous to a view displayed in the Upaniṣads in which philosophers and mystics began to question both the efficacy of Vedic ritual and the soteriological goal of *svarga* ["heaven"].) While the human state with its more "neutral" or ambivalent *kamm*ic (*karm*ic) inheritance is most ideal for the encountering and grasping of *dhamma,* theoretically, even the inauspicious births among the lower classes of beings and demons (among them, yakkhas) offer more potential for spiritual advancement than the supernal births where the mind becomes sheltered from reality behind a seductive veil of pleasure. Demonic creatures are favored, as it were, by a detached compulsion to commit evil acts that they have secured in their previous lives and now experience as their very natures. This tendency to evil is still more readily transformed than the evil that demonic humans display, always founded on an unwillingness to be fully human. The violence of yakkhas is lacking in emotional prejudice and functions more impersonally and retributively, as in the Eumenides, who serve blindly to attack and punish injustice in Aeschylus' *Oresteia.* This function of the yakkha is seen particularly in the *Dhonasakha Jātaka,* where the evil ambition of a king, inspired by his even more wicked priest, entails plucking out the eyes and entrails of a thousand kings and offering them a *rukkha devatā.*

> The king readily agreed and having placed powerful wrestlers behind a curtain, sent for the kings, one by one. Just by squeezing them, the wrestlers rendered them unconscious and having torn out their eyes, the king had them killed and took their flesh and had their corpses carried off by the Ganges. Then he made the offering he was told to and had the drum beaten and went to battle. Then, a certain yakkha came from his watchtower and tore out the right eye of the king. Great pain set in and, driven mad by the agony, he laid down flat on his back on a bed prepared for him at the foot of a *nigrodha* tree. At

> that time, a certain vulture picked up a sharp, pointed bone and perched at the top of a tree to eat the meat from it. He dropped the bone which fell like an iron stake upon the left eye of the king and destroyed it as well. At that moment, he remembered the words of the Bodhisatta and said, "Our teacher, when he said, 'These mortals reap the consequences of their deeds just as the fruit is created by the seed,' must have seen all of this as he spoke."[9]

In this case, the yakkha functions as an instrument of retribution who, because his nature is violent and the very embodiment of cruelty, may be employed as a sort of "hit man," punishing the more egregious evil of the king whose violation of his charge as just ruler has drawn the impersonal rebellion of nature against his deadly excesses.

In the early Buddhist conception, the greatest ethical responsibility comes down squarely on the shoulders of the human being. It is the human being whose consciousness most clearly serves as a window into the truth. In the hierarchy of beings, his is the pivotal position from which to move up or down. Any other placement on that hierarchy or *maṇḍala* (as it is conceived in later Buddhist art of northeastern India, Nepal, and Tibet) is characterized by a proclivity for stagnancy. The mass conversions of yakkhas and *nāga*s that are described in the Vijaya legends, seem to dispute this assumption, but these conversions are of a different order from those attested to in the *Theratherīgāthā* (*Psalms of the Elders*). As it is only humans who are practically susceptible of enlightenment (though all beings are theoretically susceptible), it is only humans who are welcomed into the *saṁgha* or order of monks and nuns. This is illustrated in a Pāli legend[10] where a *nāga* disguises himself as a human and enters the *saṁgha*. While sleeping, however, he reverts to his true form and terrifies the other monks. The Buddha banishes him from the order and makes "a rule that all candidates for admission to the order should be asked, among other matters, if they are real human beings or *nāga*s in manly disguises."[11]

The fundamental problem in the establishment of a basis for hierarchy within Buddhism, a problem that takes form in the mythology as well as in the social organization, revolves around this blurring and refocusing of distinctions among humans, gods, and demons. Gautama Buddha's mission—to become himself fully "awakened" and to pass on the method for achieving that psychic wakefulness, responsibility, and freedom from unhappiness and rebirth to all others who would listen and learn—is a challenge to the gods and to the caste system. Merely through reflection and control of the senses, the Buddha was able to accomplish feats not only of ascetic prowess, but of paranormal insight and omniscience, qualities that could only be attributed to the gods in both the Vedic and post-Vedic contexts. In the former period, such mastery on the part of humans was unexplored; in the latter period, ascetical power had come to be desired and feared, but, for the most part, was dichotomized as magical and bad or gnostic and unconcerned with displays of magical power and therefore good. In the personality of the Buddha, a synthesis of gnosis, power, and compassion is made. The Buddha is preeminently human, yet through insight and asceticism he has developed the power and cosmic centrality of a god. That he has done this in defiance, not only of caste restrictions, but also of the many basic tenets of Vedic Hinduism, confers upon him the status of a demon with respect to Hindu orthodoxy.

This notion of the demonic heresy of the Buddha receives an interesting interpretation in the Vaiṣṇava myths dealing with the "Buddha *avatāra*" of Viṣṇu. The Buddha, though conceived as arch heretic, is styled as an *avatāra* or incarnation of the Hindu god Viṣṇu because of a convoluted and clever notion that states that the Buddha's (i.e., Viṣṇu as the Buddha's) mission in coming to earth was to convert the demon races to his sacrilegious doctrine, thus drawing them away from and purifying the sacrosanct teachings of Vedic Hinduism. Of course, the equation of Buddhists with demons resolves the paradox of how formerly good Hindus could believe such heresies, and the casting of the Buddha as a Hindu *avatāra*[12] addresses the problem of how such a heretic could become so powerful, a problem that is confronted also in the many myths that tell of the boons and powers conferred upon ascetic demons.[13]

Outwitting the Yakkhas

The symbolization of power in the relationship between the Buddha and the various demigods who are known from Buddhist art and mythology takes the form of the subordination of the lesser demons and deities of local cult to the dominating ideology and image of Buddhism. In this regard, we encounter the many tales of the *bodhisatta*'s outwitting and vanquishing of wicked yakkhas and yakkhinīs, *rakkhasas* and *rakkhasīs*, nāgas and *nāginīs*. In the *Mahāvaṁsa* and the

Dīpavaṁsa, we have the Buddha routing and converting entire troops of *nāgas* and yakkhas who have overrun the island of Laṅkā, making it unfit for human habitation (i.e., for Buddhist practitioners). The narratives that pit the Buddha or the *bodhisatta* against hostile demons in his diverse births clearly afford him the opportunity to absorb and assimilate their powers and the territories over which they rule. Demonic power is manifested and transmitted in the Jātaka tales principally through fear and ignorance, and in all cases, the *bodhisatta* represents a still center of wisdom and fearlessness that invariably overcomes his demonic adversaries.

The outwitting of the yakkha may occur, as we have seen in the preceding chapter, in a "testing" episode, a genre that is related to the dialogic style of the philosophic and parabolic religious *sūtras* (*suttas*) of Hinduism and Buddhism. In the Buddhist texts particularly, the interrogative mode is employed to test the Buddha in order to discover his superiority and the truth of his teaching. This testing is conducted by a variety of personages and beings, and in the *Yakkha Suttas* of the *Saṁyutta Nikāya,*[14] there are stories of the contacts of the enlightened Buddha with various yakkhas, both benign and hostile. In the *Hemavatasutta* of the Uragavagga of the *Sutta Nipāta,* two yakkhas, Hemavata and Satagira, go to see the master, Gautama, and observing his luminous qualities, discuss these virtues in detail and finally question the master himself about the Dhamma, which results in their conversion and the conversion of one thousand of their kind to Buddhism and their vow to preach the Dhamma throughout the countryside.

In the *Āḷavaka Sutta* of the *Sutta Nipāta*[15] the motif of the fierce, testing yakkha is clearly seen.

> At one time, Bhagavat (the Buddha) lived in Āḷavī in the place of the yakkha, Āḷavaka. Then, Āḷavaka approached the place where Bhagavat was staying and, having approached, said this to Bhagavat:
>
> "Come out, samana!"
>
> "Very well, friend."
>
> "Enter, samana."
>
> "Very well, friend." And so saying, the Bhagavat entered. For the second time, Āḷavaka Yakkha said,
>
> "Come out, samana."

"Very well, friend." And the Bhagavat came out.

"Enter, samana."

"Very well, friend." And the Bhagavat entered. For the third time, Āḷavaka Yakkha commanded,

"Come out, samana!"

"Very well, friend." And the Bhagavat came out.

"Enter, samana."

"Very well, friend." And the Bhagavat entered. For the fourth time, Āḷavaka Yakkha said,

"Come out, samana."

"No, indeed, friend, I will not come out. Do whatever you wish."

"I shall ask you a question. If you cannot answer it, I will either scatter your mind or split open your heart or take you by the feet and throw you across the Ganges."

"Friend, I do not see how anyone in the world of the devas, of Māra, of Brahmā, of the families of either brāhmans and samanas or gods and men, can scatter my mind, split my heart, or take me by the feet and fling me across the Ganges, but go ahead and ask me whatever you wish."[16]

Āḷavaka proceeds to ask the Buddha several questions about the true religious path, which, as the Buddha indicates, must be followed with faith (*saddha*) and adherence to Dharma, the truth of which Āḷavaka then embraces and vows to promote.

> For my sake, the Buddha has come to live at Āḷavī. Today I understand how a gift may bear fruit. I will go about from village to village, from town to town, worshipping the Enlightened One and the perfected Dharma.[17]

The concurrence of threats and interrogation is the familiar form of religious trial that is also known in other contexts, in which the hero or king must face the sphinx, dragon, or oracle in order to win some piece of intelligence or cultural wisdom that is to be integrated into his life and repertoire of powers. In these examples, an important aspect is the transition from the frightening and emotive to the rational and didactic.

In the Buddhist parables, the calm, rational rigor of the Buddha in the face of terrifying threats and supernatural displays of force is sufficient to transform the demonic resistance into docile compliance. In this way, the testing genre serves to underscore the primary importance in Buddhism placed upon the cognitive skills acquired by means of intellectual, sensual, and emotional mastery. With the weapons of reason and dispassion at one's disposal, there are no enemies too daunting to overcome.

Monstrous Yakkhas

Yakkhas are encountered in Buddhist mythology primarily as fierce, implacable monsters who stalk, kill, and often eat the luckless inhabitants of a particular region, much in the way that King Kong exerted despotic control over his native island. In the *Sutano Jātaka,* a yakkha terrorizes a kingdom. The king has agreed to send him every day a man with a plate of rice to be eaten (both man and rice, that is). If the kingdom should run out of these edible couriers, the yakkha has vowed to eat the king himself. The prison, from which the king has been taking a prisoner every day to feed the yakkha, is finally depleted of its victims, and thus, the king advertises and offers a reward for someone to go to the yakkha. The *bodhisatta* steps forward and offers to face the monster. He is able to outwit the yakkha by wearing the king's slippers, thus circumventing the specific limitations of the yakkha's power that require that his victims must stand on the ground. The *bodhisatta* also takes along the king's golden bowl containing the rice and the king's parasol so that he will not stand in the shade of the yakkha's tree (thus eluding another stipulation of the yakkha's power). The *bodhisatta* is able to convince the yakkha that if he continues to terrify everyone he will lose the chance to gain any food at all. He admonishes and palliates the yakkha, saying:

> "Friend, you did evil deeds of old, you were cruel and harsh, you ate the flesh and blood of others and so were born as a yakkha: from henceforth do no murder or the like." So telling the blessings of virtue and the misery of vice, he established the yakkha in the five virtues; then he said, "Why dwell in the forest? Come, I will settle you by the city gate and make you the best rice." So he went away with the yakkha, making him take the sword and the other things, and come to Benares. They told the king that Sutana was come with

> the yakkha. The king with his ministers went out to meet the Bodhisatta, settled the yakkha at the city gate and made him get the best rice: then he entered the town, made proclamation by drum, and calling a meeting of the townsfolk spoke the praises of the Bodhisatta and gave him the command of the army; he himself was established in the Bodhisatta's teaching, did the good works of charity and the other virtues, and became destined for heaven.[18]

The blood lust of the yakkha in this fable serves as a metaphor for the unenlightened rule of the king himself, before his conversion to the Buddhist *dhamma*. Throughout these fables, the yakkha may be seen to represent a people who lie outside of the Buddhist doctrinal system, as unbelievers of various kinds. They may be forest ascetics of other philosophical schools or simply *brāhmans* whose practice of sacrifice is metaphorically rendered as cannibalism. The eating of flesh is, in the Buddhist view, both a manifestation as well as a symbol of a state of supreme ignorance, delusion, and vice. The demon's ghoulish feasting on human flesh stands in the same relationship to the ideals and precepts of Buddhism as the greatest human sin of murder. This is well illustrated in the famous tale of Aṅgulimāla ("Finger Garland"),[19] a cruel robber who terrorizes villages, killing their inhabitants and wearing the fingers of his victims in a garland around his neck. The Buddha deliberately encounters Aṅgulimāla on the half-deserted highway where he waylays, robs, and slaughters his victims. As in the encounters with the yakkha, the evil Aṅgulimāla lives on the outskirts of the village, both a guardian of the passage between the two worlds of town and wilderness and a representative of what may inhabit the mysterious, savage, forest domain.

In the case of both the monstrous yakkha and the monstrous human sinner, the phenomenon of conversion is crucial to the Buddhist rendering of these tales, many of which are drawn from a vast body of ancient folk fables and allegories. Again and again, it is the *bodhisatta*'s (or Buddha's) outsmarting logic and rational proof of the evil of the demon's actions that are the simple catalyst for the total reversal of the yakkha's or outlaw's personality. The context of Buddhist doctrine posits a totally revolutionized society where caste distinctions and hierarchies of birth are superseded by hierarchies based upon understanding, religious attainment, and service. Within this context, metaphors of otherness are employed, such as the yakkha, the criminal, the unbeliever, and the *nāga*. These metaphors serve, morally and epistemologically, in opposition to the Buddha himself as the embodiment of the Buddhist *dhamma*.

Kings and Yakkhas

As we have seen in the Hindu stories as well, the yakṣa serves as a symbol of the savage and uncultivated in opposition to the king, who embodies the highest rigors and values of society (although in the Hindu context, more often it is the Untouchable rather than the yakṣa who functions this way).[20] For both Hindu and Buddhist notions of kingship, it was necessary to accommodate a "local" appeal and power over the forces and deities of the earthly, natural realm.

> As the ideal of kingship spread or became more and more a force in the life of the common people it was forced by the strength of the local cults to associate with the potent territorial deities such as the nagās and yakṣas. . . . Through these myths, the populace could relate the king to the important factors and forces that affected their own existence. The king could, therefore, be seen not only to obtain power from the more universal and often celestial beings such as Indra, but from the local *caitya* and more chthonic deities which existed most vividly in the minds of the common people.[21]

In the Buddhist stories of similar structure, however, the Buddha or *bodhisatta* plays a role identical to the king in the Hindu tales. This is, to a great extent, a revolutionary notion, and yet knowing what we do about the legendary Śākyamuni Buddha, it seems to make sense: On the one hand, the highly intellectual sense of the "truth" or *dhamma* that the Buddha has won in his enlightenment seems, in terms of the Vedic, sacrificial image of kingship, to be an inadequate tool with which to rule an earthly kingdom with its complex economic concerns and earthly responsibilities. On the other hand, however, despite the Buddha's symbolic rejection of caste and social position, the mythic power of his *kṣatriya* caste designation prevails as the most potent symbol of the triumph of his religious insight over the world of the senses, of sin, of illusion, of rebirth, of injustice. As *cakravartin* (world monarch), he not only teaches a new philosophical system (hundreds of such teachers abounded in his time), but also institutes a new world order, with its redrawn map of human potential and religious *telos*. The ascetic, otherworldly aspect of his career gives way to the triumphant world-reforming and teaching phase, and thus, the preexistent prototypes of *brāhman* and *kṣatriya* inform the developing imagery and legend of the Buddha. The assimilation of these two prototypes to the *cakravartin* imagery associated with the Buddha occurs by means of a purification or a splitting off of certain aspects of both figures. The "seer" characteristic of the *brāhman* is split off from the ritual practitioner and assimilated to the transcendent and mystical insight of the Buddha. The wise and responsible ruler aspect of the *kṣatriya* is split off from its fierce, warrior aspect and employed within the corpus of Buddhist *sutta*s and legends as the ultimate symbol of the compassion and total concern of the Buddha.[22]

This transformation is to a large extent realized in and symbolized by a movement away from the primary, static world of maternal sustenance, well-being, and erotic indulgence. The symbolic testings of the king that we have cited are encounters with paternal images of authority and ritual claimings of patrimony. Yudhiṣṭhira, significantly, is tested by his divine father, the ultimate patriarch of the world order, Dharma. The sojourn in the forest of the many important rulers of Indian legend seems to serve in part as a movement away from the feminine as symbolized by the palace and court, filled with its lascivious courtesans (in the case of the Buddha), scheming queens, or at the very least, cloyingly powerful queen mothers. In the examples we have adduced, the transformation of the yakṣa in the water serves as a potent metaphor for the transformation of the king himself who, through his ritual peregrinations in the wild, absorbs the potency and power inherent in nature and yet must control or "renounce" the wilderness just as he has "renounced" his kingdom, in order once again to assume his rightful place in the socially generated hierarchy.

In the Hindu Epics and Purāṇas, the seeking out of, encounter with, and ultimate homage to yakṣas become elements of the heroic narrative, as they were in the Buddhist Vijāya legends, the *Mahāvaṁsa* and *Dīpavaṁsa*. In these latter territorial myths, and in the Epic legends of the peripatetic heroes as well, yakṣas are part of a forest sojourn that establishes and reestablishes the sovereignty of the *kṣatriya* heroes and religious champions. They are, in fact, a vital element in the *bhakti* world that is portrayed in the Epics and Purāṇas. Yakṣas, as *kṣetrapāla*s ("protectors of the field") or *dvārapāla*s ("door guardians" or "keepers of the way"), are signposts on the pilgrimage trail and guardians of ancient, sanctified grounds and pools. The Pāṇḍavas are enjoined by the sage Pulastya to honor these *devatās* on their tour of the holy *tīrtha*s of northern India:

> For, if a man goes to Kurukṣetra filled with faith, he obtains the fruit of a Royal Consecration and a Horse Sacrifice. Then, having saluted the Dvārapāla, the Yakṣa Macakruka, one obtains the reward of a gift of a thousand cows.[23]

> Then, continuing to the mountain of the wise Great God, named Munjavata, and staying there for one night, one achieves the status of Gaṇapati. In the same area there is a world-renowned Yakṣi; if one is intimate with her, one attains to auspicious worlds.[24]

> Then the pilgrim should go to Rājagṛha; by touching the hot springs, he rejoices like Kakṣivat. There, a pure man should dally with the Yakṣiṇī regularly; and by the favor of the Yakṣiṇī, he will be absolved of the sin of abortion.[25]

The king, in his close association with the sacred and physical geography of his kingdom, is responsible for the institutionalization and propagation of local cult.[26] The king's encounter with the yakṣa serves, in part, as a particularly clever syncretic device. Through his triumph over these local guardian figures, two important themes are coalesced: On the one hand, the king is thought to sustain cosmic harmony through his interaction with ancient and popular chthonic deities, and on the other hand, from a purely Buddhist point of view, the king is thought to exhibit his righteousness through his own conversion and his ability to convert others to the logocentric religion, Buddhism. The syncretic process involved the homologization of the Cakravartin-Buddha (World-liberator) with the Cakravartin-king (World-ruler), whose demonstration of sovereignty depended upon his religious and political assimilation of parochial cults.

Through the symbolism of the *caitya,* the king's presumed hegemony over both wilderness and civilization is established. In his victory over the yakṣa or *nāga,* he symbolically becomes them, which is signified by the stone or arboreal *caitya-vṛkṣa* itself.[27] The ultimate unity of the two different sovereigns—the king (social divinity) and the yakṣa (wilderness divinity)—is seen in the Hindu context in the previously cited Yakṣapraśna, the tale of the Pāṇḍavas' encounter with King Dharma, disguised as a yakṣa. The tremendous importance of the yakṣa legends as paradigms of the sovereign's creative and custodial relationship to nature is seen in the Buddhist tale of the yakkhinī-mare (*vaḷavā-rūpa* or *vaḷavā-mukha*) in the *Mahāvaṁsa*.

> Her name was Cetiya, and she used to wander about the Dhumarakka mountain in the form of a mare, with a white body and red feet. Pandukabhaya [the king] bored her nostrils and secured her with a rope; she became his adviser, and he rode her in battle. When at last established on the throne (in Anuradhapura) Pandukabhaya "settled the Yakkha Kaluvela on the east side of the city, the Yakkha Cittaraja at the lower end of the Abhaya tank. The slave-woman who helped him in time past (as foster-mother) and was (now) reborn as (or of) a Yakkinī, the thankful (king) settled at the south gate of the city. Within the royal precincts he housed the Yakkhinī having the face of a mare. Year by year he had sacrificial offerings made to them and to other (Yakkhas); but on festival days he sat with Cittaraja beside him on a seat of equal height, and having gods and men to dance before him, the king took his pleasure in joyous and merry wise. . . . With Cittaraja and Kalaveva who were visible, the prince enjoyed his good fortune, he that had those that had become Yakkhas for friends.[28]

The king's capture of the wild mare is linked with the Vedic symbolism of the lascivious mare's threat to the horse sacrifice. As we will see, birth into the form of a yakṣa or yakṣī is often a punishment for sexual transgressions. In this case, the king's relationship to the beast-yakṣī suggests the theme of the monarch's responsibility to protect other classes as well, since the yakṣī-mare is the embodiment of the slave woman who was his guardian in a previous life. Coomaraswamy interprets the "visibility" of the yakṣas as their being painted or sculptured images with which the king has adorned his throne in order to symbolize his close relationship with the ancient elemental deities. The yakkha Cittaraja is mentioned also in the *Kurudhamma Jātaka* (no. 276) as the ritual witness of an ancient rite, in which the king would shoot arrows to the four quarters.[29]

The terrifying proximity to savagery of the king in his potential for the abuse of martial powers and prerogatives is graphically represented in the *Mahāsutasoma Jātaka* (no. 537), where the conversion of a wicked king follows precisely the form of the conversion of the yakkha. In this story, a certain Prince Brahmadatta of Benares is instructed in the "arts" (*sippagahana*) by another precocious prince, Sutasoma, who is the *bodhisatta*. The vows he enjoins his students to keep are imperiled by Brahmadatta's unfortunate habit of taking meat with his rice every day. One day, when meat is not available, the king's cook, desiring above all else to please his sovereign, visits a cemetery and takes the flesh from a dead human body to roast for the king. The taste of the human flesh sends a thrill through his entire body (*sakalasariram khobhetvā*) and excites an uncontrollable desire for more of this unholy food. This strange fetish is attributed to his having been a yakkha in the life previous to his current one, when he consumed quantities of such flesh. In pursuit of this reawakened pleasure, the king empties the prisons of their prisoners, having them slaughtered one by one, to feed his escalating cannibalism. When the prisons are exhausted, his cook takes to roaming the city by night, killing its citizens and cooking them for his ghoulish master. Ultimately, the cook is discovered in his wrongdoing, the king is revealed for the abomination he is, and he takes to the open road, completely abandoning his kingdom in order to be a man-eating robber. He dwells in and around a banyan tree whose spirit (*rukkhadevatā*) he honors with bloody offerings, which the *devatā* does not desire and is appalled by. Finally, the aid of the cannibal-king's former friend and teacher, the *bodhisatta,* Sutasoma, is sought, and through the subtlety of his reasoning, he is able to convince the king to shed his wickedness and embrace the *dhamma,* comprised of teachings that are distinguished from the *kṣatriya* code, which the king, even in the extremity of his mad orgy, may still be seen somehow to obey.

In the Buddhist stories in which we encounter yakkhas and other demonic beings, it appears that their demonism resides in something other than their simply being linked with nature and natural symbols and myths. It is not nature that spawns the demonic, but humans, in their ignorance and the gross indulgence of their pleasures and senses. In all cases, even the most guilty sinners are capable (with careful persuasion) of the reasoning that can lead to conversion and the subsequent commitment to Buddhist ideals of compassion and noninjury. In his dialogue with Sutasoma, the wicked king claims that he is not capable of refraining from cannibalism because of his lust for human flesh. The conversion of the king is a reeducation of his will, an instilling in him of the understanding that he is capable of controlling his passions and that no desire is stronger than his resolve to adhere to truth and goodness.

The difficulties inherent in kingship underlie all of the stories we have been discussing. In the *Sutasoma Jātaka,* however, we have the most graphic illustration of the virulent assault on the will and righteousness of the king, an assault to which the life of royal indulgence gives rise. In one part of the Jātaka, the king's commander-in-chief attempts to dissuade his sovereign from indulging his vile practices and uses the example of a prince who had been undone by his addiction to alcohol and, because of it, let his kingdom go to ruin. Here we have, of course, two of the major vices of the Hindu Rājputs, the eating of meat and the unbridled consumption of liquor. It is thought that the latter vice particularly is responsible for the decay of many Rājput (*kṣatriya*) families. It is the conversion to Buddhist vegetarianism and the positive stylization of nature by means of vegetal imagery (as seen in the pacific righteousness of the *rukkhadevatā*) that is being enjoined in the *Sutasoma Jātaka* particularly.

In contrast to the demonic aspect of the king fallen from righteousness, in the story of Maitribala from the *Jātakamāla* (in Sanskrit) we are presented with an image of the superior ethical merit of the king in relationship to the yakṣa representatives of the demonic world. In this tale, several "*ojohara*" yakṣas ("vigor-stealing" yakṣas) enter a town, having been exiled by their king, Kubera, from the proper domain of the yakṣas. The yakṣas are amazed at the prosperity and freedom from disease and sorrow that they discover in the kingdom. Though they try their hardest, in vampire fashion, to take away the "vigor" of the inhabitants, they are not able to do it. They disguise themselves as *brāhman*s and question a cowherd boy as to why he displays no fear of yakṣas, *rākṣasa*s, and other demons. He replies that the people of the country are protected by a mighty "*svastyayana,*" or power and blessing of the king that has been acquired through virtue. The king hears of the visiting *brāhman*s, and he orders them to be fed and entertained. The yakṣas assume their true forms and refuse the food offered to them, requesting instead raw human flesh. The king gives them flesh from his own body so that they will be satisfied as guests and not offended. The yakṣas are so impressed by this unprecedented generosity and sacrifice that they beg the king not to mutilate himself further, and they go away peacefully (though not before having consumed a share of his flesh and blood). In this case, the steadfast virtue of the king in the face of the demonic provides the example to mirror the previous tale, in which the moral descent of the king is a nightmare threatening to plunge the entire kingdom into chaos and ruin. It is the righteous controlling and defining principle that the king provides that protects his subjects from even the fear of the demonic orders of beings. His rational and benevolent rule is a safeguard against a destructive mixing of the orders of the cosmos: humans remain human and yakṣas stay where they belong.[30]

The belief that the king must found his kingdom upon perfect virtue in order to insure its prosperity is prevalent within Indian thought in general, but has special pedagogic utility within Buddhism: If the king can be converted to the social and moral principles of Buddhism, his subjects will likely follow suit. This connection of the sovereign with his subjects and the ancient cultic sources of his kingdom is underscored in the *Dummedha Jātaka,* where the *bodhisatta* in the guise of a prince weans his subjects from the practice of animal sacrifice to local deities.

> One day, the prince mounted his chariot and drove out of the city. At that time, he saw a crowd assembled at a banyan tree, near a Devatā who had been reborn in the tree. They worshipped the Devatā, desiring to obtain all of the sons and daughters, fame and wealth they wanted. Getting down from his chariot, the Bodhisatta approached the tree and made a pūjā with fragrant flowers and an ablution with water and then circumambulated the tree.[31]

Pretending to worship these local gods himself, the *bodhisatta* claims to have made a vow to the tree *devatā* that he will punish all those who slaughter living creatures for the purpose of offering their flesh, blood, and entrails on the *devatā*'s altar. In this way, he adopts the strategem of "fighting fire with fire," and instead of condemning the ancient cultic practices, he purifies them by ridding them of their bloody aspect.

This particular fable throws the Buddhist appreciation of local cult into question. The prince-*bodhisatta* does not appear actually to share with his subjects a belief in these deities (yakkhas). He adopts the demeanor of a believer as an expedient to effect his moral and political aims. This is a motif found in Buddhist aesthetic theory and representation, where it is often difficult to determine the precise stance of the author or artist vis-à-vis popular, pre-Buddhist symbols and rituals. In the employment of aesthetic irony, the Buddhists were able to include very subtly the practices of the dominant tradition, Hinduism, within the scope of their satirical depiction. It is not the worship of the ancient *devatās* that is anathema to Buddhism, but rather the sacrifice of flesh as the prevailing form of worship, a practice that was certainly common in "mainstream" Hinduism at that time. By implication, Hinduism is equated with these barbaric cults because of its employment of blood sacrifice. This issue is an undercurrent in religious debate in India for centuries and certainly contributes to the ambiguity with which the yakṣa and other demigods are viewed. As prime recipients of bloody offerings, they are a threat to the claims made by both Hinduism and Buddhism to being moral and universal religions.

> The word yakkha, which is one of the commonest terms for a demon, is explained by the Pāli Buddhist commentators as being derived from the root *yaj,* to sacrifice, so that a yakkha is understood as a being to whom sacrifice is offered. The etymology may be unsound, but it indicates that there was some connection between yakkhas and sacrifice in common practice. The Jātakas contain several direct references to sacrificial offerings made to demons.[32]

The etymology of yakkha put forward by the Pāli Buddhist commentators contrasts significantly with that found in the *Rāmāyaṇa* passage cited in Chapter 1.[33] In that text, the etymological connection with "sacrifice" (*yaj*) is also maintained, but yakṣas are thought to be sacrific*ers,* not the recipients of the sacrifice. This contrast probably reflects the difference of emphasis and attitudes between Hindu and Buddhist sources toward demons and sacrifice. The *Rāmāyaṇa* passage, in which yakṣas along with *rākṣasa*s are Prajāpati's vice-regents, protecting and consecrating the waters, focuses on the Hindu employment of demigods and demons as local extensions of bigger, more powerful gods. In their positioning the yakkha on the receiving end of bloody offerings, the Buddhist commentators emphasize the "barbarism" of the yakkha. Inevitably, they conceive of sacrifice as primitive and immoral rather than creative, as it is in the Hindu context. Without the legitimation of sacerdotal ritual, the base elements of sacrifice seem debauched. Still, the employment of flesh and blood as appropriate for sacrifice receives sanction because of its more powerful provocation of the primal spirits and the stimulation of their graciousness in the form of rainfall, offspring, or material goods.

The Yakṣa in Jainism

In the literature of Jainism, we find an employment of the yakṣa-*devatā* imagery similar to that of the Buddhists. Yakṣas are mentioned throughout Jain texts in either of two ways: as narrative devices and minor characters in the Jain legends about the development of the religion and the hagiography of the *sthaviras* (elders of the early Jain church) or in iconographical texts that discuss in detail the whole pantheon of yakṣas who are attendants of the twenty-four Tirthānkaras or saints of the Jain tradition.[34]

The antiquity of the yakṣa (or "jakkha" in Jain texts) shrines or *caityas* is referred to in the *Antagaḍa Dasāo,* and the power of these shrines and the deities they honor is never underestimated. Elsewhere in the same text, an incident concerning the yakṣa, Moggarapāṇi, is recounted—in which a devoted follower of his, Ajjunae, a garland-maker, is attacked by a band of louts who tie him up and rape his wife. This happens in front of Moggarapāṇi's shrine, and Ajjunae, in a crisis of faith with respect to his beloved yakṣa, is prepared to curse him, but the yakṣa bestirs himself and enters his devotee's body, empowering him to kill his captors and oddly enough, his wife as well. This sudden infusion of aggression triggers an orgy of revenge that Ajjunae now wreaks upon the inhabitants of the city of Rayagihe (Rājagṛha), in which he kills six men and one woman every day. Finally, a follower of Jainism, a certain merchant, Sudaṁsane, encounters the yakṣa at his shrine and without fear prays to Mahāvīra to protect him from the yakṣa's iron mace that is being swung by the yakṣa-possessed Ajjunae. His prayer consists of the monk's *mahāvratas* in which he renounces forever the taking of life, sexuality, the possession of goods, and the telling of lies. The strength with which he is imbued by virtue of his vow makes him invulnerable to the yakṣa, who abandons the body of the garland-maker and leaves him in a heap at the feet of Sudaṁsane. When he awakens, he is converted to Jainism by the merchant and prepares to enter the order of Jain monks. After his conversion, he goes about the city, deliberately exposing himself to the rebuke and punishment of the families of those he has killed when possessed by Moggarapāṇi.

Like the Buddhist tales of the conversion of yakṣas, this Jain legend embodies the central relationship of ancient indigenous gods and their worshippers to the teachings and moral values of the new, ascetically based religious tradition. There are two important movements in this ultimately syncretic encounter between the older and newer cults: an acknowledgment of the real power of the ancient forest deity and the righteous supersession by the power of asceticism and *dharma* over the crude power of magical propitiation and invocation. Again, it is possible that the critical depiction of the cultic worship of the yakṣa encodes a more threatening critique of Hindu sacrificial and magical manipulations of power.[35] These Jain and Buddhist texts and legends serve simultaneously to dissever their traditions from the *brāhmani*cal and Hindu traditions *and* to establish a common mythical and folkloric provenance with them by reference to a nondenominational substratum of popular stories and beliefs. By virtue of age alone, the folk beliefs with which the yakṣa myths and legends are linked provide a foundation upon which to build later revisions and transformations of religious legend. The attributions of domain and power to the various yakṣas of legend serve as a basis for indubitable folk wisdom: In the *Pariśiṣṭaparvan,* II, the eighth story, an adulterous woman offers to establish her truthfulness by stepping under the legs of a yakṣa (presumably, a yakṣa statue). She outwits her examiners and the yakṣa himself by vowing that no man other than her husband had ever touched her. Before she performs the truth act, her lover, disguised as a madman, rushes up to her from the crowd and clings to her neck. When he has been pushed aside, she is forced to change her vow before completing the act, saying that "no man other than my husband and this madman have ever touched me." The yakṣa is confused by this sophistry and helplessly allows the woman to go between his legs.

These Jain and Buddhist tales articulate a special relationship between the still vital remnants of a polytheistic imagination and a growing cult of monistic rationalism and institutional mysticism. It is in this uniquely fertile soil that the genre of the folk tale, to which the Buddhist and Jain Jātakas belong, is able to flourish and proliferate. The tension between the ideological one-pointedness and the multiplicity of ancient folk beliefs both reduces the scope of those beliefs, so that a new religious mythology is never able to develop, and, at the same time, expands the need for their telling. The transformative scope of the folk narrative is diminished in comparison with the sweep of the Epic narrative, while the pragmatically illustrative quality of the genre entails a huge proliferation of discrete episodes and tales that explain and illuminate every aspect of human life and interraction.

The supreme, nonworldly goals of Buddhist and Jain liberation and the turning away from the world of the senses (which especially in Jainism is an essential part of the profession of faith) leave a gap in the explanatory power of the dominant ideology, to be filled by the lessons and examples of the folk tale. We assume that a similar process has obtained in the proliferation of European fairy tales, in which numerous archaic fears and desires that lie outside the professed higher interests of institutional Christianity are indulged and explored. (A number of these Indian tales, in fact, found their way into the European repertoire in the Middle Ages by means of traders and merchants traveling from India through Persia.) One Jain yakṣa tale from the *Pariśiṣṭaparvan* of Hemacandra (twelfth century A.D.) clearly follows a folkloric pattern familiar to us from the huge corpus of European folk tales. In this tale, an old woman, Buddhi ("Intelligence"), living in a village worships the yakṣa Bhola in order to receive material blessings, and indeed, finally, he bestows them upon her. Her old friend, Siddhi ("Success"), is very curious about the source of her newfound wealth, and learning that yakṣa worship is responsible, she herself begins to worship Bhola and also reaps the material benefits, having asked him to grant her double what he has given Buddhi. Buddhi becomes jealous and asks for double what has been granted Siddhi. Finally, Siddhi, wishing to eliminate the competition, asks the yakṣa to blind her in one eye, which he does, and when Buddhi returns to the yakṣa's shrine, she, of course, unwittingly asks for double what her friend has just received and is promptly blinded in both eyes.[36] The familiar theme of the discovery, use, and abuse of magical power can be seen in such European fairy tales as Grimms' "The Fisherman and His Wife" and "Little Klaus and Big Klaus," in both of which escalating greed and envy cause the downfall and reversal of the good fortune that had recently been won as a boon from a magical figure. Unexpected guardians of power may be encountered, appeased, and gratified, but as we have seen, this power is difficult to control. Once it has been aroused, its bounty seems inexhaustible but impossible to direct or manipulate. The yakṣa, like the magic fish of the Grimms' fairy tale or the genii of the *Arabian Nights,* is a doorway to riches, but a doorway that cannot be closed at will or barred to others.

There is a tendency in these Jain tales that employ the yakṣa to depict him rather more positively than in either the Buddhist or Hindu myths. This is due, in part, to the Jain cosmological classificatory system that subsumes the yakṣa under the category of Vyantara, a kind of *deva*. In this system, there are four kinds of gods: (1) Bhaumeyikas (including *asuras*, *nāgas*, *suvarṇas*, *vidyuts*, *agni*-beings, *dvīpa*-beings, *udadhi*-

beings, *vāta*-beings, and *ghanika*-beings or "*kumāras*"); (2) Vyantaras (consisting of yakṣas, *piśācas*, *bhūtas*, *rākṣasas*, *kinnāras*, *kiṁpuruṣas*, *mahoragas*, and *gandharvas*); (3) Jyotiṣkas (consisting of the moons, the stars, the suns, the *nakṣatras* ["lunar mansions"], and the planets); and (4) the Vaimānika gods.[37] The shifting kaleidoscope of life envisioned by Indian poets, philosophers, and sages, in which beings pass through many, diverse life-forms in the process of reincarnation, perfecting their selves or souls to achieve some version of absolute transcendence, is a particularly prominent concept in Jain philosophy and cosmology.

> For according to the Jaina conception of the law of rebirth and transmigration, the roles and masks of all the gods and demons in the universe are enacted and bodied forth, in turn, by each life-monad in the course of its progress toward perfection. As a consequence of good and evil deeds, individuals pass from role to role, through many lives, and so appear now as this god or demon, now as that: the roles remaining constant but the life-monads inhabiting or enacting them continually changing.[38]

Like Buddhist cosmology, which envisions otherworldly beings as a full complement to the human sphere, Jain thought also conceives of a vast array of beings occupying every stratum of the cosmos, yet centered always upon the human as the important state in which true release may be achieved. Both traditions may be considered to be "humanistic," in the sense that it is the human faculties that are eminently capable of comprehending the laws of causation, the first step on the road to total release from the bondage of worldly existence or *saṁsāra*. In Jain cosmology, yakṣas, as one class of gods, occupy that special and precarious position, which they share with others of their class, of living lives so pleasant that they are in constant danger of moral and spiritual blindness, which may cause them to "fall" from their high estate and be reborn as humans or something lower.

> The Yakshas who are gifted with various virtues (live in the heavenly regions, situated), one above the other, shining forth like the great luminaries, and hoping never to descend thence.
>
> Intent on enjoying divine pleasures and changing their form at will, they live in the upper Kalpa heavens many centuries of former years.

> The Yakshas, having remained there according to their merit, descend thence at the expiration of their life and are born as men.[39]

The Jain texts are clear in their depiction of yakṣa *caityas*, images, pilgrimages to yakṣa shrines, oblations, and magical practices of various kinds.[40] In the *Antagaḍa-Dasāo,* there is a description of just such a place of popular worship, a *caitya* set up in the forest, near the sanctuary, Punnabhadde, surrounded by implements of worship and offerings and decorated elaborately, as the throne of some forest-deity.

> Underneath this fine asoka-tree, somewhat closer to its trunk was, it is related, a large dais of earthen blocks. It was of goodly proportions as to breadth, length, and height; and it was black, with the hue of the anjana, a cloud, a sword, a lotus, the silken robe of the Ploughsharebearer, an akaśa-keṣa, a soot-collector, cart grease, a section of a horn, a ristaka gem, jack-fruit, an assanaga, a sana-stalk, a mass of blue lotus-petals, or the flower of flax, with the colour of a heap of emeralds, sapphires, kaditra-skins, or pupils of the eye. It was smooth and massive, eight-cornered, like the face of a mirror, very delightful, and variously figured with wolves, bulls, horses, men, dolphins, birds, snakes, elves, ruru-deer, sarabha-deer, yak-oxen, elephants, forest-creepers, and padmaka-creepers. It felt as though it were of deer-skin, of ruta, of bura, of butter, or of tula. It was shaped like a throne, and was comforting . . . comely.[41]

Despite the multifaceted cosmos of the Jains, in which yakṣas and other *devas* are given their due worship and respect, the Jain view that focuses on asceticism as the desired mode of human life and behavior at times envisions threats to that asceticism emanating from other high-placed but nonascetical beings. In one tale from the *Uvasagadasāo,* a certain unspecified "*deva*" behaves very much like the yakṣa we know from other contexts and is displayed here in all of his terrible viciousness and hideousness, having assumed a terrifying magical form in order to shake the ascetic resolve of a follower of Mahāvīra's, Kāmadeva ("Love-god," a strange name for an ascetic).

> . . . its belly was rotund like the dome of an iron smelting furnace; its navel in depth looked like the rice-water bowl of a weaver; its penis in length was fashioned like the rope netting of a meat-safe; its two testicles were fashioned like the sacks for holding yeast; its two thighs were fashioned like a pair of shafts of smelting furnaces; its

> knees were like the cluster of blossoms of the Ajjuna tree, excessively tortuous, and an aspect disgusting and hideous; its shanks were lean and covered with hair; its two feet were fashioned like large grinding slabs; the toes of its feet were fashioned like the rollers of large grinding slabs; and its nails were fashioned like the valves of the oyster shell.[42]

In this form, the *deva* threatens the ascetic with many weapons and takes on as well the forms of wild elephant and serpent, all to no avail. Just as Indra (Sakka) has predicted, this practitioner is not to be shaken from his discipline nor his commitment to *dharma*. With his talent for shape-shifting and testing, his potbelly, and so forth, this deity fits very well within the yakṣa typology we have established and also assumes a role analogous to Māra's in the Buddhist myths and legends. The identification of this clearly demonic being as "*deva*" and his grouping with the other celestial beings under the rulership of Indra are perhaps a not so subtle *śramaṇ*ic ("ascetical"—including Buddhist, Jain, and Upaniṣadic) caricature of the gods of Vedic Hinduism. The heavenly realm, which is so central to Vedic eschatology, assumes an inverted position in the Buddhist and Jain cosmic hierarchy. Heaven, with its temptations to forget *dharma* and to cast aside spiritual effort for the enjoyment of *karm*ic rewards, is actually a kind of hell, and gods are, in reality, demons who are unable to use the power that they have accrued through sacrifice and meritorious deeds for anything truly *dharm*ic. Their magical abilities are like so many fireworks that have not the power to move the meditating human monk one iota. This view offers an interesting footnote to O'Flaherty's previously mentioned analysis of the "three stages of alignment of gods, demons, and men."[43] As she has said, in this second, post-Vedic stage, in which ascetical power comes to the fore to challenge the ritual power of *brāhman*s in their siding with the gods against the demons who threaten to defile the sacrifice and to assume its benefits, the ascetics become the new demons in opposition to gods and *brāhman*s whose pivotal role in the sacrifice has made them essentially like gods. However, from the point of view of the ascetical establishment, namely, the Upaniṣadic *ṛṣi*s and the heterodox religious practitioners (Buddhists and Jains), the gods have become functional demons, more virulent in their thorough opposition to meditative and ascetical mastery than the categorical demons, yakkhas, *rakkhasa*s, *piśāca*s, and so forth. While the latter, as we have seen, are frequently characterized as the enemies of Buddhism, especially in the legends and Jātaka tales, in most cases they retain the capacity for repentance and conversion, and in this sense, they have more in common with humans. In fact, the institutionalization of ascetic *dharma* within Buddhism and Jainism clearly maps out a revised ethical scheme, in which the lone ascetic opposes and battles all of the temptations and obstacles created by *māyā,* whether pleasant or unpleasant, soothing or fearful, divine or demonic.

In the later popularization and iconization of these new religious traditions, the achievement of the Buddha or Mahāvīra becomes symbolic of the totality of human achievement. In the Mahāyāna cosmos, the Buddha has been raised to the position of god, occupying as he does (along with the Buddhas of all realms) in later pictorial representations, the central focus of a swirling, Bosch-like *maṇḍala,* the still point in the moving pageant of the internally differentiated though uniformly illusory world of *saṃsāra.* All about him in this hierarchy beings act out their parts in ignorance of the central axis, where all dualities, classes, and categories are dissolved. The formal, structural opposition between gods and demons in the Vedic texts has been replaced in the *śramaṇ*ical texts by a rational and ethical opposition between *dhamma* or *nibbana* (Sanskrit *nirvāṇa*) and *saṃsāra.* The Buddha is central in the scheme because he embodies *dhamma* and because he was the man who put an end to *saṁsāra* (birth and death). In some senses, this view has complicated the ethical blueprint and in the other senses mentioned above has simplified it. Thus, it serves as prolegomenon to the ethical relativism that obtains in O'Flaherty's third stage of alignment, in the *bhakti* stage of Indian religious ethics. In relationship to the one central point of truth, the Buddhist (or Jain) *dhamma,* all beings are freed of ultimately binding categories, castes, and notions of privilege, freed to embrace or not to embrace the truth, yet thoroughly hampered by the single, monistic view of the truth to be embraced. In this scheme it is no longer a given that demons will fundamentally oppose the *dhamma.* Their demonic propensity indicates that they will be compelled to test the *dhamma,* given as they are to magic and illusion, but in the triumphant proof of its veracity, they slink away or convert to the rational truth that has been revealed. The one persistent, eternal foe of *dhamma* is Kāmamāra, the god of sexuality and death who clearly embodies the conflation of the demonic and the divine within the revised ethics of Buddhism. He is a god because he has total power over a particular domain of human experience, and yet is a demon in his compulsive antagonism toward the Buddha and his teachings. Power is not evoked by Buddhists as a manifestation of the divine, as it is by Hindus; it must be harnessed by reason and truth, otherwise those who display it are in danger of lapsing into unregenerate demonism. In fact, there are startling comparisons to be made between Māra and the yakkha, with whom he is equated in various texts.[44] Yet it is an ambiguous relationship that the Buddha enjoys with the yakkhas and other demigods/demons, particularly the *nāga*.[45] Not only is Māra assimilated to the mythology of the yakkha, so is the Buddha at least on one occasion.[46] As a figure of supernatural power, the yakkha is subordinated to the power of the *dhamma* that the *bodhisatta* embodies; as one of the potent examples of power and efficacy in the popular mythology, the image of the yakkha, along with other figures, is absorbed by Buddhist cult.

In this chapter, which has focused on Buddhist and Jain characterizations of the yakṣa, I have attempted to account for the more demonic portrayal of the yakṣa in: (1) the Jātaka tales vis-à-vis early sculptural depictions and (2) Buddhist cosmology and myth vis-à-vis Hindu cosmology and myth. The folk literary genre, which has been employed in Buddhism and Jainism, draws upon a nondenominational collection of ghost, animal, and demon stories; the yakkhas and *rakkhasa*s, yakkhīs and *rakkhasī*s have been employed in the Jātakas as suitably frightening representatives of the folk genre. In the background of the Buddhist demonic characterizations of the yakṣa, I would contend, is a cosmological view that is distinctly dualistic, envisioning creation and the evolution of the world of matter as a negative process, a "fall" rather than a further emanation of the absolute, as it is in Vedic, Upaniṣadic, and Purāṇic cosmologies. This dualism also seems to be reflected in the mythological encounters of the *bodhisatta* and the yakkha in the Jātaka tales.

The dualistic opposition of light and dark, *bodhisatta* and yakkha, is offset by the potential for enlightenment that is shared by all beings, demonic and otherwise. Following from this, we can formulate a comparison of two ethical views: a view found in the Pāli Jātakas and Suttas as opposed to a view found in Hindu mythology of a comparable period (Epics and early Purāṇas). In the Buddhist view, the enlightened being is dialectically opposed to the demon, who is the apotheosis of carnality, delusion, and ignorance. This dialectical opposition is mediated by the act of conversion to the Buddhist *dhamma,* by means of which the two categories, *bodhisatta*/enlightened being and yakkha/demon, come closer together. In the classical (not Upaniṣadic) Hindu view, the concept of *dharma* expresses not just one standard of "truth," "reality," or "knowledge," but a spectrum of knowledge and truths relative to a hierarchy of beings and classes. In this system, "evil" and the "demonic" are not just that which oppose the truth, but also that which undermine the maintenance of the hierarchical categories of distinct beings and classes. From this point of view, the *bodhisatta*'s conversion of the yakkha is itself a demonic act because it abrogates the ordering principle inherent in the Hindu concept of *dharma* that underpins the whole cosmosocial order of Hinduism.

Psychologically, politically, and doctrinally, early Buddhism was a religion of assimilation. Despite the centrality of the human being within Buddhist theory, the multidimensional cosmos, in which gods, humans, and demons revolved around one another in a *maṇḍala,* was a welcome inheritance from the *brāhman*ical tradition. To serve Buddhist purposes, that cosmic model was simplified and reinterpreted in key ways. The challenge to Buddhist philosophy and mythology lay in the dual necessities of *both* preserving the basic hierarchical model of the cosmos shared with *brāhman*ical Hinduism *and* asserting the primacy of *human* nature and perception. The task was one of simplification. As I have mentioned in the Introduction, the liberating notion of the personal conquest of ontological evil through introspection implied a coming to terms with the profusion of external threats and demons. The demons were not eliminated from the cosmological map, but their *essential* power for destruction was defused through assimilation. Specifically *conceptual* or *intellectual* as opposed to *ritual* means were employed to achieve this assimilation.[47] Through an intellectual analysis and simplification of the essential constituents of the cosmos, the individual is able to identify divine and demonic characteristics within himself. In his internal mastery of them, it is implied, he is able to exert an irresistible moral and rational power over the "actual" demons outside.

Chapter 5

YAKṢĪS

Introduction

While the sculptural treatments of yakṣīs (or yakṣiṇīs) display images of benign female sexuality and rampant fertility, the literary examples, both Hindu and Buddhist, exhibit an aspect that is almost entirely frightening or demonic. The benevolent yakṣī is frequently encountered in the form of dryad or aquatic nymph, in which case she is practically indistinguishable from the celestial nymph, the *apsara*s. One prevalent motif (as we have already noted) is the *śālabhañjikā* or "woman and the tree" sculptural style, denoting an early fertility festival or system of rites. The yakṣī and yakṣa pillar reliefs at Bhārhut, Sāñcī, and Mathurā depict similar primeval dryadic motifs. Misra has described a famous one of these fertility deities at Bhārhut, the yakṣī Candrā:

> She is carved on the middle face of a pillar (0.5 Calcutta Museum), bearing the label *Cadā-Yakkhī*—"The Yakshī Cadā (Candrā)"; she stands under a Nāga-tree (Mesua ferrea) entwining it with her left arm and leg. In the left hand she holds a branch of the tree with flowers and leaves. By her right hand, she is bending the branch of the tree; her right foot is put straight on a pedestal. The pedestal carries a figure variously described as "a sheep or ram with hind part of a fish" (Luders), or as a horse-faced *makara* (Banerjea and Barua). The Yakshī's hair is beautifully decorated with different bands of decorative designs. She wears large square *kuṇḍala*s, necklaces, bangles, armlets, *mekhalā* and anklets. An ornament with bead and reel design is worn by her in *upavita* fashion, and on her forehead appears a round *ṭikulī* with star design. Her left upraised foot is on the head of her *vāhana*.[1]

In contrast to the sculptural images of yakṣīs, which tend to reflect a more positive dimension of female sexuality, the literary examples serve in many contexts as projections of violent, paranoic fears of menace by the Indian male upon the Indian female. The yakṣī (or yakṣiṇī) and the other female demigoddesses, such as *nāginī*s, rākṣasīs, and *apsaras*es, share with their male counterparts the quality of changing physical form and employment of illusion to effect their desires upon hapless humans. This characteristic of shifting, indefinite form cooperates well with the need or desire to project evil upon an amorphous female presence.

Especially in her wanderings in the forest, a human female may be compared to any one of a number of forest-dwelling females.[2] The confusion about her identity stems in part from the strangeness of seeing an "undomesticated" woman, that is, a woman apparently detached from a man. For it is the formal attendance upon husband and family that is the unmistakable sign of the "good" woman. Her solitary wanderings divorce her from a safe image of the bound and the maternal and immediately evoke for a chance male beholder the embodiment of sexual license.

The Buddhist Yakkhinī

In the respect of her jurisdiction over the wild places, the yakṣī or yakkhinī is, of course, like her male counterpart, the yakṣa or yakkha. Stories abound, particularly in the Buddhist Jātaka tales, about the encounter with the yakkhinī, usually occurring in the forest or at sea. The devouring tendencies of the yakkhinī are, unlike the yakkha's, however, strongly sexual as well as alimentary. The *Telapatta Jātaka* (no. 96) tells the story of the *bodhisatta*'s journey from Benares to Takkasila, taking him through a forest of yakkhas and yakkhinīs.

> There in the precinct of the demons, yakkhinīs make houses appear in the middle of the road and, having prepared a costly bed with a canopy painted overhead with golden stars and enclosed with silken curtains in many colors, they decorate themselves with celestial ornaments and go to sit down in the houses from whence they ply men with sweet words, saying: "You seem tired; come here, sit down, and have a drink of water before going." When they have summoned them, they give those who come seats and seduce them with the charm of their wanton beauty. But, having excited their lust, they have intercourse with them and then they kill them and eat them while the blood flows. They take hold of men's aesthetic sense with

> their beauty, their sense of sound with sweet words and songs, their sense of smell with divine odors, their taste with all kinds of delicious food, their sense of touch with red cushions of supernal softness. But if you can restrain your senses and remember not to look at them, then on the seventh day, you will be king of the city of Takkasila.[3]

Since it is the beauty of the female that is employed as the lure to seduce and entrap the male, the beauty of women in general is linked to the demonic. The power of this connection is particularly explored in Buddhist literature and imagery, where the fusion of the erotic and the demonic is extraordinarily potent. By means of his superior insight, Siddhārtha Gautama was able, literally, to see through the exterior beauty of women to the hideous darkness at the core of everything female. The preceding passage follows a well-established paradigm for the depiction of erotic females of all species. In Aśvaghoṣa's later poetic biography of the Buddha, the *Buddhacarita,* the famous scene that precedes Siddhārtha's renunciation of the palace life involves the indecorous seductiveness of a group of female musicians. In this passage, the underside of female sensuality and beauty is seen to be a demonic, ogresslike capacity to enslave and destroy men. The frequent use of this demonic feminine imagery in the Jātaka tales makes sense within the metaphorical structure that governs imaginative expressions of Buddhist ideals and thought: Asceticism is male and must defend itself rigorously against the seductive demands of, and attachment to, the world of the senses, which is conceived of as female.

The "island of the sirens" is a motif that is employed to depict the enslaving power of the feminine as embodied in the yakkhinī. In the *Valāhassa Jātaka* (no. 196), the *bodhisatta* tells the tale of a yakkha city on the island of Ceylon, named Sirisavatthu. It is inhabited by yakkhinīs who, when a ship is wrecked, "in glorious array, take food and drink and, surrounded by an entourage of maid servants, with their children on their hips, they approach the merchants." They entice the shipwrecked men into their city, saying that their husbands are dead. When they get them there, they "bind them with magic chains" (*devasaṁkhalikāya bandhitvā*) and cast them into "houses of torment" (*karanaghare*). They force the men to marry them and then proceed to eat some of them. Two hundred and fifty of the five hundred men are saved by the *bodhisatta* in the form of a white horse, but the others are eaten. The motif of the island of the sirens is repeated in the *Ma-*

hāvastu, in the story of "The Five Hundred Merchants," and has much in common with the Circe episode of *The Odyssey,* where, again, sexuality is linked with alimentary consumption, and artifice and illusion are central to the female's mesmerizing hold over the male.

It is the femaleness of these yakkhinīs that is the source not only of their power but also of their undoing. There is always a possibility that their sexual appetites may lead them to fall in love with their captive lovers, as it does for Calypso (another of the demonically divine females of *The Odyssey*) in her attachment to Odysseus. The animal forms that these yakkhinīs and *rakkhasī*s assume seem particularly expressive of the conflation of power and powerlessness, or domination and devotion, that is characteristic of them. In the *Mahāvaṁsa,* one of Vijāya's men follows the yakkhinī, Kuvanna, who is disguised as a bitch:

> She bewitches him and all those who follow him but cannot devour them, as they are protected by charmed threads. Vijāya follows, overcomes the Yakkhinī and obtains the release of the men; Kuvanna takes the form of a beautiful girl and Vijāya marries her. . . . She enables him to destroy the invisible Yakkhas who inhabit the land, and he becomes king. Later he repudiates her and marries a human princess. She returns to the Yakkhas, but is killed as a traitress. Her two children become the ancestors of the Pulinda (perhaps the Veddas, who are still worshippers of Yakkhas; perhaps as ancestors?).[4]

The thwarted effort of the besotted nonhuman female to penetrate the human world and live with her beloved is a familiar aspect of many of these myths and legends.[5] It is her tragedy that, despite her efforts to disguise herself and become acceptable to a human community, she is doomed ultimately to the rejected and disappointed. Often, she is even deprived of her half-human children, who, as the rules of Indian kinship dictate, must go with their father, for it is he who confers legitimacy and social status upon them. In the rather literal symbolism of the Buddhist Jātakas, the demonic has become equivalent to everything that opposes the awakening of the understanding of Buddhist doctrine. Conversely, the human is symbolic of a potential for true wisdom, so that, in the case of the "half-breeds" or mixed orders of beings, the demonic side is seen as a pollutant, obscuring the *human* capacity for goodness.

An important variant of the devouring yakkhinī is the horse-faced yakkhinī (*assamukhī*), who has her mythological roots planted deeply in the soil of Indo-European symbolism through her connection with the powerful and extremely widespread mythology of the mare-goddess, whom O'Flaherty has termed, "the phallic mother."

> The mare in Indo-European mythology becomes symbolic of the evil mother, the dark mother, the erotic and devouring mother, the whore, in contrast with the good mother, the white mother, the milk-giving chaste cow. Instead of feeding her child (as the cow does), the mare eats her child. Moreover, like the female praying mantis, she devours her husband as well; she eats his substance and power even as she drinks his seed. In extreme cases, the furious goddess actually devours the testicles of the god, as an alternative to devouring young children and pregnant women, her usual food.[6]

In the *Padakusalamāṇava Jātaka* (no. 432), the devouring equine mother is seen in the softened, mitigated form in which we often encounter the yakkhinī-lover of a human beloved. In this tale, a horse-faced yakkhinī captures a *brāhman* and lives with him in a cave. Though the strange lovers commingle sexually, they remain separate in their eating habits: The *brāhman* must continue to be fed "regular" human food (foraged by his yakkhinī wife), while she can only eat raw human flesh. In time, the yakkhinī gives birth to a son, the *bodhisatta,* who tries to escape outside of the boundaries of her authority (the familiar magic circle within which the yakṣa is powerful) with his weakened, ineffectual father on his back.

> When she returned, she missed them and followed after them. The Bodhisatta picked up his father and brought him into the middle of the river. She came and stood on the river bank, and when she saw that they had passed beyond her boundaries, she stopped where she was and cried, "My dear child, come here with your father. What is my offence? Have you not prospered because of me, my husband? Come back, my lord." Thus, she pleaded with her child and husband. So the Brāhman crossed the river. She begged her child also, saying, "Dear son, don't do this to me; come back!" "Mama, we are men; you are a yakkha. We cannot live with you forever."[7]

When the *bodhisatta* refuses to remain with his mother, she reluctantly gives to him the only magical skill she has, an arcane knowledge enabling him to follow for twelve years in the footsteps of those who have gone away. So overcome is the yakkhinī with the departure of her son that she dies of sorrow on the spot and is cremated by her deeply saddened son.

This yakkhinī's tenderness toward her son is paradoxical in terms of that race's infamous slaughter of human children, expressing the inversion of maternal succor. This diabolical penchant of the yakkhinīs for consuming babies is demonstrated vividly in the *Jayaddisa Jātaka* (no. 513), in which, in a fit of jealous rage, a rival queen in the harem of a king cursed the head queen, saying, "Some day I shall be able to eat your children alive," whereupon she was turned into a yakkhinī. "Then she seized her chance and, grabbing the child in full view of the queen she crunched and devoured it as if it were a piece of raw flesh, and then ran off." In this fashion, she killed another of the queen's newborns, but in her attempt to devour a third, the queen's guards diverted her, and not having time to devour the child, she hid him in a sewer.

> The infant, thinking she was his mother, took her breast in his mouth and she conceived a love for this son, and went to the cemetery where she placed him in a rock cave and looked after him.[8]

She continued to feed her adopted son human flesh, thus transforming him into a quasi-yakkha who, despite his royal birth,[9] took to haunting the local forests, searching for edible human prey. Some time after the yakkhinī's death, his true identity was discovered by his brother's son (the *bodhisatta*). This brother was born after the prince-yakkha was carried off and now occupied the throne. Unaware, as they all were, that the marauding yakkha was, in fact, their own relative, the *bodhisatta* set out to confront the fiend and persuade him to cease his grisly activities. Having impressed the yakkha-man with his virtue and bravery, the *bodhisatta* tested the yakkha and determined that he was, in fact, no demon.

> "The eyes of yakkhas are red and unblinking. They cast no shadow and are free from all fear. This is no yakkha; it is a man. It is said that my father had three brothers who were carried off by a yakkhinī. Two of them must have been devoured by her, but she must have looked after one with a mother's love. This must be that one. I will take him and proclaim him to my father and establish him on the throne." And so thinking, he exclaimed, "Bho! You are no yakkha; you are my

father's elder brother. Come with me and raise your parasol in your ancestral kingdom."[10]

The yakkha was convinced of his true birth, but his descent into savagery had been too great for him to recover his nobility fully. He told his *bodhisatta*-nephew, "Dear friend, please go home: as for me, I am born with two natures in one form. I have no wish to be a king. I'll become an ascetic." Thus, we see another aspect of the link between morality and food. The prince had been corrupted by being fed on unholy food, and even his conversion couldn't effect a complete reversal of the alimentary pollution. Females and mothers, as the purveyors of food within a family, shoulder heavy responsibilities for the moral purity of their children.

The mythology of the yakkhinīs (and *rakkhasīs*) has lent itself to an assimilation of folk legends concerning demonic local goddesses. The famous figure of Hārīti, known in connection with a variety of geographical locations and attendant myths, was gathered into the Buddhist corpus as early as the *Vinaya Piṭaka.*[11] Among her many epithets, locales, and legends, there are a few themes that appear to be basic to her mythology: She is obviously a fertility figure, associated with the generation as well as the destruction of children. In most of the versions, she is the mother of five hundred demonlike sons, one of her names being "Bahuputrikā," "having many sons," who are thought to be, in some versions, bearers of pestilence and responsible for the deaths of many (i.e., other people's sons). In the *Vinaya Piṭaka,* she is called "Huansi," "Joy," (Sanskrit Ānanda) and lives in Rājagṛha. Originally, she was a protectress of the people there, but "as a result of a spiteful wish in a previous life, she started stealing and killing the children of the city for herself and for her five hundred children," the name "Hārīti" meaning "thief." "The Buddha ultimately brought her under control by hiding her youngest child, Piṅgala, in his alms-bowl. He ordained a share of food in every monastery to provide for her and her children."[12]

In various Gandharan sculptures, she is paired with a consort, Pāncāla,[13] and both are depicted as harbingers of abundance and embodiments of charity. The two are important in the development of the "potbellied" yakṣa iconographic type, that is, the yakṣa figure associated specifically with symbols of material wealth. Becoming purified of their link with images of disease and malevolence, Hārīti became transformed in some representations into Bhadrā, Lakṣmī, or Vasudhārā, all auspicious and gentle goddesses, while Pāñcika was absorbed into the growing iconography of Kubera or Jambhala, a Jain saint and deity. Surely, this exemplifies the extremity of the moral transmogrification that we associate with the yakṣa deities and types.

In their manifestation as tutelary deities of the Buddhist pantheon, Hārīti and Pāñcika were probably preceded by the pair, Bahuputrikā and Maṇibhadra, two figures who enjoyed some cult prominence and worship. The meaning of "*bahuputrikā*" becomes expanded and generalized in the way that often happens in popular expressions, so that, losing her diabolical characteristic of eating children, Bahuputrikā-Hārīti becomes a figure to be prayed to for the birth of sons. This is not surprising since both the possession and the destruction of sons seem conflated in her original iconography and mythology as well. Though a minor figure in the endless proliferation of popular deities, she fuses, however precariously, the two sides of the maternal character: procreative abundance and vengeful destruction, madonna and ogress, two facets that are rarely combined in a single manifestation of the Goddess (with the possible exception of the Hindu goddess Durgā, who, though both benign and martial, cannot really be considered to be "maternal").[14] The unlikely marriage of oppositions can probably be explained as one deity's assimilation of another's traits, through geographical and/or ethnic encroachment.

The devouring of children seems to constitute a special, drastic punishment of women who, through curses, misconduct, or jealous resentment (as we have seen in the *Jayaddisa Jātaka*), may be reborn as, or take the form of, these grotesque harpies. The devouring of offspring is the formal and ethical opposite of the usual maternal function of discharging rather than physically withholding infants. N. Peri recounts the well-known legend found in the Chinese Tripiṭaka of Hārīti, who, in a previous birth as Abhirati, a herdsman's wife, has been forced to dance while pregnant. She decides to avenge herself by assuming the form of the yakṣī, Hārīti, and in this guise, devouring the children of Rājagṛha. She continues her ghoulish vengeance despite the efforts of the citizens to appease her with offerings and worship, until the people seek the aid of the Buddha, who hides Hārīti's youngest and favorite child under his begging bowl.[15] The impact of her loss moves her to understand the evil of her ways, and she converts to

Buddhism. The Buddha restores her child and establishes a regular worship of her in various monasteries of which she becomes the protectress.[16] Once converted, it is then that Hārīti is worshipped extensively as a giver of children (another example of conversion as a transformation of demonic propensities, in this case, those inherent in the female). As we have seen, the withholding of male offspring and the prevention of their embarkation upon the path of asceticism acquire additional resonance within the Buddhist context. The conversion of these Buddhist demonesses to the way of *dhamma* purges them of the grasping, holding, devouring maternalism that is anathema to the spirit of Buddhist asceticism.

The etiology of the demonic aspect of these yakṣīs and other related female spirits, such as *rākṣasī*s and *nāgī*s, in the folk logic that surrounds their mythology, rooted in abrogations of the feminine nature. Women, it is believed, are defined and compelled by overwhelming reproductive needs that, when denied or truncated, result in their actual transformation into a demonic form. Or as we have seen, when they allow their passions and jealousies to override their fixed social duties, their failure is often depicted metaphorically as a descent into the demonic. The necessity of palliating their unquiet spirits bespeaks the power inherent in their rebellion against the norms of society.

More than the yakṣa mythology, the mythology of the yakṣī is interwoven with village lore about female ghosts and spirits. Untimely death is most often the reason for the development of a spirit-cult, but in the case of female spirits and ghouls, other factors as well contribute to their continued propitiation and cultic worship. Widows are known to be an unsettling force in village life. They, as well as other women whose natural fulfillment of their domestic potential has been cut off, either through death in childbirth or within the period of postpartum pollution or prior to marriage, are natural candidates for transformation into haunting spirits or demonesses. Locally, these creatures are known by a variety of names: *churel, churail, chudail, alivantin,* and so forth. In the Deccan, the Jakhin (a word related to "yakṣī") is the uneasy spirit of a married woman who "haunts bathing and cooking rooms, attacks her husband's second wife and children, takes her own children from their stepmother," or steals babies. The spirit of such a woman may be controlled by mutilating her corpse, cutting out the dead child if she has died in childbirth, breaking her ankles and turning the feet around, and burying her deeply, facedown, with the bones of an ass, while reciting incantations.[17]

Yakṣīs as *Śakti*s

In the Jain, Buddhist, and Hindu Tantric traditions, the use of yakṣas and (more numerously) yakṣīs/yakṣiṇīs as tutelary deities and devotional objects is prevalent and among the earliest examples of the enshrinement and employment of demigods as instruments of power.[18] The use of yakṣīs in this regard is a tradition that responds to the growing use of female *iṣṭadevatā*s (deities chosen by a worshipper to aid him in his practice) in Tantric-style rites. In this respect, yakṣīs become assimilated to the burgeoning pantheon of *śakti*s (female energies, powers, aspects, or individual manifestations of the Goddess).[19] The magical subjection of yakṣas and yakṣīs is a theme that finds its way into the later Śaivite legends, where trafficking with demons becomes an aspect of "left-handed" unorthodoxy. The *Karpūramañjarī* 1. 25 mentions a Śaivite *kāpālika* "who is able to call forth yakṣīs to do his bidding when and wherever he chooses."[20] Yakṣas and yakṣiṇīs appear (in the case of the former) as the twenty-four *upāsaka*s and (in the case of the latter) as the *sāsanadevatā*s (tutelary deities) of the various Jain Tirthāṅkaras. As such, they are widely represented in the temples and sites of Jain art and architecture.[21]

Coomaraswamy has linked the worship of yakṣiṇīs with the medieval cult of the Sixty-four Yoginīs, a Tantric sect that encompassed a spectrum of loosely related aspects, ranging from local village goddesses, to the witchlike Dākinīs, to the seven (or eight) *mātṛkā*s, who were *śakti*s of the Goddess. Both *yoginī*s and yakṣiṇīs have fierce and benevolent aspects; both are connected with trees and occasionally inhabit them.[22] In medieval and Tantric texts, a yakṣa or yakṣiṇī *sādhana* is known, in which the deities are invoked and persuaded to render service to the devotee.

> The devotee attracts the Yakshī, by living on *bhiksha* [alms] for three months and offering *guggula* [a perfume or fragrant resin] and chanting mantras 8000 times for the same period. On completion of the rites she appears before the devotee as mother, sister, or friend and gives him nectar which produces long life and strength like that of Yakshas.[23]

Rites for taming yakṣīs are mentioned in the *Kathāsaritsāgara,* chapter 49. Here, the *brāhman,* Adityaśarman, serves both Hindu and Buddhist ascetics to win the secrets of these rites. For his efforts, he wins the beautiful and powerful yakṣī Sulocanā, who favors him by marrying him, granting him all that he desires, and taking him off to the yakṣa heaven, Alakā, where he sires upon her a son, Gunaśarman, and continues to live in luxury until he is cast out by a curse from the peevish visiting Indra.

In the Tantric context, the symbolic domestication of the wilderness, which the yakṣa embodies, takes the form of a sexual subjugation of the wild (i.e., erotic) yakṣī by the male practitioner. Her undomesticated sexuality is brought to heel and transmuted into familial goodwill, serving simultaneously and conversely as a metaphor for her actual sexual enslavement by the practitioner (a motif that is perhaps latent in the Muslim tales of geniis as well).[24]

Chapter 6

THE *MEGHADŪTA*

The vast compendium of mythological and iconographical prototypes has served to quicken the traditionally attuned imaginations of Indian literary and visual artists. In this sense, the works of the poets may be considered to be "popular," that is, the symbols and images that the poets habitually employ are drawn from a shared and immediately recognizable representational vocabulary. In the sense that their depictions are fashioned in terms of a lexicon of highly cultivated, polished, and elite aesthetic conventions, these works are not "popular," but presuppose a learned readership. But in the sense that these urbane, Sanskrit classics, however, create new variations on traditional themes that then find their way back into a populist context through vernacular adaptations, they still qualify as "popular" works.

There are profuse examples of the ornamental use of yakṣas, *gaṇas*, *gandharvas*, and so forth, in both literary and sculptural contexts, but also one potent instance of the employment of the yakṣa as a central or pivotal figure in a poetic work. In the long dramatic poem, the *Meghadūta* (*Cloud Messenger*), by the fifth-century poet Kālīdāsa, the entire work is delivered as a monologue by the central figure/narrator, who is a yakṣa. The poem was written in the *mandakrānta* meter, which was thought to be especially apt for the depiction of the sentiments of pathos and tenderness. The setting and inspiration for the yakṣa's extended monologue are summed up in the first three verses of the poem.

> A certain yakṣa who had neglected his duties was separated from his beloved by his *guru*, whose curse had robbed him of his greatness. He endured a whole year away from her. He took up residence among the *āśramas* of Rāmagiri, in the dense shade trees, where the waters were made sacred by Sītā's ablutions.

> Weakened by the separation, his shrunken forearm emptied of its fallen golden bracelet, he spent some months on that mountain. On the first day of the month of Aṣādḥa, he saw a cloud that, in its resting against a mountain peak, reminded the lover of a charging elephant, playfully butting with its horns.
>
> Standing somehow in front of it, that lord pledged his admiration and mused: If the thoughts of a happy man are turned at the sight of a cloud, how much more those of people [like me] who live far away and long to fall upon their beloved's neck.[1]

Kālīdāsa has used the stock figure of the yakṣa to symbolize and embody the extremity of the sensual, poetic temperament. Indeed, sensuality and Sanskrit poetry are inextricably bound up with one another. In his employment of the yakṣa, he has concentrated on that side of the creature's character, which is linked with nature and fertility, and has ignored completely all hint of the yakṣa's demonic tendencies. Being a poet and not a religious historian, Kālīdāsa has not attempted to deepen our phenomenological understanding of yakṣas. Rather, he has extended the use of the symbol through one more permutation of expression. For the poet, the fluidity and ambiguity of the historical characterization of the yakṣa are distinctly advantageous for his creative purposes, for they allow him a fairly blank canvas upon which to fix his poetic conceits. The very mention of the yakṣa stirs in his audience nebulous images of fanciful creatures, existing in distant, mythical dimensions where anything is possible.

The underlying connection of the yakṣa with the waters in particular provides the subtle basis for his affinity with the cloud. The appearance of the cloud sends the yakṣa into a romantic reverie in which he charges it to take a message to his lover.

> Cloud, you who are the refuge of the tormented, please take a message from me to my beloved. I am separated from her on account of the anger of the Lord of Wealth [Kubera]. You are to go to the seat of the Lord of the Yakṣas, which is called Alakā—where the palaces are lit by the crescent moon on Śiva's head as he stands in the garden outside the city.[2]

In his monologue, addressing the cloud, the yakṣa floridly describes the sights and occurrences it will encounter on its way to

Alakā. The abode of the yakṣas is finally invoked in the latter part of the poem and offered as an image of the most exquisite paradise.

> If you haven't seen it, you will not recognize Alakā, as if in the embrace of a lover, with the rushing Ganges for its raiment. In your season [the rainy season], that city supports high palaces with roaring water and encircling puffs of clouds like the ropes of pearls that girls bind in their hair.
>
> Where the palaces with their frolicking women, their paintings, their drums beaten musically, and their clouds which kiss the mountain peaks standing in their bejeweled ether, can be compared to you with your lightning, your rainbow, and your friendly thunder which bursts with water.
>
> Where the moonstones, which are like clear drops of water suspended in networks of webs from the moon at night with its white rays obstructed by you, remove the passion-induced langor in the bodies of women whose lovers have released them from their once embracing arms.
>
> Where the paths of lovers taken at night are revealed at sunrise, by the *mandāra* flowers which have fallen from the women's hair because of their trembling gait, by cut leaves, by the golden lotuses which have dropped from their ears, and by fallen shells and garlands of pearls broken by friction with their breasts.
>
> Where tears are due to joy and no other causes. And there is no other sorrow except that which is born of love and cured by union with the beloved. Where there is never any reason for separation except for a lover's quarrel and certainly no other stage of life but youth is found there among the yakṣas.
>
> Where the trees are always full of flowers and swarms of drunken bees. And the lotus plants always bear lotuses that have as their girdles rows of *haṁsa* birds. And the house peacocks with their ever-luminous plumage lift up their necks to screech. And the nights are amiable, their darkness dispelled by eternal moonlight.
>
> Where women have lotuses in their hands to play with and fresh *kunda* flowers sprinkled in their hair. And the luminosity of their faces is made pale by the pollen of the *lodhra* blossoms they wear. And in the clasps of their topknots, there are fresh *kurabaka* flowers, and in their ears, lovely *śirīsa* flowers, and in the parts of their hair, fruits, engendered by your approach.

In which place yakṣas, along with the most beautiful women, came to the palaces made of crystal containing the images of flowers like the reflections of stars. They enjoyed the "fruit of love" [*ratiphalam*] wine, produced by the wishing tree, while the beaten drums were as pleasant as the deep sound of your thunder.

Where the linen garments of women with lips like *bimba* fruit are loosened by the unbinding of the cloth ties of their undergarments which are removed by lovers with hands emboldened by lust.

And the handful of powder thrown by the women who are flustered by their shame, though intended for the flames, is flung in vain and reaches only as far as the jeweled lamps.

Where those clouds brought by the wind, which have as their target the palaces, produce blemishes on the paintings with drops of their water, seeming to have discharged their rain as if seized with alarm. Dissolved into drops, they escape through the windows, skillful at imitating the rising smoke.

Where girls who are desired by the gods are attended by the Maruts with the waters of the Ganges and protected from the heat by the shade of *mandāra*s growing in water on the banks and play with jewels which are concealed by being thrown by handfuls into the golden sand.

Where everyday the lovers, possessed of endless wealth inside their houses celebrate with song, accompanied by the sweet-voiced *kinnāra*s, the fame of Dhanapati [Kubera] and enjoy the outside garden in the company of courtesans, immortal damsels who enthrall with their conversation.

Where wine like clear perfume, skillful in teaching the rolling of the eyes; the budding of flowers and young shoots; a variety of ornaments; and red dye suitable for the painting of a lotus foot are all produced solely for the ornament of the weaker sex by the *kalpa vṛkṣa* ("wishing tree").

Where horses dark as foliage are like the proud steeds of the sun and the elephants are as tall as mountains and, like you, spray water, but in the form of ichor. And the best of warriors, who have stood against Rāvaṇa in battle, have the splendor of their uniforms overshadowed by the marks of the wounds inflicted by their scimitars.

Where, having known that Śiva is dwelling in person as Kubera's friend, Manmatha [Kāma, the god of love, similar to Cupid],

> through fear, does not carry his bow which has bees for a string. His work is accomplished merely by the playfulness of clever women whose eyes shoot frowning glances which unfailingly reach the target of their lovers.[3]

Thus, the world of the yakṣas is celebrated, a mythical haven in which all of the metaphors known to *kāvya* (Sanskrit poetry) are freely displayed. The yakṣa-hero ends his long soliloquy with the speeches that the cloud has been charged to deliver to his yakṣiṇī-beloved, conveying to her his amorous longing and desolation.

> "When Viṣṇu arises from his serpent-bed, my curse will end. Spend the last four months with your eyes closed and afterward we will enjoy that desire which is increased by separation—in the moonlit nights of the latter part of autumn.
>
> When you go to sleep, you will soon be embraced by me in your bed and, being awakened, you will cry out loudly, suppressing a smile, and repeatedly interrogating me: 'You devil, I saw you in my dream giving pleasure and making love.'
>
> Knowing from this token that I am well, O Dark-Eyed One, do not mistrust me on account of some rumor. Moreover, they say that love is decreased in separation but, rather, in the desire resulting from abstinence the pent-up affection is intensified."
>
> "Having consoled your friend, O cloud, stung by sorrow in our first separation, and returning from those peaks which have been dug out of the mountain [Kailāsa] by Śiva's bull, restore my life, which is like a wilted jasmine flower at daybreak, with her words, sent to me and accompanied by a token.
>
> Have you decided, friend, to do this service for me? Indeed, I don't consider your present impassivity to be a rejection of my appeal. Even though you are silent, you send the water requested by the *caraka* birds; for, just accomplishing a thing is a reply to your petitioners.
>
> Having done this strange favor for me because I asked you, whether out of friendship or with intentional compassion for me in my separation, roam anywhere you like, cloud. Your beauty enhanced by the rainy season, may you never be separated from lightning in the way [that I am from my beloved], even for a moment."[4]

Kālīdāsa's yakṣa may be seen to embody an aesthetic manipulation of the mythological prototype. Aesthetic appreciation, linked as it is in Sanskrit poetics with religious experience, provides a valuable conduit for carnal transformation. Within *kāvya* in general, sexual imagery is used "counterphobicly," expressing exclusively within an artistic context what cannot be freely explored within society at large. Sexual ethics in India are socially pragmatic rather than "puritanical." The exquisite enjoyment of sexuality and the women who embody it is celebrated by the poets whose works reflect remote, courtly, sexual license. Kālīdāsa's use of the yakṣa to embody that delight in sexual imagery underscores the exotic and rarefied conception of sexual abandon. The characteristic mountainous or wilderness setting for the activities of yakṣas provides the occasion for the extravagant application of the lush natural imagery that is the poet's stock-in-trade.

That the yakṣa functions here as a neutral romantic symbol is seen particularly in the seventeenth-century illustrated manuscript of the *Meghadūta,* in which the yakṣa and yakṣī are depicted as "love-lorn Rājput prince and princess."[5] An illustration of the projected reunion of the yakṣa lovers sets them in a lavish courtly apartment where they look and behave in ways that are not dissimilar to myriad other effete, romantic lovers.

> In the spacious sitting room below, painted passion-red, the lovers celebrate their reunion under a sea-green *vitāna* decorated with tassels. The yaksha, represented as a charming ebullient prince dressed in a green turban, pink *jama* and red *pyjamas* and *patka,* is seated on pillows and holds in the hands a drinking bowl and a *pan* obviously offered by his beloved. The Yakshi stands at attention fanning her lover with one hand and holding a wine jar in the other. She is lavishly decked with pearl jewelry adorned with pompons and is charmingly dressed in a transparent *odhani,* blue *choli,* and striped green Chanderi skirt with red *pallu.* The happy meeting of the lovers is being amusingly witnessed by a pet monkey who climbs a large shady tree, perched upon by a peacock, in the courtyard.[6]

As we have seen, the yakṣa has functioned mythologically as a potent fertility image, as an embodiment of mystery and wildness, as a reflection of various dimensions of social and religious anomy, and as a broad metaphor for evil. In the various literary genres in which demonic yakṣas and yakṣīs have appeared, their evil propensities have been countered by having them defeated, destroyed, converted, appeased, exorcised, and worshipped. In the *Meghadūta,* the yakṣa has been aestheticized and thus, in yet one more way, divested of his dangerous wildness and demonic license.

CONCLUSIONS

The yakṣa has never been amenable to precise location. His mysterious and protean formulations are central to what he is. We discovered that, from the beginning, the yakṣa was both manifest and unmanifest (*vyakta* and *avyakta*). Thus, the theistic incorporation of both dimensions within a single deity that was adumbrated in the *Śvetāśvatara Upaniṣad*[1] and that later became central to Viśiṣṭadvaita and Śaiva Siddhāntha theologies, has some of its earliest, however shadowy, expressions in the Vedic yakṣa references. His dual nature confers an intermediate status upon the yakṣa, in which he shares the attributes of celestial deities such as the *gandharva*s as well as the qualities of the lower, purely demonic beings such as the *rākṣasa*s and *piśāca*s. The potential earthiness of the yakṣa and yakṣī provided a basis for their employment as sculptural motifs and popular religious icons. The early and frequent visualization of the concept/personality of the yakṣa in sculpture perhaps contributed to the withering away of his early *avyakta* significance. His aura of mystery, we decided, persisted in a more circumscribed form—as the mystery in nature. Through the fusion of nature, mystery, and magic, the yakṣa's demonic persona was more steadily forged.

In the discussion of the symbolic background of the yakṣa, which was undertaken in Chapter 1, the second section, a basis for his ethical ambiguity was established—in his association with the mixed blessing of fertility and the potent, transformative waters that confer it. In section three the yakṣa's powerful link with other, less ambiguous but prevalent demons was underscored.

On the basis of this short catalogue of demons and the analysis of the mythological relations of the yakṣa, I have extrapolated a functional definition of evil or disvalue (*pāpa, adharma,* etc.), as it has been embodied by the yakṣa and yakṣī and their kindred demons. I submit this multifaceted definition, knowing that there are other possible axes along which to delineate the conceptual categories of evil in Indian culture and that the distinctions can and must overlap and regroup in many ways.

The dimensions of evil or disvalue

1. A structural concept of opposition to the good (*dharma*)

2. An obscuring of knowledge or reality by means of illusion or delusion (*māyā*)

3. An impediment to the correct performance of ritual

4. An abuse or misuse of power

5. A disturbance of social hierarchies and relationships

6. An existential or innate aspect of suffering and/or frustration that pervades both life and death

7. A total otherness or unknown conceived of as enemy and threat

8. A frightening but temporary initiatory obstacle to union with the gods.

In all of these categories, yakṣas and other demons have been active, representing and effecting evil.

1. As formal, structural opponents to the good, they are encountered, on the one hand, as the *asura*s, the traditional rivals of the Vedic *deva*s, and, on the other hand, as the hordes of yakṣas and *rākṣasa*s of the Epics, who are slain by the thousands when they cross the paths of the Pāṇḍava heroes.

2. As possessors of *māyā,* yakṣas are known by their abilities to assume various shapes and disguises and, particularly in the Jain and Buddhist texts, as heretics whose unconverted status casts them as demonic opponents to the tradition.

3. The demons constitute a threat to the sacrifice through their pollution of the physical elements, thus invalidating the ritual; their improper seizure of the fruits of the sacrifice; or in the popular texts, their ancient, unorthodox, and by some accounts, heretical receiving of sacrifices and gifts of worship.

4. Scores of demons have gained dangerous power through the performance of difficult feats of asceticism. In the classical literature, the ensuing threat can be combated only through the agency of the strongest god's most potent weapons of resistance. In some of the popular myths about local gods, this ill-gotten power is responsible for a total transformation of status, from demon to god. This theme was exemplified in Chapter 1 in the variant tales of the yakṣa Harikeśa and the *rākṣasa* Sukeśin.

5. The demonic disturbance of social hierarchies and relationships may be seen particularly in the domain of the transgression of dietary and sexual injunctions: Yakṣas and other demons often eat improper foods (such as human flesh) and scavenge the remains of other people's meals and sacrifices; they steal other people's wives, and their own females assume human forms and seduce human males and bear their children.

6. Village demons and *devatās* are actively involved in the whole *saṁsāric* character of human existence: They govern the vital and magical transpositions by which health may become disease, and they preside over the village boundaries through which malevolencies of all sorts may pass or be rebuffed. They inhabit trees, wells, and wooded spots in the form of the ghosts of erstwhile villagers (particularly females) whose disembodied spirits have become disquieted through violent or untimely death and now disrupt the activities of their progenitors.

7. As representatives of the unknown, the tribal, the foreign, the uninhabited, yakṣas, *rākṣasas*, and *nāgas* resist the rationalizing and civilizing influences of *brāhmans* and Buddhists, especially in the latter context, terrorizing whole islands as ghoulish sorcerors and cannibals.

8. As *dvārapālas* or "door guardians," yakṣas and related figures in art and mythology test and hinder improper or threatening suppliants to the god within the sanctum.

The subtle diminution of the yakṣa was obvious in certain references in the Brāhmaṇas, Upaniṣads, and Gṛhya Sūtras. Like Varuṇa and Yama, the yakṣa was a "divided deity" whose close affiliation with the watery element devalued his status and importance when that element became more inextricably associated with the underworld. By the time of the Epics, the image of the underworld had, as we have seen in our examination of Varuṇa, undergone a radical reimaging, losing its Vedic reputation as the welcoming abode of the *pitṛs* and becoming more tainted by the fearful pollution of death. As with Varuṇa, the yakṣa's peculiar synthesis of vengefulness, sexuality and fecundity, secrecy and magic, the mysteries of birth and death, and the association with the ambiguous figure of the king, all contribute to his growing demonic characterization. The yakṣa came to possess a central role in the shift of emphasis from the Vedic opposition of *devas* and *asuras* to the Epic opposition of the earthly heroes and subterranean demons. In this role, the yakṣa confronts the hero, challenges his knowledge of *dharma,* and helps to redefine the balance between *dharma* and *adharma,* the socialized and the untamed.

One important aspect of my investigation became the comparison of Hindu versus Buddhist images of the yakṣa. Although they share a common basis, certain vital cosmological departures in the Buddhist context may be responsible for that tradition's greater demonization of the yakṣa. Within Buddhism, cosmogonic myths display a fundamentally negative view of matter and nature. In the Buddhist debasement of nature, as a manifestation of human weakness and ignorance, the Indian nature deities are also debased, losing their capacity (within this new system of *dharma*) for "*dharm*ic" behavior. Water, in particular, has lost its cosmic and ritual significance within Buddhist literature, retaining, virtually, a "social" significance as a metaphor for the righteous rule of the king. Deprived of the cosmically well-rounded image of demonic figures found within Hinduism, the Buddhist yakkha became a metaphor for the human being gone astray rather than for an ambivalent nature divinity. Ironically then, within Buddhism, the yakkha was, on the one hand, more demonic but, on the other hand, closer to the human realm, since humans have more in common with demons than they do with gods (the latter being susceptible to becoming fixed on the wheel of *saṁsāra* because of their experience of perpetual pleasure).

Particularly important to our emerging picture of the yakṣa was the way in which he and other mythical demons (beginning with the Vedic *asura*s) have played a vital role in sustaining human capacities for understanding and coping with misfortune. They do this in an oscillating economy in which their powers to effect evil expand and diminish according to historical, social, and theological pressures. This economy, we discovered, was handled differently within the *brāhman*ical and *bhakt*ic traditions as opposed to the ascetical traditions. Inherent to the ethical monism of the latter was the mitigation but not obliteration of the imagined power of yakṣas. The latter were converted to the doctrines of Buddhism and Jainism rather than combated and annihilated, only to regroup and rise again in power as they do in Vedic mythology and the mythology of the Epics and Purāṇas.

Two explanatory principles that are most often employed to attribute meaning to human misfortune are, on the one hand, angry deities, demons, or ghosts and, on the other, the concept of *karma.*

The choice of one or the other of these to explain any single event is conditioned primarily by the human needs most pressing at the moment, and rarely does the application of one preclude the use of the other. We have seen how the intractability of *karma* and the agency of demons cooperate in many Epic and Purāṇic Hindu texts. The demons are ultimately wicked because humans are wicked, and it is the evil *karma* and ritual neglect of the latter that compel the intervention of the former.

> "We are hungry and eternally devoid of dharma," said the Rākṣasa. "We do not do all the evil that we do because of our own desire; it is because of your evil karma, and your disfavor toward us. Our faction increases because of the Brāhmins who behave like Rākṣasas, and our ranks are swelled by the sexual sins of evil women."[2]

This same circularity exists in popular beliefs about ghosts in Sinhalese causal systems, where orthodox Buddhist ethics are brought in to justify the misbehavior and torment of the unquiet spirits.

> The concept of *karma* is implicit in Sinhalese beliefs about ghosts (*preta*) and their malign effects on the living. Human beings doomed to become ghosts are those who, through wrong action or extreme attachment, craving, and desire for worldly things (wealth, power, property) have failed to proceed to one of the Buddhist heavens or to be reborn in another existence. They remain in limbo, haunting their living kinsfolk or the residents of the house they once inhabited. . . . Through ghosts, therefore, living kin or house residents can be afflicted by the results of actions, of *karma* in effect, that accrued to another in his or her life.[3]

The categorical fluidity implied in the above considerations, in which the demonic agents may be seen to be either the cause or the effect of evil, bespeaks the complex ethos of a society in which ritual and caste purity and abstract ethics mirror one another in endlessly ricocheting reflections. The absolute fear of pollution tempers the potential ethical egalitarianism (or anarchy) inherent in the more ascetical and mystical aspects of Hinduism. The mystical abolition of personal boundaries may be opposed to the institutions of caste and rituals of purity that seek to establish an ever more precise definition of appropriate social contact and to regulate dangerous bodily "overflows."

The yakṣa, like other Indian deities and spirits, serves as a causal nexus that may be variously construed—with philosophical, animistic, devotional, or medical schema for instance. In village life in particular, demons, ghosts, and spirits are marshaled on one end of the "organic—mechanical" continuum of village explanation traditions. In Paul Hiebert's exploration of a particular village, Konduru, he finds that at the "organic" end of the continuum,

> "the world is seen in terms of living beings of one or more kind in relationship to each other:" Konduru and its vicinity is inhabited not only by people and animals, but also by ghosts, by *rākṣasas*, *dayamulu, apsaras,* and many other types of spirits, and by more than a hundred different female goddesses who reside in trees, wells, fields, and the nearby forest. In addition, the Hindu gods and their consorts leave their heavenly abodes to minister to their devotees in the temples and shrines. All of these beings influence human affairs in certain ways. Spirits possess humans, driving them mad. Female *apsaras* lure men into their lairs and draw out their life forces. Goddesses bring plagues of disease, drought, and fire. And high gods punish people in their anger. Human responses to these beings are analogous to interpersonal relationships and include offerings, confessions, supplications, and prayers.[4]

The author further makes the point that the self-same villagers employ such "mechanical analogies" as the stars, the planets, *karma,* and nature as alternative means to explain a range of events and behaviors. In this sense, mechanistic, theistic, and demonic causal schemes function almost interchangeably, their efficacy resulting from a dynamic internal to the particular metaphorical scheme employed. As we have seen, potent, deeply rooted metaphors may function in all of these ways, simply by means of a process of linguistic reformulation.

One question that I proposed in the Introduction was whether it was "necessary or even possible to resolve ethical, rational, emotional, and aesthetic paradoxes in order to develop and sustain a consistent notion of the demonic."[5] My analysis revealed that the question begs the real issue. As the question stands, it conflates the moral and the hierarchical. What I discovered was that there was no necessary correlation between the two. Taxonomical texts obey a logic that pertains to utilitarian, sectarian, and authorial dictates. It is certain that one class of beings will be at the top of the hierarchy and another class will be at the bottom. In most cases, gods of some description will occupy the topmost rung and demons of some description will occupy the lowest rung, but the details of this arrangement will vary from text to text, and in the space between the two poles, there are infinite possibilities for enumeration and variation. Rarely is it the point of these texts to create permanently exclusive categories; rather, like caste (or more specifically, *jāti*), the categorical stability and exclusion mask a tendency to subdivision and proliferation. The acknowledgment of demonic groupings in cosmological hierarchies does not perforce establish any particular notion of evil as normative.

Time and geography play important roles in this upward mobility. As purely local deities or demons acquire a mythology and ritual history through time, their status is enhanced, their domain of power is widened, and their local application vis-à-vis any one village is diminished. Other, even cruder, even less well articulated divinities rise to prominence in their wake. Upon being asked in one village I visited near Benares what a yakṣa was, several villagers answered, "*dev*" ("god"). Ironically, his more recent demonism had been forgotten, and his archaic status somewhat restored. His immemorial beginnings had conferred a moral sanction and religious venerability upon him, rather like a mafioso who, in managing to reach old age, is remembered for his contribution of the new wing of the opera house rather than for his early misdeeds and mayhem. Fierceness, cruelty, and ugliness are transformed through devotion and consequently seen as vaguely beautiful, benignly powerful.

Like the taxonomies of class, caste, and kinship, conceptions of the demonic contribute to the fabrication of a hierarchical cultural mosaic. And like these other classificatory systems, hierarchical value is derived from complex, if loose, patterns of social contact, alliance, and intermarriage. And also like these other systems, demonic hierarchies function as paradigms of inclusion and identification or paradigms of exclusion and repudiation vis-à-vis adjacent cosmoses of humans and gods.

In general, Hindu society deals with anomaly by means of reinterpretation and assimilation. The taxonomic method of caste constantly propagates subcategories to account for incongruity. Moslems and Christians cannot be assessed because, not being Hindu, they are not casted and therefore do not exist on the rational map of what can be known about people. To account for their existence, new caste categories are created. To say that one is a "Moslem" or "Christian" is meaningless in hierarchical India; to say that one is "Moslem caste" or "Christian caste" (or one of the subgroupings thereof) gives one a voice in a complex society where caste is the real lingua franca. As we have seen, in many texts demons are a class of beings who are also subsumed by caste, in many cases their strangeness being softened or mediated by the additional qualities and relationships inherent in being a "*brāhma rākṣasa,*" for instance.

It is not correct, however, to suggest that caste is the only system of classification in Indian thought; although as a matrix for establishing human excellence, it is in the background of all other Indian hierarchical contexts. There are, in fact, countless explanatory schemes and methods for organizing the raw data of the phenomenal world. In philosophical texts, classes of beings are derived from the interaction of principles. In *The Laws of Manu* (12. 41–50), human castes, animals, demons, and deities are lumped together and then graded according to their embodiment of the metaphysical constituents of being, the *guṇa*s, rather than their species, so that *śūdra*s are classed with horses, elephants, and other animals; hypocrites are grouped with *rākṣasa*s and *piśāca*s.[6] A similar gradation of beings is adopted in the Pāli Buddhist literature[7] to account for perceptible differences in nobility, behavior, and morality. Here, the descriptive principle also cuts across other categorical systems, often grouping together ghosts and gods, since both occupy lower rungs of the Buddhist cosmos and exist within the general category of the nonliving/nonhuman.

> There are various grades among the dead. A broad distinction is made between two classes, the *deva*s and the *peta*s. The *deva*s generally have a preponderance of good and meritorious deeds in their favour, though they are tainted at least in the lower ranks, with some stain of evil which they have got to work out. The highest among them who have made . . . gifts while on earth on an immense scale, are born in the *Tavatiṁsa* heaven, but even here there are innumerable grades.[8]

Between the *deva*s of the heavenly palaces, the *vimāna deva*s, and their counterparts among the ghosts, the *vimāna peta*s, there is practically no distinction at all. The latter are the most fortunate among the *peta*s, they have been able in past lives to add "some good to their account," though it is not "unmixed with some evil which subjects them to suffering and torture. Below them is the great mass of *peta*s and *peti*s that suffer intolerable miseries"[9]

The philosophical component of archaic Buddhism, for which the supreme desideratum is truth and for which the most abhorrent quality is illusion, places low value on the manipulation and propitiation of demons. For this sensibility, there is a hatred of the "low arts."[10] While Sanskritic and popular Hinduism are distinct (though parallel) traditions in many ways, both of them focus on ritual efficacy and purification as a means to control the cosmos. For the Vedic religious practitioner, this efficacy depends upon *brāhman*ical expertise and sacred textual sanction, while the vernacular counterpart often employs low-caste shamans and oracular improvisation. The Vedic ceremonies provide a broad cultural endorsement that connects individuals to an ancient religious community by means of transformatory rites or *saṁskāra*s; popular or village Hinduism focuses within local mythology and rituals upon a narrower or more immediate order of needs. Though both traditions are intensely concerned to effect the material, spiritual, and emotional well-being of the common man and both recognize the sacramental character of basic physiological and natural processes, village morality often focuses more squarely on the specific details of agricultural and bodily maintenance.

In the Vedic and *bhakt*ic stages of religious power, where theism is inherent and essential, a functional ethical dualism obtains. This dualism is opposed to the ethical monism of the ascetic stage of power, where demons and deities are subordinated or assimilated to human control through meditative mastery and doctrinal proliferation. In the theistic stages of power, gods, as recipients of either sacrifice or devotion, must be brought close to man through ritual or *pūjā*. In the intervening separation between men and gods, demons are rife and jealously covet the offerings made to the gods. Since it is the struggle between the gods and the demons that sustains the universe, the demons are always necessary. From this perspective, it may be stated that either the universe itself, depending as it does upon the existence of the demonic, is inherently evil or that the demons possess only a qualified evil.[11] It is not only the aggression of the demons that is an indispensable aspect of the organic continuation of the cosmos; *māyā,* with which they are linked, is fundamental to existence as well, since it is responsible for the *appearance* of phenomena.

As early as the *Ṛg Veda,* the origin of all sorts of human afflictions was attributed to the earthly demons, the *rākṣasa*s, who functioned to plague the ordinary existence and daily activities of men, just as their cosmic counterparts, the *asura*s, opposed the activities of the gods. The demons were counted among the various possible sources of disease; the gods and diverse astrological influences were also deemed responsible. The ritual and moral offenses of humans brought down the wrath of divinities, which then resulted in calamities for those people, but the gods themselves also indulged in moral and ritual abrogations, sometimes arbitrarily afflicting an individual or punishing him or her excessively. As the agent of divine retribution, Varuṇa, for instance, was responsible for the "fetter" of the disease dropsy, which, it was believed, tormented the unrighteous. In the *Atharva Veda,* various illnesses, such as arthritis, insanity, and barrenness, are associated with demons[12] and at *ṚV* 10. 97. 11, a kind of consumption is simply called by the name of the demon to which it is attributed, "yakṣa." In this particular verse, which praises the many healing herbs employed by the priestly physician, divine propitiation, the prescription of curative plants, and the use of magical spells to vitiate demonic effect all seem to be viable methods for counteracting disease.

In the *Mahābhārata* and other sources[13] the *graha* ("grasper") etiology of disease is expounded. In this traditional view, a demonic spirit contained within any deity or particularly associated with the deity may possess humans, causing diverse physical effects. These *graha*s are also thought to be planets that exert inauspicious influences upon human beings. At *Mbh* 3. 219. 25–60, two basic kinds of *graha*s are recognized: those who afflict children up to the age of sixteen and those who afflict adults. The origin of the former is attributed to a boon given to the *matṛ*s (mothers of the world) by their son, the war god Skanda. In the form of various demonesses, these "mothers" are thought to control primarily the dangers that may befall the fetus. Adults may be victimized by the *graha*s of yakṣas, *rākṣasa*s, *gandharva*s, *piśāca*s, and so forth. These demons possess their victims with various sorts of insanity, according to their specialty.

The classic medical text, the *Cāraka Saṁhitā,* also proposes a complex etiology and treatment of disease. Insanity, the infirmity that is most often engendered by spirit possession, is thought to be of two types: innate (*nija*) and exogenous (*agantu*). The former type is thought to arise from dietary imbalances, moral or ritual oversights or infractions, or emotional excesses. The latter is caused by possession by gods, ghosts, sages, *gandharva*s, yakṣas, *rākṣasa*s, *brāhmarākṣasa*s, or *piśāca*s. Each of these *graha*s produces a particular set of symptoms, and each is drawn to a particular sort of person.

*Gandharva*s, for instance, are thought to possess people who are fond of the pleasures of music and sexual promiscuity. Yakṣas possess the person who is "strong, attractive, and egotistical," and who is fond of "garlands, jokes, and too much talking. *Brāhmarākṣasa*s possess the person who dislikes study, asceticism, religion, fasting, celibacy and worship of the gods, ascetics and gurus," is unclean and rather arrogant. *Rākṣasa*s and *piśāca*s attack the person who "has a weak mind, is two-faced, a thief, and greedy and wicked. . . ."[14] The *agantu* insanity is treated with herbal medicines as well as by pious deeds and offerings.

Historically, the Indian ethical economy has depended upon a balance of powers to achieve a workable moral dialectic between self and others. As we have seen, demons are psychologically and morally useful in the pragmatic dispersion of the causes of misfortune. On the individual, emotional level, the Indian metaphysical recognition of the consubstantiality of good and evil is of positive value. The demons are an inescapable aspect of life. This fact is inherent in the popular cults of guardian, protective spirits. They are, in practically every case, barely tamed demons whose powers of evil have been transformed into positive forces for good. Power and goodness are united in the Judeo-Christian god; for the Indian sensibility, they are separate qualities that are contained in every being, including the gods, in a different proportional admixture. Since there is no absolute good or evil in Hindu theology, the demands of individual moral life are great, what with the necessity of avoiding polluting activities and relationships as well as satisfying the perverse whims of innumerable relatively powerful beings who lurk, literally, behind every rock and tree. The yakṣa is a unique figure in the crowded compendium of such divinities because of his tendency, from ancient times, to display universal as well as local sovereignty. In his complexity and spectrum of applications, the yakṣa remains a potent example of that persistent Indian striving to fashion images of the formless which may be imagined, the wildness which may be tamed, and the forbidden which may be approached.

NOTES

Introduction

1. Throughout this book, I have used both the Sanskrit (yakṣa, yakṣī, yakṣiṇī) and Pāli (yakkha, yakkhī, yakkhinī) versions of central terms. I have varied the usage according to which terms are applicable to the literary and/or religious tradition under immediate scrutiny. In general, I use a genderized pronoun (he, she, his, her) to refer to the yakṣa or yakṣī, except in a few cases where the use of "it" or "its" alleviates awkwardness or clarifies syntactical ambiguities. Unless otherwise noted, all translations are my own.

2. Ananda Kentish Coomaraswamy. *Yakṣas,* 2 vols. in 1. (New Delhi: Munshiram Manoharlal, 1931).

3. See "The testing yakṣa," above, p. 88.

4. Wendy O'Flaherty, *The Origins of Evil in Hindu Mythology* (Berkeley: University of California Press, 1976), p. 83.

5. Ibid., p. 82.

6. Mary Douglas, *Implicit Meanings, Essays in Anthropology* (London: Routledge & Kegan Paul, 1984), p. 54.

Chapter 1

1. Heinrich Zimmer, *The Art of Indian Asia,* 2 vols., completed and ed. Joseph Campbell, Bollingen Series, no. 39 (Princeton, N.J.: Princeton University Press, 1968), pt. 1, p. 12.

2. F. D. K. Bosch, *The Golden Germ: An Introduction to Indian Symbolism* (The Hague: Mouton & Co., 1960), pp. 99–216.

3. Ibid., p. 33.

4. Coomaraswamy, *Yakṣas,* pt. 1, p. 33.

5. Dietrich Seckel, "Early Buddha Symbols," in David L. Snellgrove, ed., *The Image of the Buddha* (New Delhi: Vikas Publishing House Pvt. Ltd., 1978), pp. 32–33.

6. Ibid., p. 24.

7. Ibid.

8. Ananda Coomaraswamy, *History of Indian and Indonesian Art* (New York: Dover Publications, 1965), p. 41. See also Benjamin Rowland, "Religious Art East and West," *History of Religions,* vol. 2, no. 11 (Summer 1962), pp. 11–33.

9. The aesthetician Carl Hausman speaks of this creative freedom and independence of the culturally adopted metaphors: "Thus creative metaphors are faithful or appropriate to more than established concepts and language. These extra-linguistic conditions are individuals that provide independent constraints on our systems. At the same time, the individuals creatively designated are unique." (Carl R. Hausman, "Metaphors, Referents, and Individuality," *The Journal of Aesthetics and Art Criticism,* vol. 2 [Winter 1983], pp. 181–97.)

10. Douglas, *Implicit Meanings,* pp. 44–45.

11. Mircea Eliade refers to this in his consideration of the "Greatness and Decadence of Myths". ". . . privileged religious experiences, when they are communicated through a sufficiently impressive and fanciful scenario, succeed in imposing models of sources of inspiration on the whole community. In the last analysis, in the archaic societies everywhere else, culture arises and is renewed through the creative experiences of a few individuals. But since archaic culture gravitates around myths, and these are constantly being studied and given new, more profound interpretations by the specialists in the sacred, it follows that the society as a whole is led toward the value and meanings discovered and conveyed by these few individuals. It is in this way that myth helps man to transcend his own limitations and conditions and stimulates him to rise to 'where the greatest are.' " (Mircea Eliade, *Myth and Reality* [New York: Harper Colophon Books, 1975], p. 147.) What Eliade fails to mention in the preceding passage is that the same process of revisioning myths in ever more fanciful modes has also produced a descent to the lowest common denominator as well as the occasional rising to "where the greatest are." Again, India may be unique in having lived with and out of its myths so long that they are the framework in which all popular narrative of any sort is sustained. In the case of the charming Amar Chitra Katha children's comic books, depicting the major myths of Indian literature, this is a delightful phenomenon. Various gods of the Indian pantheon, however, are frequently invoked to promote products, in the way that we in America hire celebrities to flog unlikely consumer items. I myself noted a store in Benares that sold toilet seats endorsed by the god Hanuman, whose reputation for extraordinary strength accrued to the aforementioned items.

12. *Mahad yakṣam bhuvanasya madhye tapasi krantam salilasya pṛṣṭhe tasmin śrayante ya u ke ca deva vṛkṣasya skandhah parit iva sakhah* (*AV* 10. 7. 38).

13. See *Mahābhārata* 1. 15–17 and *Viṣṇu Purāṇa* 1. 9. 75–115.

14. For a discussion of the relationship of the poison to other vital fluids and the shifting ethical application of "ambivalent milk," see Wendy O'Flaherty, *Women, Androgynes, and Other Mythical Beasts* (Chicago: University of Chicago Press, 1980), pp. 53–57.

15. Coomaraswamy, *Yakṣas,* pt. 2, pp. 25–26.

16. Heinrich Zimmer, *Myths and Symbols in Indian Art and Civilization,* ed. Joseph Campbell, Bollingen Series, No. 6 (Princeton, N.J.: Princeton University Press, 1972), p. 34. Cf. Wendy O'Flaherty, *Dreams, Illusion, and Other Realities* (Chicago: University of Chicago Press, 1984), pp. 81–89.

17. *Matsya P* 166. 18–21.

18. Ram Nath Misra, *Yaksha Cult and Iconography* (New Delhi: Munshiram Manoharlal Publishers, 1981), p. 9.

19. F. B. J. Kuiper, "Cosmogony and Conception: A Query," *History of Religions,* no. 10 (November 1970), p. 108.

20. *Śatapatha Brāhmaṇa* 11. 1. 6. 1–2. See the discussion by Kuiper, "Cosmogony," pp. 100–1.

21. For a thorough treatment of the development of the *hiraṇyagarbha* demiurge, see Bosch, *Golden Germ,* and Greg Bailey, *The Mythology of Brahmā* (Delhi: Oxford University Press, 1983), pp. 86–106.

22. Bosch, *Golden Germ,* p. 55, referring to *ṚV* 10. 82 and *AV* 10. 7. 39.

23. *AV* 10. 2. 33.

24. See Mircea Eliade, *Patterns in Comparative Religion,* trans. Rosemary Sheed (New York: New American Library, 1974), pp. 266–67.

25. Above, p. 21.

26. Lowell W. Bloss, "Ancient Indian Folk Religion as Seen Through the Symbolism of the Nāga" (Ph.D. dissertation, University of Chicago, 1971).

27. "It has been suggested that the burning and resuscitation of Kāma has its basis in a fertility ritual in which either Kāma's image or a tree is burnt. The significance of the burnt tree, and of its relationship with the Dionysian aspect of Śiva, may be seen in the parallels between the phallic Indra-pillar,

the Śiva-*liṅga,* and the tree of Kāma." (Wendy O'Flaherty, *Śiva: The Erotic Ascetic* [London and New York: Oxford University Press, 1981], p. 160.)

28. Coomaraswamy, *Yakṣas,* pt. 2, p. 11.

29. Ibid., pt. 2, p. 21, citing *AV* 19. 31. 12.

30. Ibid.

31. Abel Bergaigne, *La Religion védique d'après les hymnes du Rig-Veda* (Paris: Librairie Honore Champion, 1963), p. x. See also O'Flaherty, Śiva, pp. 90–110.

32. Semen falls from the clouds as "rain no doubt, but as rain, regarded especially as containing the male element itself, that is to say, fire. . . . This fire enters the plant at the same time as its nourishing saps, then passes along with it into the body of man and thence into that of his children. According to these very ideas, we may hold that fire constitutes the real principle of life, of which rain is some sort of envelope or vehicle, and that this principle of life always descends from heaven." (Bergaigne, trans. Maurice Bloomfield [Delhi: Motilal Banarsidass, 1978], p. 33.)

33. See Albert Grunwedel, *Buddhist Art in India,* ed. James Burgess, trans. A. C. Gibson (Spain and England: Susil Gupta, 1965), p. 181, n. 2, and M. S. Randhowa, *The Cult of Trees and Tree-Worship in Buddhist Hindu Sculpture* (New Delhi: All India Fine Arts and Crafts Society, 1964), p. 13.

34. Coomaraswamy, *Yakṣas,* pt. 2, p. 7.

35. Aśvaghoṣa, *Buddhacarita* 5. 52.

36. Jean Philippe Vogel, "The Woman and the Tree or Śālabhañjikā in Indian Literature and Art," *Acta Orientalia,* vol. 7 (1929), pp. 201–31.

37. Bosch, *Golden Germ,* p. 55.

38. The *Viṣṇu Purāṇa* 9. 99–104 contains a particularly vivid portrait of the lotus goddess, Śrī, arising from the cosmic waters during the churning that the gods and demons have undertaken to produce the elixir of immortality (*amṛta*). In this version of the myth, her generation is preceded by the arising of: the magical wishing cow, Surabhi; the goddess of wine, Varuṇī; the sweet-smelling celestial Pārijāta tree; the divine nymphs (*apsaras*es); the moon; the virulent poison (*viṣa*), which is then taken by the serpent gods, the *nāga*s; and the physician of the gods, Dhanvantari.

39. Zimmer, *Art of Indian Asia,* vol. 1, p. 165.

40. Zimmer, Myths and Symbols, p. 98.

41. Ananda Coomaraswamy, "Early Indian Iconography—II, Śrī Lakṣmī," *Eastern Art,* vol. 1, no. 2 (October 1928), pp. 175–89.

42. Ananda Coomaraswamy, "Sir Gawain and the Green Knight: Indra and Namuci," *Speculum,* vol. 19 (1944), pp. 109–11.

43. Examples of this are yakṣa sculptures from Parkham, Pawaya, Patna, Bhārhut, and Sāñcī.

44. For a summary, see Coomaraswamy, *Yakṣas,* pt. 2, p. 47 ff.

45. ". . . we gather that from its first appearance in Indian art, over the entrance to the cave of Lomas Rishi in Bihar (ca. 350 B.C.), the makara was pictured as a fantastic quadruped with a crocodile-like head, a snout curled backwards and a scaly crest on the tail. In the next stage of development, represented e.g. at Bharhut (ca. 150 B.C.), the crocodile with curled up snout is maintained but the mouth is now wide open; the jaws are provided with sharply pointed teeth, the hind legs have disappeared and the body is transformed into a scaly tail rolled up volute wise. But for some minor details, like the addition of ram's horns and the replacement of the tail by the body of a fish with caudal fin, this type has also been used at Mathura (50–200 A.D.) and at Amaravati (150–300 A.D.), but when after some centuries the monster reappeared, e.g. in Gupta art (300–600 A.D.), and at Seven Pagodas (7th century A.D., it has under-gone an important metamorphosis. The fish-like tail is replaced by a luxuriously developed bush tail, the front legs have disappeared, and the head is provided with an elephant's trunk with the tactual organ curling forward. In its South-Indian mediaeval form the makara finally appears as a monster with ornate bush tail, elephantine head with trunk and the body of an elephant, rhinoceros, or some other pachyderm." (Bosch, *Golden Germ,* p. 22.)

46. Ibid., p. 34.

47. Zimmer, *Myths and Symbols,* p. 63.

48. "The slabs can be seen in temple-courtyards, at the entrances of villages and towns, near ponds (the waters of which are supposed to be populated with nāgas), or under trees (which from immemorial times have been associated with the worship of serpents, since trees indicate that there is water in the ground). When their reliefs have been carved, the nāgakals are placed for a period of six months in some pond, to become imbued with the life-force of the watery element, and then are consecrated with a ritual and with sacred formulae (*mantras*), after which they are set up beneath two trees, a pippala and a numba. These are often found together, and are looked upon as a married couple. The nāgas, whose blessing is being invoked, are supposed to dwell among the roots." (Zimmer, *Art of Indian Asia,* vol. 1, p. 49.)

49. See Diana Eck for a description of particularly interesting *nāgapañcāmī* rites in Benares, centered around the ancient well of Nāg Kuan: "One of the deepest wells in Kāshi is called Nāg Kuan (Karkotaka Vapi in the *Kāshi Khanda*). It is in the ancient and now dilapidated part of northern Kāshi, and it is said to have been the home of the great Sanskrit grammarian Patañjali, over two thousand years ago. On Nāga Panchamī this well, in part of the city not usually frequented by most Hindus, comes to life with a great *mela*. Here thousands of people bathe in the deep well, honor its serpent deities, and watch the daredevil young men from this district plunge from the top of the wall surrounding the well into the waters some thirty feet below. These waters, they say, are very deep because they emerge from the netherworlds, *pātāla,* which is the realm of the *nāga*s. In the late afternoon, as the festivities wane, a great crowd will gather under an enormous banyan tree to listen to speeches in honor of Patañjali, who is said to have been an incarnation of Vishnu's serpent, Shesha." (Diana L. Eck. *Banaras City of Light* [Princeton, N.J.: Princeton University Press, 1982], p. 264.)

50. Mānasā's poisonous glance is strongly reminiscent of the Greek Gorgon Medusa, whose glance will paralyze anyone who falls in its sway and whose hair is a mass of swarming snakes, a state that was inflicted upon her as the result of a curse of Athena, whose sanctuary she had defiled. The compelling power of the poisonous glance and other serpentine aspects (secrecy, unpredictability, subtle sexual prowess) are attributed to females whose sexual charisma is particularly powerful and dangerous to men.

51. See Pradyat Kumar Maity, *Historical Studies in the Cult of the Goddess Manasā* (Calcutta: Punthi Pustak, 1966), p. 52. For further treatment of the goddess, see Edward C. Dimock, "Manasā, Goddess of Snakes: The Ṣaṣṭhī Myth," in *Myths and Symbols: Studies in Honor of Mircea Eliade* (Chicago: University of Chicago Press, 1969), pp. 217–26; "The Goddess of Snakes in Medieval Bengali Literature 1," *History of Religions,* vol. 1 (Winter 1962), pp. 307–21; and Edward C. Dimock and A. K. Rāmānujan, "The Goddess of Snakes in Medieval Bengali Literature 2," *History of Religions,* vol. 3, no. 2 (Winter 1964), pp. 300–22.

52. "Poison as the inverse of Soma appears throughout the mythology; a fiery poison is said to devour the world—like the doomsday fire—in contrast with Soma or milk, that is itself devoured in the genitals of the destructive erotic woman, the poison damsel (Penzer 1924, pp. 275–313). In the Bengali *Manasāmaṅgal*, Lakhindara is fated to die on his wedding night (the recurrent myth of fatal sexuality); when he flies in the face of the prophecy, he is bitten by the snake damsel and dies of her poison. Snakes (often symbolizing women) perform an alchemy in which milk is transmuted into poison, the inverse of that alchemy that women perform by turning blood into milk. In the village

ritual, milk is fed to a snake; the snake then turns this into poison, which in turn is rendered harmless by Soma (or by the shaman, who controls Soma, drugs, and snakes)." (O'Flaherty, *Women*, p. 54.)

53. Edward Washburn Hopkins, *Epic Mythology* (Varanasi: Indological Book House, 1968), p. 26.

54. The elephants of the four quarters (*diggaja*s or *dinnaga*s) support the world and so does the serpent, Śeṣa, the theriomorphic support and counterpart to the god Viṣṇu. It is in the symbolism of the elephant that we can see particularly the conjunction of terrestrial and aetherial mythologies through the neutral medium of the water. Through both their physical form and their function as bearers of rain and water (spraying it from their trunks), elephants are linked with clouds and even called *megha* ("cloud"), being thought to be a rain cloud walking on the earth. For an analysis of the ophidian and elephantine dimensions of the term *nāga,* see Elena Semeka-Pankratov, "A Semiotic Approach to the Polysemy of the Symbol, *Nāga,* in Indian Mythology," *Semiotica,* vol. 27 (1979). For a discussion of the waters above and below the earth in Vedic cosmology, see F. B. J. Kuiper, "The Basic Concept of Vedic Religion," *History of Religions,* vol. 15 (November 1975), p. 107.

55. *Mahāvaṁsa,* trans. William Geiger (London: Oxford University Press for the Pali Text Society, 1912), 1. 58–63.

56. *Dīpavaṁsa,* trans. Herman Oldenburg (London: Williams & Norgate, 1874), 1. 54.

57. Bloss, "Ancient Indian Folk Religion," p. 62.

58. Coomaraswamy, *Yakṣas,* vol. 1, p. 13.

59. In several instances, the Buddha himself is called a yakkha: *Dīpavaṁsa* 1. 54; *Majjhima Nikāya* 1. 383.

60. *Mahāvagga* 1. 3, discussed in Jean Philippe Vogel, "Serpent Worship in Ancient and Modern Asia," *Acta Orientalia,* vol. 1 (1923), p. 295, and Bloss, "Ancient Indian Folk Religion," pp. 197–98.

61. Ibid.

62. Ibid.

63. Lowell Bloss, "The Taming of Māra: Witnessing to the Buddha's Virtues," *History of Religions,* vol. 18 (November; 1978), p. 169.

64. Zimmer, *Myths and Symbols,* p. 66.

65. Ananda Coomaraswamy, "Angels and Titans, an Essay on Vedic Ontology, JAOS, vol. 55 (1935)," p. 392. The image of the divine serpent is

first memorialized in the Indian religious context in the Vedic hymns about the *asura* Vṛtra, whose celebrated slaying by Indra is responsible for the release of the cosmic, fructifying waters that he withholds. The cosmic dragon has its counterpart in Avestan and Sumerian mythology, where it is known, respectively, as Azhi and Mushussu, who later becomes the dragon-mother, Tiamat, slain by the hero Marduk, who carves out the cosmos from her parts. (See Coomaraswamy, "Sir Gawain," p. 390.) Vṛtra's slaying seems to relate in part to the cosmogonic dismemberment of Tiamat, the Vedic analogy being the "Puruṣa Sūkta" (*ṚV* 10. 90), in which the prototypical human being is sacrificed in Vedic style and carved up into the elements of the physical and social universe. The Vṛtra myth seems most obviously to relate to the *nāga* mythology in the matter of the control and release of the vital waters in the form of rainfall and in the ethical delineation of the dark, demonic Vṛtra, slain by the representative of light and Vedic nobility, Indra. The ethical dialectic between the two figures is attended by many complexities and ambiguities that echo the shifting status of the *nāga*. The specifically snakelike nature of Vṛtra is adduced from various Vedic citations (*ṚV* 1. 32. 5; 1. 32. 8; 1. 3. 10; 1. 61. 8; 1. 103. 7), where Vṛtra is referred to as "*ahi,*" a word denoting serpent.

66. The multivalency of the *nāga* symbol is displayed in the further connection of the dragon-slaying, thunder-bolt god, Indra, with the elephant; the milk-white elephant chief, Airāvata, is the mount or *vāhana* of Indra. Thus, Indra rides one *nāga* to slay another.

67. This story is found, among other sources, in the *Śatapatha Br* 1. 8. 1. 1–6; the *Mahābhārata* 3. 187; the *Matsya P* 1–3; and the *Bhāgavata P* 8. 24.

68. 3. 314. 27–46.

69. Only in the "lower-case" sense of "demonic," as distinguished from the "upper-case" "Demonic" to be found in the Western conception of the sacred and that which opposes it.

70. A number of Vedic hymns praise and invoke the blessings of various rivers, among them the Sarasvatī, Sindhu, Sarayu, Yamunā, Gaṅgā, and Sutudrī. Most beloved for her power and beneficence is the Sarasvatī, known as a "mother of streams." One of seven such "mothers," she bestows wealth, offspring, and immortality and, like all rivers, purifies those who bathe in her, granting healing and release from sin. The adoration of the holy waters in the form of the river goddesses, as mothers or sisters, is augmented in the later Epic literature by a strain of earthy or perhaps pre-Āryan piety that lauds above all spiritual practices, the pilgrimage or *tīrtha-yātrā* in which devotees of both sexes and all classes and castes visit the sacred points on the cosmological map of India. These points of intensified contact with the divine are

conceived of as places "where one launches out on the journey between heaven and earth"; they are "a threshold of time, or space, or ritual." (Diana Eck, "India's Tīrthas: 'Crossings' in Sacred Geography," *History of Religions,* vol. 20 (May 1981), p. 328.) As Eck has ably summarized, the concept of the *tīrtha* subsumes a multilayered network of metaphors bridging notions of the safe crossing of monsoon-swollen rivers; the traversing of the trileveled cosmos consisting of the heavens, the atmosphere, and the earth; and the individual experience of the transcendence of earthly bonds and illusions. The multivalence of the term involves two spatial notions having to do with both the horizontal and vertical axes of the universe. The spatial extent of a river, covering large areas of land, is obviously one dimension of the flow of a river (and its attendant symbolism); the vertical flow of a river, as it springs from its mountain source, is conceived as a metaphor for the "vertical" flow of the river from heaven to earth, the gift of the gods to the earth.

71. *Mbh* 104–109 and *Rām* 1. 37–43.

72. The Gaṅgā, Yamunā, Godāvarī, Sarasvatī, Narmadā, Sindhu, and Kāverī rivers.

73. See especially chapter 3 below.

74. O'Flaherty, *Evil,* p. 199.

75. *Markandeya P* 45. 18–40. Cf. *Viṣṇu P* 1. 5. 59–65, in O'Flaherty, *Evil,* p. 52.

76. Hopkins, *Epic Mythology,* p. 38.

77. *Jātakamālā,* trans. Speyer, fn. p. 61.

78. Hopkins, *Epic Mythology,* p. 38.

79. *Mahābhārata* 1–5, trans. Van Buitenen, vol. 2, pp. 201–2, referring to *Mbh* 2, 258 ff.

80. *Mbh* 3. 154. 1 ff.

81. Ibid., 3. 154. 8–12.

82. See Misra, *Yaksha Cult,* p. 3.

83. Ibid., pp. 3–4.

84. Ibid., p. 4.

85. Hopkins, *Epic Mythology,* p. 39, quoting *Mbh* 3. 139. 10.

86. *Rām* 7. 4. 9–13.

87. See *Bṛhadāraṇyaka Up* 1. 2. 1.

88. *Mbh* 1. 60. 1 ff.

89. Ibid.

90. According to Coomaraswamy, Śiva's connection with yakṣas is shown by the "existence of numerous temples dedicated to him under names which are those of Yakṣas, e.g., the Virupakṣa temple at Paṭṭadakal. Śiva's followers—called 'Pariśādas' are huge-bellied like Yakṣas." (Coomaraswamy, *Yakṣas,* vol. 1, p. 12, fn. 2.)

91. *Matsya P* 180. 5–19.

92. *Matsya P* 180. 96–97.

93. *Vāmana P* 11–15, in O'Flaherty, *Evil,* pp. 129–30.

94. Ibid., p. 130.

95. See for instance, *Chāndogya Up* 8. 7–9, where both the gods and the demons become disciples of Prajāpati's in order to discover the nature of the true self.

96. *Vāmana P* 6. 50–53, in Stella Kramrisch, *The Presence of Śiva* (Princeton, N.J.: Princeton University Press, 1981), pp. 320–21.

97. Cf. the yakṣa who takes on Śikhandin's femaleness in the *Mbh,* Udyoga Parvan.

98. Hopkins, *Epic Mythology,* p. 38.

99. Misra mentions texts in which the similarity between the two is made obvious: *AV* 5. 29. 9 ff.; *Visuddhimagga* II, p. 665; *Gilgit MSS* I, p. 5. 3; Jātaka 3, no. 132; 5, no. 257 (*Yaksha Cult,* p. 4).

100. "The only reputable Piśācas are those that have ceased to be piśitāśana and act as guards of the White Mountain, a troop devoted to Skanda ([*Mbh*] 3. 225. 11). These become vegetarian and abandoning their usual diet live on the fruit of the tree (called Mahāśaṅkha) which grows there." (Hopkins, *Epic Mythology,* p. 45.)

101. *Vāmana P* 11–15, in O'Flaherty, *Evil,* p. 129.

102. Again, Misra has correlated the shared qualities of yakṣas and *gandharvas*: They both like fragrance (g: *RV* 10. 85. 40–44, y: *Dhammapada Commentary* 3. 208 ff; 6. 194); they possess women; they are both prayed to for the granting of offspring (g: *Pañcaviṁśa Br* 19. 3. 1; y: *Vipāka Sūtra* 7. 28: p. 84 ff); have the same habitat (*gandharvasya dhruve padam* [*ṚV* 1. 22.

14], interpreted by Sāyaṇa as the "antariksa"); are repositories of secret knowledge (*AV* 2. 1. 2; *Mbh* 3. 296–97; *Sutta Nipāta,* Hare 1); possessors of beauty; and music lovers. (Misra, *Yaksha Cult,* p. 3.)

103. "This is the magic of seeing everything which Manu gave to Soma, Soma gave to Viśvasu, and Viśvasu to me. If, given by a guru, it falls into the hands of a coward, it is lost. I have told you about the origin of this magic; learn from me its power. With this magical vision, one can see anyone in the three worlds that one wants to see. One obtains this knowledge by standing on the same foot for six months. I myself, according to my vow, will win you over to this knowledge. For, by being led by this knowledge, we are different from men and, propelled by its authority, we are not unlike the gods. (*Mbh* 1. 158. 40–44.)

104. Coomaraswamy, *Yakṣas* vol. 1, p. 34.

105. Although, in the Jātakas, Kubera is afforded a nominal rulership over the spirits of trees and water ([1: 25, 182; 3: 201] and *nāga*s [7: 133, 147].)

106. *Āśvalāyana Śrauta Sūtra* 10. 7. 6.

107. *Śat Br* 13. 4. 3. 10.

108. For a thorough account of the various etymologies of Kubera's aliases, see Misra, *Yaksha Cult,* pp. 59–70.

109. 5. 96; 7. 4.

110. *Mbh* 3. 258. 10–260. 1.

111. The question of why Rāvaṇa has chosen this selective group of beings to be protected from is not addressed in the text. Prajāpati does mention, however, that men are specifically excluded from the boon. This tendentious point is scoffed at by Rāvaṇa, whose arrogant lack of respect for the race of humans blinds him to the danger they potentially represent. No one, seemingly, notices the flagrant omission of yakṣas, the group with which Kubera is associated.

112. "He who shall kill you in battle shall ride on it. And as you have shown me, your elder, contempt, you shall soon cease to be." (*Mhb* 3. 259. 35, trans. van Buitenen, vol. 2, p. 730.)

113. See Misra, *Yaksha Cult,* pp. 80–85.

114. Ibid., p. 85, citing V. S. Agrawala, *India as Known to Pāṇini,* pp. 359 ff.

115. For references to Kubera in other Jain sources, see the *Antagaḍadasão*, the *Aupapātika Sūtra*, and the *Rayapasenaiyam Sūtra* 14, among others. See Misra, *Yaksha Cult*, p. 86.

116. "The earliest assignments of deities to the four quarters are those of *Yajur Veda* 1, 8. 7. where we get Agni (E), Yama (S), Savitṛ (W), and Varuṇa (N), Bṛhaspati (Zenith), and *YV*, 2. 4. 14. Indra is guardian of the East. In *AV* 1. 3. the immortal guardians are praised, but not named. The *Ṣadviṁśa Br, LV* 4 and *Śatapatha Br* 3. 6. 4. have Agni (E), Yama (S), Varuṇa (W), Soma (N); and other schemes occur, those of the Buddhists and Jainas differing, usually with Kubera in the North." (Coomaraswamy, *Yakṣas*, vol. 2, p. 31.)

117. Zimmer, *Art of Indian Asia*, p. 47.

118. Ibid.

119. 30. 123.

120. L. A. Waddell, "Evolution of the Buddhist Cult, Its Gods, Images and Art," *Imperial and Asiatic Quarterly* (January 1912), p. 126.

121. Zimmer, *Art of Indian Asia*, p. 47.

122. See Joseph Masson, *La Réligion Populaire dans le Canon Bouddhique Pāli* (Louvain: Bureaux du Museon, 1942), pp. 39 ff.

123. See Waddell, "Buddhist Cult," pp. 124 ff.

124. Ibid., pp. 125–26.

125. *Mbh* 12. 274. 5–17.

Chapter 2

1. Misra, *Yaksha Cult*, p. 10.

2. For the origin of this speculative strain, see: *ṚV* 10. 129. 6–7.

3. Arthur Anthony Macdonell, *The Vedic Mythology* (Varanasi: Indological Book House, 1963), p. 23.

4. Coomaraswamy, *Yakṣas*, vol. 2, p. 2.

5. *AV* 10. 2. 32.

6. *AV* 8. 9. 8.

7. *AV* 10. 8. 15.

8. *AV* 8. 9. 25.

9. *Tait Br* 3. 3. 12. 3. 1.

10. *Gopatha Br* 1. 1.

11. *Bṛhadāraṇyaka Up* 5. 4.

12. *Maitri Up* 7. 8.

13. Cf. *asura/ahura* versus Ahura and *daimon* versus demon, and so forth.

14. See Misra, *Yaksha Cult*, p. 20.

15. See *Gobhila Gṛhya Sūtra* 3. 4. 28; *Āśvalāyana Gṛhya Sūtra* 3. 4; *Śāṅkhāyana Gṛhya Sūtra* 4. 93.

16. See *Parāskara Gṛhya Sūtra* 1. 8. 2. and *Śāṅkhāyana Gṛhya Sūtra*. In *ṚV* 10. 85, the marriage hymn of Sūrya, a *gandharva* named Viśvavāsu is invoked and begged to surrender his *droit de seigneur* over the bride. (See O'Flaherty, trans. *ṚV*, p. 269.)

17. Their names have a common derivation, from the root, vṛ, "to cover," "conceal," "surround," "obstruct."

18. Mircea Eliade, *Images and Symbols*, trans. Philip Mairet (New York: Sheed & Ward, 1961), p. 96.

19. This link is now challenged; see O'Flaherty, *Dreams*, p. 118, citing Thomas Burrow, 1981.

20. Paul Ricoeur, *The Symbolism of Evil*, trans. Emerson Buchanan (Boston: Beacon Press, 1969), p. 27.

21. Ibid., p. 31.

22. Kuiper, "Cosmogony and Conception," p. 27, citing *ṚV* 8. 69. 12.

23. For instance, Rāvaṇa; See Kuiper, "Cosmogony and Conception," p. 90.

24. Ibid., p. 115.

25. See Coomaraswamy, "Angels and Titans," pp. 390–91, for his enumeration of the Varuṇa-*nāga* comparisons: *AV* 12. 3. 57, Varuṇa is a "*pṛdaku*," an adder, viper, snake; Varuṇa's domain, the ocean, is *nāgānām alayam, Mahābhārata* 1. 21. 6 and 25. 4; at Bhārhut *nāga*s are depicted among the *deva*s of the western quarter, the *loka* that Varuṇa rules ("Varuṇa-*pāñcamī* replaces the more usual expression Nāgapāñcamī in the *Nīlamāta Purāṇa;* in Buddhist cosmology, Virupakṣa, as regent of the West, corresponds to Varuṇa and both are nāgarājas, etc.").

26. See the *Mahābhārata* 3. 100 version of the slaying of Vṛtra, in which the gods en masse endeavor to kill the *asura,* with Indra at their head. They consult with Brahmā, who tells them to fashion a *vajra* weapon from the bones of the seer Dadhica, who will abandon his body on request. With this weapon, they are able to kill Vṛtra. With the destruction of their chief, the Daityas enter the water to hide from the powerful gods. The ocean or "Varuṇaloka" conceals them by day and by night they emerge to slaughter gods and *brāhmans*. They are defeated only when Agastya, the son of Varuṇa, drinks up all of the waters.

27. See Varuṇa as bringer of death to his son as object lesson in Wendy O'Flaherty, *Tales of Sex and Violence: Folklore, Sacrifice, and Danger in the Jaiminiya Brāhmaṇa* (Chicago and London: University of Chicago Press, 1985), pp. 32–36.

28. See O'Flaherty, *Evil,* "The Birth of Death" and "Crowds in Heaven," pp. 212–72.

29. Lourens P. Van Den Bosch, "Yama—The God on the Black Buffalo," in *Visible Religion,* vol. 1, eds. H. G. Kippenberg; L. P. Van Den Bosch; L. Leertouwer (Leiden: E. J. Brill, 1982), pp. 28–29.

30. *Śatapatha Br* 13. 3. 65.

31. Van Den Bosch, "Yama," p. 30.

Chapter 3

1. Nancy E. Falk, "Wilderness and Kingship in Ancient South Asia," *History of Religions* vol. 13 (August 1973), pp. 1–15.

2. For another example of this modality, see the *Rāmāyaṇa* for Rāma's encounter with Tātakā (1. 23 ff.) as a "rehearsal" for the meeting and slaying of Śūrpaṇakhā (Āraṇya Kāṇḍa 5).

3. *Mbh* 3. 177. 31.

4. *Mbh* 3. 178. 28–45.

5. *Mbh* 3. 314. 27–46.

6. *Mbh* 3. 314. 46–63.

7. The basic format of these stories entails that the main character, whoever (or whatever) he might be in the particular story, is always the *bodhisatta* in disguise. His true identity is revealed by means of introductory or epilogic explanation by the Buddha himself.

8. Supernatural beings living in the Himālayas.

9. Yakṣas, like various magical beings, have the gift of *kāmarūpa,* the ability to take any form they wish.

10. My translation, from *The Jātaka,* ed. V. Fausboll (London: Trübner & Co., 1877), vol. 1, no. 6, p. 129.

11. Ibid., p. 132.

12. Ibid., p. 133.

13. "*. . . le lieu sacré, quand la brousse est défrichée et organisée en une 'campagne' agricole, est souvent un bois, residu de la forêt primitive, de ses dangers et de ce que la mauvais vouloir des génies, possesseurs anciens du terroir, ferait courir aux nouveaux occupants, si ceux-ci ne prenaient pas leurs précautions. La plus évidente de ces anciennes dans une sorte de 'réserve' de l'eau habitat primitif. Les aborigènes réfugiés plus loin dans la forêt sont fréquemment appelés à participer symboliquement à ce genre de culte propitiatoire.*" (Jeannine Auboyer, *Le Trône et son Symbolisme dans L'Inde Ancienne* [Paris: Presses Universitaires de France, 1949], p. 4.)

14. *Mbh* 13. 139. 9–31. Cf. the rape of Utathya's wife by his lascivious brother-in-law, Bṛhaspati, at *Mbh* 1. 98. 7–17, and the abduction of Bṛhaspati's wife by Soma at *ṚV* 10. 109. The motif of gods hiding in the waters is seen at *ṚV* 10. 51, where Agni is coaxed out of hiding by the gods, and at *Mbh* 5. 9–15, where Indra hides after sinning.

15. Lowell W. Bloss, "The Buddha and the Nāga," *History of Religions,* vol. 13, no. 1 (August 1973), p. 45.

Chapter 4

1. For references to benevolent yakkhas, see Misra, *Yaksha Cult,* pp. 40–41.

2. See Zimmer, *Art of Indian Asia,* vol. 1, p. 44.

3. For a discussion of Bhārhut yakkhas and yakkhīs, see especially Misra, *Yaksha Cult,* pp. 114–20 and Waddell, "Evolution of the Buddhist Cult," pp. 132–44.

4. Misra cites a stone head that may be Suciloma in the Mathurā museum (no. 281), having hair pointed upward and bearing a skull on the side of the hair above the forehead. (Misra, *Yaksha Cult,* p. 118.)

5. See A. K. Warder, *Indian Buddhism* (Delhi: Motilal Banarsidas, 1970; revised, 1980), p. 158 ff., and O'Flaherty, *Evil,* pp. 32–33.

6. Indra (Sakka) is elsewhere referred to as a yakkha. See *Majjhima Nikāya* 1. 252.

7. *Ayakūṭa Jātaka* (no. 347), stanzas 3 and 4.

8. Wendy O'Flaherty has spoken of this in her analysis of the three stages of "alignment" of gods, men, and demons: "Asceticism introduces ambiguities into the post-Vedic alignment of loyalties: while Vedic gods want men to be good (sacrificial), post-Vedic gods do not want men to be good (ascetic). The sacrifice helps the gods, creating mutual dependence; asceticism hurts the gods, producing a challenge from men which breaches the basic Vedic relationship of human dependence on the gods or demonic inferiority to the gods. Asceticism negates the distinction between the categories of the gods, demons, and men, producing a problem which can be resolved in either of two ways: one can negate the negation (destroy the ascetic power of the man or demon) or negate the categories (make the ascetic man or demon into a god). The first solution is usually adopted by post-Vedic mythology; the second occurs in the devotional mythology of the third period, the bhakti period." (O'Flaherty, *Evil,* p. 82.)

9. *Dhonasakha Jātaka* (no. 353) 5–20.

10. *Vinaya Piṭaka,* in *Mahāvagga* 1. 63, *Sacred Books of the East,* vol. 13, pp. 217–19.

11. Zimmer, *Art of Indian Asia,* vol. 1, p. 59.

12. The Buddha as a Hindu *avatāra* is described in the *Viṣṇa Purāṇa* 18. 21. 30.

13. For examples, see O'Flaherty, *Evil,* chapter 5.

14. Cf. many parallel versions found in the *Sutta Nipāta*.

15. Cf. its parallel text, *Āḷavī,* in the *Yakkha Sutta*s of the *Saṁyutta Nikāya* and the *Suciloma Sutta,* also of the *SN*.

16. *Ālavaka Sutta,* Introduction.

17. Ibid., 11–12.

18. *The Jātaka or Stories of the Buddha's Former Births,* ed. and trans. E. B. Cowell (London: Luzac & Co., for the Pali Text Society, 1973), vol. 3, no. 398, pp. 201–4.

19. *Majjhima Nikāya* 86. 2. 97–105 (*The Collection of the Middle Length Sayings,*) trans. I. B. Horner [London: Luzac for the Pali Text Society, 1954–59], 86. 2. 97–105.

20. See O'Flaherty, *Dreams,* pp. 132–65.

21. Bloss, "Ancient Indian Folk Religion," p. 127.

22. This purification of the kingly image of all taint of its violent and erotic moorings is highly reminiscent of the renunciation or sublimation of instincts involved in the Freudian concept of the transformation of the "pleasure principle" into the "reality principle," the necessary psychic process undergirding the development of civilization out of its archaic beginnings in unrestrained eros. See especially Herbert Marcuse, *Eros and Civilization* (New York: Vintage Books, 1955), throughout.

23. *Mbh* 3. 81. 9.

24. Ibid., 3. 81. 19.

25. Ibid., 3. 82. 90.

26. "A king who worships at a local *caitya* and can be said to receive his authorization from a nāga or yakṣa, might also be likened to Indra or Varuṇa and receive the royal consecration mentioned in the *Yajur Vedas.* Nevertheless, there is a difference in emphasis between the parochial and Brahmanic perspectives of kingship." (Bloss, "Ancient Indian Folk Religion," p. 80.)

27. For a description and analysis of yakṣa *caityas,* see Coomaraswamy, *Yakṣas,* vol. 1, p. 23, and Misra, *Yaksha Cult,* pp. 88–97, where he enumerates the varieties of yakṣa *caityas:* "structured" temples, stone daises or platforms, stone chairs, four-legged stools, city gates, sacred trees, mountains, and streams.

28. Coomaraswamy, *Yakṣas,* vol. 1, p. 16, summarizing *Mahāvaṃsa,* chs. 9 and 10. See also O'Flaherty, *Women,* p. 216, where she notes that the name, "Vaḷavāmukhī," "Mare-mouth," is "the same term used for the underwater doomsday fire." She also notes the king's ability, in this case, to channel the yakkhī-mare's aggression "into martial power," instead of being "overpowered by her" (p. 217).

29. Coomaraswamy, *Yakṣas,* vol. 1, p. 16.

30. The issue of the conversion of yakṣas is, interestingly, not addressed here.

31. *Dummedha Jātaka,* p. 259.

32. Trevor O. Ling, *Buddhism and the Mythology of Evil: A Study in Theravāda Buddhism* (London: George Allen & Unwin, 1962), p. 19.

33. P. 55.

34. See especially *Jaina Iconography,* eds. Jyotindra Jain and Eberhard Fischer (Leiden: E. J. Brill, 1978).

35. *The Antagaḍa-Dasāo and Anuttarovavaiya-Dasāo,* trans. L. D. Barnett (London: Royal Asiatic Society, 1907), p. 13.

36. Cf. the use of the blinding motif in the above-mentioned Buddhist story, pp. 113–14.

37. For a complete breakdown of the Jain cosmology, see *Jaina Sūtras* II: *The Uttaradhyāyana Sūtra and the Sūtra Kritanga, Sacred Books of the East,* vol. 45 (Delhi: Motilal Banarsidas, 1968), p. 206 ff.

38. Zimmer, *Art of Indian Asia,* vol. 1, p. 58.

39. *Uttaradhyāyana Sūtra,* in *Jaina Sūtras,* pt. 2, pp. 16–17.

40. See Misra, *Yaksha Cult,* pp. 50–52 for a description of the varieties of yakṣa worship.

41. *Antagaḍa-Dasāo,* from *The Antagada-Dasāo and Anuttarovavaiya-Dasāo,* p. 7.

42. *Uvasagadasāo,* trans. A. F. Rudolph Hoernle (Calcutta: Baptist Mission Press, 1888), pp. 65–69.

43. O'Flaherty, *Evil,* pp. 78–93.

44. See *Sutta Nipāta,* p. 72; *Dīgha Nikāya* 1.93; *Mahāvastu* 2. 260.10; 2.261.2

45. This is thoroughly explored in Bloss, "The Buddha and the Nāga."

46. *Majjhima Nikāya* 1. 383. "Elsewhere the Buddha finds it necessary to say that he is not a Deva, Gandhabba, or Yakkha. (*Aṅguttara Nikāya;* II, 37)." (Coomaraswamy, *Yakṣas* vol. 1, p. 4, fn. 2.)

47. Although it could be argued that conversion to Buddhism is ultimately ritualistic and Vedic ritual is ultimately transformative.

Chapter 5

1. Misra, Yaksha Cult, pp. 115–16.

2. See *Mbh* 3. 265. 1–3a: "Who are you who stands shining alone in the hermitage, bending down the branch of a Kadamba tree, glowing in the night like a flame trembling in the wind? Oh fair browed one, possessed of exceeding beauty, you could never frighten anyone in the forest, so how could you be a yakṣī or a Dānavī or an apsaras or a lovely limbed Daitya maiden or a beautiful daughter of a nāga king or a rākṣasī roaming in the woods?"

3. *Telapatta Jātaka,* ed. Fausboll, no. 96, pp. 395–96, my translation.

4. *Mahāvaṁsa,* ch. 7, trans. Coomaraswamy, *Yakṣas,* pt. 1, pp. 13–14.

5. See Calypso's speech to Odysseus, Hans Christian Anderson's, "The Little Mermaid," and so forth. In Indian mythology, the prototype for this motif is to be found in the Vedic variant of the marriage of the *apsaras,* Urvāśī, and the human king, Pururāvas. See O'Flaherty, "Immortal Woman and Mortal Man," in *Women,* p. 180 ff.

6. O'Flaherty, *Women,* p. 207.

7. *Padakusalamāṇava Jātaka* (no. 432), 15–21.

8. *Jayaddisa Jātaka* (no. 513), 17–20.

9. Again, the paradox of the demonic ruler. See above, chapter 4, "Kings and yakkhas."

10. *Jayaddisa Jātaka* 13–20.

11. For a full list of her many aspects and legends, see Misra, *Yaksha Cult,* p. 73 ff., and N. Peri, "Hārīti, la Mère-de-Démons," *Bulletin de l'École française d'Extrême-Orient* (1917), pp. 1–15.

12. Misra, *Yaksha Cult,* p. 74.

13. See Ibid., p. 77 ff.

14. In the *Mahāvastu,* "it is not Kuṇḍalā but her five hundred children who are the bearers of the pestilence which strikes the whole population, including the children. Hāritā, as a malevolent goddess responsible for killing and devouring children, is introduced only later." She has come to be identified with other malevolent disease goddesses such as Jarā, Jyeṣṭhā, Revati, and Śītalā. (Misra, *Yaksha Cult,* p. 74.)

15. Cf. the bowl of the Buddhist goddess, Manimekhalai. See especially, Paula Richman, "Religious Rhetoric in Manimekalai" (Ph.D. dissertation, University of Chicago, 1983).

16. Peri, "Hārīti," pp. 1–15.

17. James Hastings, *Encyclopedia of Religion and Ethics* (New York: Charles Scribner's Sons, 1912), p. 604.

18. See Misra, *Yaksha Cult,* p. 127.

19. "The regular *sādhakas* invoke the help of Yakshīs for killing their enemies during a specific time limit. This practice in Andhra Pradesh is known as *Seṭhabaḍi.* But the remedies to it have also been described. A

person under *Seṭhabaḍi* loses health and vomits blood but can alleviate the danger to his life by worshipping Adiśakti Mahākālī. If the person escaped from the malevolence of the charm, it is necessary for the *upāsaka* to provide an alternative sacrifice; otherwise he, it is believed, was himself devoured by the Yakshiṇī. It is also said that Yakshiṇīs do not harm pious men." (Ibid., p. 163.)

20. Ibid., p. 101.

21. "In the Central Indian iconography of these demi-gods, Deogarh (Jhansi distt.), Pathari (Vidisha distt.), Simhapur (Shadol distt.), Tripuri and Sohagpur (Jabalpur distt.), are important. Deogarh alone, as an important centre of Jain art, has yielded more than two dozen such sculptures in round or relief. The place is scattered with some thirty-one Jain temples and, on the temple no. 12, twenty Yakshiṇīs along with their Jinas have been represented. They are all inscribed:

> Four-armed Cakreśvarī (Jina Rishabha), two-armed Saraswatī (Jina Abhinandana); Sulocanā (Jina Padmaprabha); Sumālini (Candraprabha); two-armed Bahurupi (Pushpadanta); four-armed Srīyadevī (Śītala); two-armed standing Vahni (Śreyāṁsanātha); two-armed Abhogarohiṇi (Vāsūpujya); two-armed Sulakshaṇā (Vimala); two-armed Anantavīryā (Ananta); two-armed Surakshitā (Dharma); two-armed Śrīyadevī and similar Anantavīrya (with Jina Śānti); four-armed Arakarabhi (?) Kunthu) [sic]; two-armed Tārādevī (Ara); two more unnamed Yakshiṇīs (Munisuvrata and Nimi) and four-armed (Padmāvatī, Varddhamāna)." (Ibid., pp. 126–27.)

22. See Coomaraswamy, *Yakṣas*, pt. 1, p. 9, and Vidya Dehejia, *Yoginī Cult and Temples: A Tantric Tradition* (New Delhi: National Museum, 1986), pp. 36–38.

23. Misra, *Yaksha Cult*, pp. 100–1, citing the *Jayakhya Saṁhitā*, p. 295, and the *Mañjuśrīmūlakalpa* 2. 293; 3. 720. See also *Sādhanamāla* 2; *Bhūtadamaratantra; Vāmakeśvarimatam* 2. 13.

24. The providing of sexual pleasure by yakṣis for their devotees is referred to in the *Mañjuśrīmūlakalpa* 2. 293 and *Vāmakeśvarimatam* 4. 39, Misra cites modern texts that refer to arcane methods for controlling yakṣīs: *Yakshadamaram, Yakshiṇīkalpa, Yakshiṇīsādhana Vidhi,* and *Yakshiṇīprayogah.*

Chapter 6

1. *Meghadūta* 1–3 (my translation).

2. *Md* 7.

3. *Md* 65–79.

4. Md 115–20.

5. Krishna Deva, "Illustrated Manuscript of Meghadūta Dated A.D. 1669," in *Dr. Moti Chandra Commemoration Volume of the Journal of the Indian Society of Oriental Art,* eds. Umakant P. Shah and Krishna Deva (Calcutta: Mrs. Shrimati Tagore, 1978), p. 91.

6. Ibid., pp. 95–96.

Conclusion

1. *Śvetāśvatāra Upaniṣad* 1. 8.

2. *Vāmana Saromahātmyam* 19. 31–35, (O'Flaherty, trans., *Evil,* p. 77).

3. Bruce Kapferer, *A Celebration of Demons: Exorcism and the Aesthetics of Healing in Sri Lanka* (Bloomington, Indiana: Indiana University Press, 1983), p. 16.

4. Paul G. Hiebert, "Village Explanation Traditions," in *Karma: An Anthropological Inquiry,* eds. Charles F. Keyes and E. Valentine Daniel (Los Angeles: University of California Press, 1983), p. 120.

5. Above, pp. 1–2.

6. "Immovable beings: insects, both small and great, fishes, snakes and tortoises, cattle and wild animals, are the lowest conditions to which the quality of Darkness (*tamas*) leads. Elephants, horses, *Śūdra*s, and despicable barbarians, lions, tigers, and boars are the middling states, caused by the quality of Darkness. *Caraṇa*s, *Suparṇa*s and hypocrites, *Rākṣasa*s and *Piśāca*s belong to the highest rank of conditions among those produced by Darkness. *Jhalla*s, *Malla*s, *Nata*s, men who subsist by despicable occupations and those addicted to gambling and drinking, form the lowest order of conditions caused by Activity [*rāja*s]. Kings and *Kṣatriya*s, the domestic priests of kings, and those who delight in the warfare of disputations constitute the middling rank of the states caused by Activity. The *Gandharva*s, the *Guhyaka*s, and the servants of the gods, likewise the *Apsaras*es, belong to the highest rank of conditions produced by Activity. Hermits, ascetics, *Brāhmaṇa*s, the crowds of the *Vaimānika* deities, the lunar mansions, and the

Daityas form the first and lowest rank of the existences caused by Goodness [*sattva*]. The sages declare Brahmā, the creator of the universe, the Law, the Great One, and the Undiscernible One to constitute the highest order of beings produced by Goodness." (*Manu* 12. 41–50, quoted by Bimala Churn Law, *The Buddhist Conception of Spirits* [London: Luzac & Co., 1936], pp. 13–14), brackets mine.

7. *Dīgha Nikāya* 3. 262 and *Khuddakapatha Commentary* 86–87, cited in ibid., pp. 12–13.

8. Ibid. p. 108. 2.

9. Ibid.

10. See Ling, *Buddhism*, p. 27.

11. "Sin is necessary for the balance of earthly society; it is necessary for there to be Untouchables in order for there to be Brahmins; purity depends on impurity. Goddesses of disease and filth are worshipped throughout India; the Hindus recognize the necessity of coming to terms with evil." (O'Flaherty, *Evil*, p. 47.)

12. *AV* 2. 9. 1; 6. 3. 3; 6. 81. 1.

13. *Bhāgavata P* 7. 9; *Brahmā P*, *Hitopadeśa* 2. 1. 20.

14. My retranslation of *Cāraka-Saṁhitā*, ed. and trans. Priyavrat Sharma (Varanasi: Chaukhamba Orientalia, 1983), pp. 163–64.

BIBLIOGRAPHY

Abel Bergaigne's Vedic Religion. Translated by Maurice Bloomfield. Delhi: Motilal Banarsidass, 1978.

Agrawala, Vasudeva Sharana. *India as Known to Pāṇini: A Study of the Cultural Material in the Ashṭadhyāyi*. Lucknow: University of Lucknow, 1953.

Ahern, Emily Martin. *The Cult of the Dead in a Chinese Village*, Stanford, California: Stanford University Press, 1973.

Aiyangar, K. *Manimekhalai in Its Historical Setting*. London: Luzac & Co., 1928.

"Animaux fantastiques de l'Indochine, de l'Insulinde et de la Chine." *Bulletin de l'École française d'Extrême-Orient* 36 (1936): 427 ff.

Aṅguttara Nikāya. Translated by F. L. Woodward and E. M. Hare, 5 vols. London: Pāli Text Society, 1932–1936.

The Antagaḍa-Dasāo and Anuttarovavaiya-Dasāo. Translated by L. D. Barnett. London: Royal Asiatic Society, 1907.

Anthropological Approaches to the Study of Religion. Edited by Michael Banton. London: Tavistock Publications, 1966.

Arbman, E. "Rudra. Untersuchungen zum altindischen Glauben und Kultus." *Uppsala Universitets Arsskrift* 1922, filosofi, sprakvetenskapoch historiska vetenskaper 2.

Archer, W. G. *The Vertical Man: A Study in Primitive Sculpture*. London: George Allen & Unwin Ltd., 1947.

Aronoff, Arnold L. "Contrasting Modes of Textual Classification." Ph.D. dissertation, University of Chicago, 1982.

Ashton, Martha Bush. "Yakshagana Badagatittu Bayalata, A South Indian Dance Drama." Ph.D. dissertation, Michigan State University, 1972.

Aśokāvadāna. Edited by Sujitkumar Mukhopadhyaya. New Delhi: Sahitya Akademi, 1963.

Aspects of Indian Art. Edited by Pratapaditya Pal. Leiden: E. J. Brill, 1972.

Attagara, Kingkeo. *The Folk Religion of Bon Nai*. Bangkok: Kurusapha Press, 1968.

Auboyer, Jeannine. *Le Trône et son Symbolisme dans L'Inde Ancienne*. Paris: Presses Universitaires de France, 1949.

Ayyar, P. V. Jagadisa. *South Indian Shrines*. Madras: 1920.

Bachhofer, Ludwig. *Early Indian Sculpture*. 2 vols. Paris: The Pegasus Press, 1929.

Bailey, Greg. *The Mythology of Brahmā*. Delhi: Oxford University Press, 1983.

Bailey, H. W. "Cognates of pūjā." *Adyar Library Bulletin* 25 (1961):1–12.

Baird, Robert D. *Category Formation and the History of Religions*. The Hague: Mouton, 1971.

Balint, Michael. *The Basic Fault*. New York: Brunner-Mazel, 1968.

Banerjea, Jitendra Nath. *The Development of Hindu Iconography*. Calcutta: University of Calcutta, 1956.

Barnsley, John H. *Social Reality of Ethics: The Comparative Analysis of Moral Codes*. London: Routledge & Kegan Paul, 1972.

Beck, Brenda E. F. "The Symbolic Merger of Body, Space and Cosmos in Hindu Tamil Nadu." *Contributions to Indian Sociology* NS. (1976):10. 2.

Becker, Ernest. *Escape from Evil*. New York: The Free Press, 1975.

Bendall, C. "The History of Nepal and Surrounding Kingdoms (1000–1600 A.D.)." *Journal of the Asian Society of Bengal* 72 (1903):1. 1.

Bergaigne, Abel. *La Religion védique d'après les hymnes du Rig-Veda*. Paris: Librairie Honore Champion, 1963.

Bernheimer, Richard. *Wild Men in the Middle Ages: A Study in Art, Sentiment, and Demonology*. New York: Octagon Books, 1970.

Bhattacharyya, Benoytosh. *The Indian Buddhist Iconography*. Calcutta: Humphrey Milford. Oxford University Press, 1924.

______. *Śaivism and the Phallic World*. 2 vols. New Delhi: Oxford & IBB Pub. Co., 1975.

Bidney, David. "Myth, Symbolism, and Truth." In *Myth: A Symposium*.

Edited by Thomas A. Sebeok. Bloomington, Indiana: Indiana University Press, 1958.

The Biographical Process: Studies in the History and Psychology of Religion. Edited by Frank E. Reynolds and Donald Capps. The Hague: Mouton, 1976.

Blackburn, Stuart H. "Death and Deification: Folk Cults in Hinduism." *History of Religions* 24. 3 (February 1985):255–74.

Bloomfield, Maurice. "The Story of Indra and Namuci," from "Contributions to the Interpretation of the Veda." *JAOS* 15 (1893):143–63.

Bloss, Lowell W. "Ancient Indian Folk Religion as Seen Through the Symbolism of the Nāga." Ph.D. dissertation, University of Chicago, 1971.

______. "The Buddha and the Nāga." History of Religions 13. 1 (August 1973).

______. "The Taming of Māra: Witnessing to the Buddha's Virtues." *History of Religions* 18. 2 (November 1978).

Boggs, Ralph Steele. "Folklore Classification." *Southern Folklore Quarterly* 13 (1949):166.

Bosch, F. D. K. *The Golden Germ: An Introduction to Indian Symbolism.* The Hague: Mouton & Co., 1960.

Boyd, James W. "Satan and Māra: Christian and Buddhist Symbols of Evil." *Studies in the History of Religions* (supplements to *Numen*) 27. Leiden: E. J. Brill 1975.

The Bṛhad-Devatā. Edited and translated by Arthur Anthony Macdonell. Harvard Oriental Series vols. 5 and 6. Cambridge: Harvard University Press, 1904.

Brown, Peter. *The Cult of the Saints: Its Rise and Function in Latin Christianity.* Chicago: The University of Chicago Press, 1981.

______. "Understanding Islam." *The New York Review of Books* (February 22, 1979).

Brown, W. Norman. "Proselyting the Asuras." *JAOS* 39 (1919):100–13.

______. "The Ṛgvedic Equivalent for Hell." *JAOS* 61 (1941):76–80.

Buddhavaṁsa with commentary. Translated by B. C. Law. The Minor Anthologies of the Pāli Canon 3. London: Oxford University Press, 1938.

Buddhist Birth Stories, Nidāna-Kathā London: George Routledge & Sons, 1925.

Buddhist Records of the Western World, Travels of Fah-huan and Sung-yun: Buddhist Pilgrims from China to India (400 A.D. *and 518* A.D.). Translated by Samuel Beal. London: Trübner and Co., 1869.

Burgess, James. *Buddhist Art in India.* New Delhi: S. Chand & Co., 1972, reprint of 1901.

Burrow, Thomas. "Sanskrit *mā,* 'to make, produce, create.' " *Bulletin of the School of Oriental and African Studies* 43 (1980):311–28; 44 (1981):85.

Caillois, Roger. *Man and the Sacred.* Glencoe, Illinois: Free Press, 1960.

Campbell, Joseph. *Historical Atlas of World Mythology.* Vol 1: "The Way of the Animal Powers." New York: Harper & Row, 1983.

______. *The Mythic Image.* Princeton, New Jersey: Princeton University Press, 1974.

Caraka-Saṁhitā. Vol. 2. Edited and translated by Priyavrat Sharma. Varanasi: Chaukhamba Orientalia, 1983.

Carnoy, Albert J. "The Moral Deities of Iran and India and Their Origins." *The American Journal of Theology* 21 (1917):58–78.

Carstairs, G. M., and R. L. Kapur. *The Great Universe of Koṭa: Stress, Change and Mental Disorder in an Indian Village.* Berkeley: The University of California Press, 1976.

Cassirer, Ernst. *Symbol, Myth, and Culture: Essays and Lectures of Ernst Cassirer 1935–1945.* New Haven and London: Yale University Press, 1979.

Chandra. Moti. "Some Aspects of Yaksha Cult in Ancient India." *Bulletin of the Prince of Wales Museum* 3 (1952–53):53–54 and 61–62.

______. *Trade and Trade Routes in Ancient India.* New Delhi: Abhinav Publications, 1977.

Chandra, Pramod. *The Sculpture of India 3000* B.C.*–1300* A.D. (A catalogue of an exhibition, National Gallery of Art, Washington, D.C., May 5–September 2, 1985). Cambridge, Massachusetts: Harvard University Press, 1985.

Charpentier, Jarl. *Die Suparṇasage.* Uppsala: Akademiska Bokhandeln, 1920.

Chatham, Doris Clark. "Rasa and Sculpture." In *Kaladarśana: American*

Studies in the Art of India. New Delhi: Oxford and I.B.H. Publishing Co. in collaboration with the American Institute of Indian Studies, 1981. Edited by Joanna G. Williams.

Chatterji, Suniti Kumar. "Race Movements and Prehistoric Culture." In *The History and Culture of the Indian People*, vol. 1. Edited by R. C. Majumdar. Bombay: Bhāratiya Vidya Bhavan, 1951, pp. 162–64.

Chaudhuri, Nirad Chandra. *Scholar Extraordinary*. New York: Oxford University Press, 1974.

Coccari, Diane M. "The Bir Bābas of Banaras: An Analysis of a Folk Deity of North Indian Hinduism." Ph.D. dissertation, University of Wisconsin, Madison, 1986.

Cohn, Norman. *Europe's Inner Demons: An Enquiry Inspired by the Great Witch-Hunt*. New York: Basic Books, Inc., 1975.

The Collection of the Middle Length Sayings (*Majjhimanikāya*). Translated by I. B. Horner. London: Luzac for the Pali Text Society, 1954–59.

Concepts of Person: Kinship, Caste and Marriage in India. Edited by Akos Östor, Lina Fruzzetti, and Steve Burnett. Cambridge, Massachusetts, and London: Harvard University Press, 1982.

Conze, Edward. *Buddhist Scriptures, A Bibliography*. Edited and revised by Lewis Lancaster. New York and London: Garland Publishing, 1982.

Coomaraswamy, Ananda Kentish. "Angels and Titans, An Essay on Vedic Ontology." *JAOS* 55 (1935):373–419.

______. "Ātmayajña: Self Sacrifice." *Harvard Journal of Asiatic Studies* 6 (1942):358–98.

______. *The Dance of Śiva*. New York: The Sunrise Turn, Inc., 1924.

______. "The Darker Side of Dawn." Smithsonian Miscellaneous Publications. vol. 94. Washington, D.C.: Smithsonian Institution, 1935, no. 1.

______. "Early Indian Iconography-II, Śrī Lakṣmī." *Eastern art* 1:2 (October 1928):175–89.

______. *History of Indian and Indonesian Art*. New York: Dover Publications, 1965, reprint of 1927.

______. "Sir Gawain and the Green Knight: Indra and Namuci." *Speculum* 19 (1944):109–11.

______. *The Origin of the Buddha Image*. New Delhi: Munshiram Monoharlal, 1972.

______. *La Sculpture de Bhārhut*. Translated by Jean Buhot. Paris: Vanoest, 1956.

______. *Spiritual Authority and Temporal Power in the Indian Theory of Government*. New Delhi: Munshiram Manoharlal, 1978.

______. *The Transformation of Nature in Art*. Cambridge, Massachusetts: Harvard University Press, 1935.

______. "Uṣṇīṣa and Chatra." *Poona Orientalist* 3. 1 (April 1938):7.

______. "The Yakṣa of the Vedas and the Upaniṣads." *The Quarterly Journal of the Mythic Society* 28. 4: 232–40.

______. *Yakṣas*. 2 parts in 1 vol. New Delhi: Munshiram Manoharlal, 1971.

Cosmogony and Ethical Order: New Studies in Comparative Ethics. Edited by Robin W. Lovin and Frank. E. Reynolds. Chicago and London: University of Chicago Press, 1985.

Courtwright, Paul B. *Ganeśa, Lord of Obstacles, Lord of Beginnings*. New York and Oxford: Oxford University Press, 1985.

Crooke, W. "Demons and Spirits (Indian)." In the *Encyclopedia of Religion and Ethics*. New York: Charles Scribner's Sons.

______. *Religion and Folklore of Northern India*. London: Oxford University Press, 1926.

Cunningham, Alexander. *The Bhilsa Topes or Buddhist Monuments of Central India*. London: Smith, Elder and Co., 1854.

Dange, S. A. *Vedic Concept of 'Field' and the Divine Fructification: A Study in Fertility and Sex-Symbols with Special Reference to the Ṛgveda*. Bombay: University of Bombay, 1971.

Dasgupta, Surendra Nath. *Fundamentals of Indian Art*. Bombay: Bhāratiya Vidya Bhavan, 1954.

Dathavaṁsa. Edited and translated by Bimala Charan Law. Lahore: Motilal Banarsidas, 1925.

David-Neel, Alexandra. *Magic and Mystery in Tibet*. London: Unwin Paperbacks, 1984.

Dayal, Har. *The Bodhisattva Doctrine in Buddhist Sanskrit Literature*. Delhi: Motilal Banarsidas, 1975, reprint of 1932.

de Coral-Remusat, Countess G. "Concerning some Indian Influences in Khmer Art." *Indian Art and Letters* n.s. 8 (1933):110–20.

______. "Influences javanaises dans l'art de Rulûoh." *Journal Asiatique* (1933, 2):190–92.

Dehejia, Vidya. *Yoginī Cult and Temples: A Tantric Tradition.* New Delhi: National Museum, 1986.

Deva, Krishna. "Illustrated Manuscript of Meghadūta Dated A.D. 1669." In Dr. Moti Chandra Commemoration Volume *of* The Journal of the Indian Society of Oriental Art. Edited by Umakant P. Shah and Krishna Deva. Calcutta: Mrs. Shrimati Tagore, 1978.

Devereux, George. *Basic Problems of Ethnopsychiatry.* Translated by Basia Miller Gulati and George Devereux. Chicago and London: University of Chicago Press, 1980.

Dīgha Nikāya. Translated by T. W. Rhys Davids and C. A. F. Rhys Davids, 3 vols. London: Pāli Text Society, 1899–1921.

Dhammapada Commentary, Buddhist Legends Translated from the Original Pāli. Harvard Oriental Series vol. 28. Cambridge, Massachusetts: Harvard University Press, 1921.

Dialogues of the Buddha. London: Pāli Text Society (pts. 1, 2, 3), 1977.

Dimock, Edward C. "The Goddess of Snakes in Medieval Bengali Literature." 1 *History of Religions* 1. 2 (Winter 1962):307–21.

______. "Manasā, Goddess of Snakes: The Ṣaṣṭhī Myth." In *Myths and Symbols: Studies in Honor of Mircea Eliade.* Chicago: University of Chicago Press, 1969, pp. 217–26.

______. and Rāmānujan, A. K. "The Goddess of Snakes in Medieval Bengali Literature 2." *History of Religions* 3. 2 (Winter 1964):300–22.

Dīpavaṁsa. Translated by Herman Oldenberg. London: Williams & Norgate, 1874.

The Divyāvadāna. Edited by E. B. Cowell and R. A. Neil. Cambridge: At the University Press, 1886.

Douglas, Mary. *Implicit Meanings, Essays in Anthropology.* London: Routledge & Kegan Paul, 1984, reprint of 1975.

______. *Natural Symbols: Explorations in Cosmology.* New York: Pantheon Books, 1982, reprint of 1970.

______. *Purity and Danger: An Analysis of Concepts of Pollution and Taboo.* Binghamton, New York: Vail-Ballon press, 1980, reprint of 1966.

Duerr, Hans Peter. *Dreamtime*. Translated by Felicitas Goodman. Oxford: Basil Blackwell, 1985.

Dumézil Georges. *Mitra-Varuṇa* Paris: Librairie Gallimard, 1948.

Dumont, Louis. *Affinity as Value: Marriage Alliance in South India with Comparative Essays on Australia*. Chicago and London: University of Chicago Press, 1983.

Dundes, Alan. *Analytic Essays in Folklore*. The Hague: Mouton, 1975.

———. *Sacred Narrative*. Berkeley: University of California Press, 1984.

———. *The Study of Folklore*. New York: Prentice Hall, 1965.

Eck, Diana L. *Banaras City of Light*. Princeton, New Jersey: Princeton University Press, 1982.

———. "India's Tīrthas: 'Crossings' in Sacred Geography." *History of Religions* 20. No. 4 (May 1981):323–45.

Edgerton, Franklin. *The Beginnings of Indian Philosophy*. Cambridge, Massachusetts, and London: Harvard University Press, 1965.

Eliade, Mircea. *Images and Symbols*. Translated by Philip Mairet. New York: Sheed & Ward, 1961.

———. *Myth and Reality*. Translated by Willard R. Trask. New York: Harper Colophon Books, 1975, reprint of 1963.

———. "Mythologies of Memory and Forgetting." *History of Religions* 2 (Winter 1963):329.

———. *Patterns in Comparative Religion*. New York: New American Library, 1974, reprint of 1958.

Elmore, Wilber Theodore. *Dravidian Gods in Modern Hinduism*. New Delhi: Asian Educational Services, 1984.

Emeneau, M. B. "The Strangling Figs in Sanskrit Literature." *University of California Publications in Classical Philology* 3 (1949):364–69.

Encyclopedia of Indian Philosophies. Vol. 2, Indian Metaphysics and Epistemology: The Tradition of Nyāya-Vaiśeṣika up to Gangeśa. Edited by Karl H. Potter. Delhi: Motilal Banarsidas, 1977.

The Essays Throwing New Light on the Gandharvas, the Apsarases, the Yakshas and the Kinnāras. Edited by N. G. Tavakar. Bombay: Tavkar Prakashan, 1971.

Evans-Wentz, W. Y. *Tibet's Great Yogi Milarepa*. London and Oxford: Oxford University Press, 1969.

Falk, Nancy E. "The Study of the Cult: With Special Reference to the Cult of the Buddha's Relics in Ancient South Asia." Ph.D. dissertation, University of Chicago, 1972.

______. "Wilderness and Kingship in Ancient South Asia." *History of Religions* 13 (August 1973).

Farquhar, James N. "Temple and Image Worship in Hinduism." *Journal of the Royal Asiatic Society* (1928):15–23.

Foucher, Alfred. *The Beginnings of Buddhist Art*. Varanasi and Delhi: Indological Book House, 1972.

______. *The Life of the Buddha: According to the Ancient Texts and Monuments of India*. Middleton, Connecticut: Wesleyan University Press, 1963.

Friedman, John Block. *The Monstrous Races in Medieval Art and Thought*. Cambridge, Massachusetts: Harvard University Press, 1981.

Fûrer-Haimendorf, Christoph von. *The Aboriginal Tribes of Hyderabad*. Vol. 3. *The Rāj Gonds of Adilabad 1: Myth and Ritual*. London: Macmillan, 1948.

______. "The After-Life in Indian Tribal Belief." *Journal of the Royal Anthropological Institute* 83, pt. 1 (1953):37–49.

______. "Caste in the Multi-Ethnic Society of Nepal." *Contributions to Indian Sociology* 4. Edited by Louis Dumont and D. Pocock. Paris: Mouton & Co., 1960.

______. *South Asian Societies, A Study of Values and Social Controls*. Delhi: Sterling Pub., 1979, reprint of 1966.

Geertz, Clifford. *The Religion of Java*. New York: The Free Press of Glencoe, 1964.

Georges, Robert A. *Studies on Mythology*. Homewood, Illinois: Dorsey Press, 1968.

Getty, Alice. *Ganeśa: A Monograph*. Oxford: Clarendon Press, 1971.

Ghoshal, Upendra Nath. "Principle of the King's Righteousness in the Pāli Canon and the Jātaka Commentary." *Indian Historical Quarterly* 32. 2–3 (January-September 1956):304–12.

Girard, Rene. *Violence and the Sacred.* Baltimore, Maryland: Johns Hopkins University Press, 1977.

Gjertson, Donald E. *Ghosts, Gods, and Retribution: Nine Buddhist Miracle Tales from Six Dynasties and Early T'ang China.* Amherst: University of Massachusetts Press, 1978.

Gokhale, B. L. *Ancient India.* Bombay: Asia Publishing House, 1952.

Gonda, Jan. *The Vision of the Vedic Poets.* The Hague: Mouton, 1963.

Greenberg, Jay R. and Stephen A. Mitchell. *Object Relations in Psychoanalytic Theory.* Cambridge, Massachusetts, and London: Harvard University Press, 1983.

Grunwedel, Albert. *Buddhist Art in India.* Translated by A. C. Gibson. Revised and enlarged by James Burgess. Spain and England: Susil Gupta, 1965.

Haldar, J. R. *Early Buddhist Mythology.* Delhi: Manohar, 1977.

Handiqui, K. K. *Yaśastilaka and Indian Culture.* Sholapur: Jaina Saṁskriti Saṁrakshaka Sangha, 1968.

Harshadeva. *Nāgānanda.* Edited and translated by M. R. Kale. Bombay: Booksellers' Publishing Co., 1952).

Hastings, James. *Encyclopedia of Religion and Ethics.* New York: Charles Scribner's Sons, 1912.

Hastyāyurveda, "The Sacred Wisdom of the Longevity of the Elephants." Edited by Shivadattasharman. Poona: The Anandāshrama Sanskrit Series 26, 1894.

Hausman, Carl R. "Metaphors, Referents, and Individuality." *The Journal of Aesthetics and Art Criticism* 2 (Winter 1983):181–97.

Hawkes, Terence. *Structuralism and Semiotics.* London: Methuen & Co., 1983, reprint of 1977.

Heesterman, Johannes C. *The Ancient Indian Royal Consecration: The Rājasūya Described According to the Yajus Texts and Annotated.* Gravenhage: Mouton and Company, 1957.

Heidegger, Martin. *Poetry, Language, Thought.* Translated and with introduction by Albert Hofstadter. New York: Harper & Row, 1971.

Hemacandra, *Sthaviravalicharita* or *Pariśiṣṭaparvan.* Edited by Hermann Jacobi. Calcutta: Asiatic Society, 1883.

Hentze, Carl. "Gods and Drinking Serpents." *History of Religions*. 4 (Winter 1965):179.

Hiltebeitel, Alf. "The Mahābhārata and Hindu Eschatology." *History of Religions* 12: 95.

Hindu Myths. Translated, edited, and with introduction by Wendy Doniger O'Flaherty. England: Penguin Books, 1982, reprint of 1975.

Hingorani, R. P. *Jaina Iconography in Rūpamaṇḍana*. Varanasi: Kishor Vidya Niketan, 1978.

Hirsch, E. D., Jr. *Validity of Interpretation*. New Haven, Connecticut: Yale University Press, 1967.

History of Nepal. (The *Vaṁśāvali*.) Translated (from Parbatiya) by Munshi Shew Shunker Singh and Pandit Shri Gunananand. Kathmandu: Nepal Antiquated Book Publishers, 1972, reprint of 1877.

Hocart, Arthur Maurice. *Kings and Councillors*. Cairo: Printing Office Paul Barbey, 1936.

Hohenberger, A. *Die Indische Flütsage und das Matsyapurāṇa*. Leipzig: Otto Harrassowitz, 1930.

Honko, Lauri. "Genre Analysis in Folkloristics and Comparative Religion." *Temenos* 3 (1968):48–66.

Hopkins, Edward Washburn. *Epic Mythology*. Varanasi: Indological Book House, 1968.

Hospital, Clifford. *The Righteous Demon: A Study of Bali*. Vancouver: University of British Columbia Press, 1984.

Ibbetson, Sir Denzil, and Sir Edward Maclagan. *A Glossary of the Tribes and Castes of the Punjab and North-West Frontier Province*, vol. 1. Lahore: The Superintendent, Government Printing, Punjab, 1919.

The Image of the Buddha. Edited by David L. Snellgrove. Paris: Serindia Publications/UNESCO, 1978.

Inden, Ronald. "The Temple and the Hindu Chain of Being." *Puruṣārtha* 8 (1985):53–73.

Jaiminiya Upaniṣad Brāhmaṇa. *JAOS* (1896):16. 1.

Jaina Iconography. Edited by Jyotindra Jain and Eberhard Fischer. Leiden: E. J. Brill, 1978.

Jaina Sūtras I: The Akarāṇga Sūtra and the Kalpa Sūtra. Sacred Books of the East 5. 22. Translated by Hermann Jacobi. Delhi: Motilal Banarsidas, 1968.

Jaina Sūtras 2: The Uttaradhyāyana Sūtra and the Sūtra Kritāṇga. Sacred Books of the East 5. 45. Translated by Hermann Jacobi. Delhi: Motilal Banarsidas, 1968.

Japanese Ghosts and Demons. Edited by Stephen Addiss. New York: George Braziller, 1985.

The Jātaka. Edited by V. Fausboll. London: Trübner & Co., 1877.

The Jātaka or Stories of the Buddha's Former Births. 6 vols. Edited and translated by E. B. Cowell. London: Luzac & Co. for the Pali Text Society, 1973, reprint of 1969.

The Jātakamālā; or Garland of Birth Stories of Āryaśūra. Translated by Edward Speyer, Delhi: Motilal Banarsidas, 1971.

Johnson, Willard. *Poetry and Speculation of the Ṛg Veda*. Berkeley and Los Angeles: University of California Press, 1980.

Jordan, David K. *Gods, Ghosts and Ancestors: Folk Religion in a Taiwanese Village*. Berkeley: University of California Press, 1972.

Kakar, Sudhir. *Shamans, Mystics and Doctors*. Delhi: Oxford University Press, 1982.

Kalhana's Rājataraṅgiṇī: A Chronicale of the Kings of Kasmir. Translated by M. A. Stein. Westminster: Archibald Constable and Co., 1900.

The Kalpa Sūtra and Nava Tattva. Translated by The Rev. J. Johnson. Varanasi: Bharat-Bharati, 1972.

Kapferer, Bruce. *A Celebration of Demons: Exorcism and the Aesthetics of Healing in Sri Lanka*. Bloomington, Indiana: Indiana University Press, 1983.

Karma: An Anthropological Inquiry. Edited by Charles F. Keyes and E. Valentine Daniel. Los Angeles: University of California Press, 1983.

The Kathākośa or Treasury of Stories. Translated by C. H. Tawney. London: Royal Asiatic Society, 1895.

Keith, Arthur Berriedale. *The Religion and Philosophy of the Veda and Upaṇishads 1.*, vol. 31 of the Harvard Oriental Series. Cambridge, Massachusetts: Harvard University Press. London. Oxford University Press, 1925.

Khuddaka Pathā. Sacred Books of the Buddhists, vol. 7. London: Oxford University Press, 1931.

The Khuddaka-Pathā with Its Commentary Paramatthajotika 1. Edited by Helmer Smith. London: The Pali Text Society, 1978.

Kirk, G. S. *Myth: Its Meaning and Functions in Ancient and Other Cultures*. Berkeley: University of California Press, 1975.

Kramrisch, Stella. "Emblems of the Universal Being." *Journal of the Indian Society of Oriental Art* 3. 2 (December 1935):160.

______. "Jain Painting of Western India." In *Aspects of Jaina Art and Architecture*. Edited by U. P. Shah and N. A. Dhaky. Ahmedabad: L. D. Institute of Indology, 1975.

______. The Presence of Śiva. Princeton, N.J.: Princeton University Press, 1981.

Kretschmer, P. *Varuna und die Urgeschichte der Inder*. Wiener: Zeitschrift fur den Kunde des Morgenlandes 33. 1926.

Krom, N. J. *The Life of the Buddha and the Stūpa of Barabudur According to the Lalitavistara*. The Hague: Martinus Nijhoff, 1926.

Kuiper, F. B. J. "The Basic Concept of Vedic Religions," *History of Religions* 15: 2 (November 1975):107.

______. "Cosmogony and Conception: A Query," *History of Religions* 10 (November 1970):108.

______. *Varuṇa and Vidūṣaka: On the origin of the Sanskrit Drama*. Verhandelingen der Koninklijke Nederlandse Akademe van Wetenschappen, Afd. Letterkunde nieuwe reeks, deel 100. 1979.

LaFleur, William R. *The Karma of Words: Buddhism and the Literary Arts in Medieval Japan*. Berkeley and Los Angeles: University of California Press, 1983.

Lahiri, Ajoy Kumar. *Vedic Vṛtra*. Delhi: Motilal Banarsidas, 1984.

Lakoff, George, and Mark Johnson. *Metaphors We Live By*. Chicago: University of Chicago Press, 1980.

Lamotte, Etienne. *Histoire du Bouddhisme Indien*. Louvaine: Publications Universitaires, 1958.

Langton, E. *Essentials of Demonology*. London: Epworth Press, 1949.

Law, Bimala Churn. *The Buddhist Conception of Spirits*. London: Luzac & Co., 1936.

The Laws of Manu. Sacred Books of the East. Translated, with extracts from seven commentaries by Georg Bühler. Delhi: Motilal Banarsidas, 1964.

Légendes bouddhistes et djainas. Traduites du Tamoul. Translated into French by J. Vinson. Paris: G. P. Maisonneuve & Larose, 1969.

Levi, Sylvain. *Le catalogue géographique de Yakṣa dans le Mahāmāyūri. Journal Asiatique*, Janvier-Février (1915): 1. 19–138.

______. *Doctrine du sacrifice chez les Brāhmaṇas*. Paris: E. Leroux, 1898.

______. *Le Népal: étude historique d'un royaume hindou*. 3 vols. Paris: Ernest Leroux, 1905.

Lin-Bodien, Carol G. "An Early Yaksha from Āktha near Sarnāth (Varanasi District, U.P.)." *Chhavi* 2. Benares: Bhārat Kala Bhavan, 1981.

Ling, Trevor O. *Buddhism and the Mythology of Evil: A Study in Theravāda Buddhism*. London: George Allen & Unwin, 1962.

Little, David, and Twiss, Sumner. *Comparative Religious Ethics*. San Francisco: Harper & Row, 1978.

Long, J. Bruce. "Life Out of Death: A Structural Analysis of the Myth of the Churning of the Ocean of Milk." In *Hinduism: New Essays in the History of Religion*. Edited by Bardwell Smith. Leiden: Supplement to *Numen* 33 (1976):171–207.

Lovejoy, Arthur. *The Great Chain of Being*. Cambridge, Massachusetts: Harvard University Press, 1961.

Macdonell, Arthur Anthony. *The Vedic Mythology*. Varanasi: Indological Book House, 1963.

MacIntyre, Alistair. "Epistemological Crises, Dramatic Narrative and the Philosophy of Science." *The Monist*. 60. 4 (October 1977): 453–72.

Mahābhārata. Edited by V. S. Sukthanker et al. Poona: 1933–1960.

Mahābhārata. Books 1–5. Translated by J. A. B. van Buitenen. Chicago: The University of Chicago Press, 1978.

Mahāparinibbana-sutta, "The Book of the Great Decease." In *Dialogues of the Buddha translated from the Pali of the Dīgha Nikāya, Part 2*. Sacred Books of the Buddhists, vol. 3–4. London: Luzac and Co., 1966 (vol. 3: 78–191).

Mahāvaṁsa. Pali Text Society. Translated by William Geiger. London: Oxford University Press, 1912.

The Mahāvastu. In Sacred Books of the Buddhists, vol. 1 and 2. London: Luzac & Co., 1952.

Maity, Pradyat Kumar, *Historical Studies in the Cult of the Goddess Manasā*. Calcutta: Punthi Pustak, 1966.

______. "Tree Worship and Its Association with the Snake Cult in India." In *Tree Symbol Worship in India: A New Survey of a Pattern of Folk-Religion*. Calcutta: Indian Publications.

Majjhima Nikāya. Translated by I. B. Horner, 3 vols. London: Pali Text Society, 1954–1959.

Malandra, Geri Hockfield. "Māra's Army: Text and Image in early Indian Art." *East and West*. New Series, 31, nos. 1–4 (December 1981.):121–130.

Malinowski, Bronislav. *Magic, Science, and Religion*. New York: Doubleday, 1954.

Mallmann, M. Th. *Les Enseignemements iconographiques de l'Agni Purāṇa*. Paris: M. Mayrhofer., 1963.

Marriott, McKim. "Little Communities in an Indigenous Civilization." In *Village India: Studies in the Little Community*. Edited by McKim Marriott. Chicago: University of Chicago Press, 1969.

Marshall, Sir John, and Albert Foucher. *The Monuments of Sāñchī*. The Government of India Press.

Masson, Joseph. *La Réligion Populaire dans le Canon Bouddhique Pāli*. Louvain: Bureaux du Museon, 1942.

Mātaṅgalīla ("*The Playful Treatise on the Elephants*"). Edited by T. Ganapati Shastri. Sanskrit Series No. 10, 1910. Trivandrum: (German translation by H. Zimmer, *Spiel um den Elefanten*, Munich and Berlin. 1929.)

Matsunaga, Alicia. "The Chinese Concept of Hell." Review of Goodrich. *History of Religions* 23. 1 (August 1983):94–96.

Maury, Kurt. *Folk Origins of Indian Art*. New York: Columbia University Press, 1969.

Mauss, Marcel. *A General Theory of Magic*. Translated by Robert Brain. New York: W. W. Norton & Co. 1975.

______, with Henri Hubert. *Sacrifice: Its Nature and Function*. Translated by W. D. Halls. Chicago: University of Chicago Press, 1964.

Meyer, Johann Jakob. *Sexual Life in Ancient India*. London: George Routledge & Sons, 1930.

______. *Trilogie altindischer Mächte der Vegetation* 2 (1937): 132.

Misra, Ram Nath. *Yaksha Cult and Iconography*. New Delhi: Munshiram Manoharlal Publishers, 1981.

Mitra, Rajendralala. *Buddha Gāya: The Hermitage of Śākya Muni*. Calcutta: Bengal Secretariat Press, 1878.

Mitra, S. C. "Village Deities of Northern Bengal." *Hindustan Review* (February 1922).

Mitter, Partha. *Much Maligned Mosters: History of European Reactions to Indian Art*. Oxford: Clarendon Press, 1977.

The Monstrous Races in Medieval Art and Thought. Edited by John Bloch Friedman. Cambridge, Massachusetts: Harvard University Press, 1981.

Müller, Friedrich Max. *Letters on the Science of Language*. New York: Charles Scribner & Co., 1866.

______. *The Science of Language*. 2 vols. London: Longmans, Green, and Co., 1891.

______. Vedic Hymns. Sacred Books of the East. Vols. 32 and 46. Oxford: 1891. Delhi: 1964.

Mus, Paul. *Barabudur*. New York: Arno Press, 1978.

Nāgānand of Harshadev. Introduction and English translation by Asha V. Toraskar and N. A. Deshpande. Sanskrit commentary by M. R. Kale. Bombay: Booksellers' Publishing Co., 1952.

Narayan, R. K. *Gods, Demons and Others*. New York. The Viking Press, 1964.

Nebesky-Wojkowitz, Rene de. *Oracles and Demons of Tibet: The Cult and Iconography of the Tibetan Protective Deities*. London: Oxford University Press 1956.

Neumann, Erich. *The Great Mother*. Bollingen Series 47. Translated by Ralph Manheim. Princeton New Jersey: Princeton University Press, 1972.

Nicholas, Ralph W. "The Goddess Śītalā and Epidemic Smallpox in Bengal." *Journal of Asian Studies* 41. 1 (November 1981):21–44.

Obeyesekere, Gananath. "The Buddhist Pantheon in Ceylon and Its Extension." In *Anthropological Studies in Theravada Buddhism.* Edited by Manning Nash. New Haven, Connecticut: Yale University Press, 1966.

———. *The Cult of the Goddess Pāttinī.* Chicago: University of Chicago Press, 1984.

———. Medusa's Hair. Chicago: University of Chicago Press, 1981.

———. "Theodicy, Sin and Salvation in a Sociology of Buddhism." In *Dialectic in Practical Religion.* Cambridge Papers in Social Anthropology No. 5. Edited by E. R. Leach. Cambridge: Cambridge University Press, 1968.

The Ocean of Story. Translation of Somadeva's *Kathāsaritsāgara.* 10 Vols. Translated by C. H. Tawney. London: Charles. J. Sawyer, 1924.

O'Flaherty, Wendy Doniger. *Dreams, Illusion and Other Realities.* Chicago and London: University of Chicago Press, 1984.

———. *The Origins of Evil in Hindu Mythology.* Berkeley: The University of California Press, 1976.

———. *Śiva the Erotic Ascetic.* New York: Oxford University Press, 1981.

———. *Tales of Sex and Violence: Folklore, Sacrifice, and Danger in the Jaiminiya Brāhmaṇa.* Chicago and London: University of Chicago Press, 1985.

———. *Women, Androgynes, and Other Mythical Beasts.* Chicago: University of Chicago Press. 1980.

Ogibenin, B. L. *Structure d'un mythe védique: Le mythe cosmogonique dans le Ṛgveda.* The Hague: Mouton 1973.

Oldenberg, Hermann. "Varuṇa und die Ādityas." *Zeitschrift der deutschen morgenländischen Gesellschaft* 50. Leipzig: 1896 (pp. 43 ff.).

Oldham, Charles Frederick. *The Sun and the Serpent: A Contribution to the History of Serpent Worship.* London: A. Constable and Co., 1905.

O'Malley, Lewis S. S. *Popular Hinduism.* Cambridge: Cambridge University Press, 1935.

Palāsa-Jātaka: Stories of the Buddha's Former Births. 6 vols. Edited by E. B. Cowell. Translated by Robert Chalmers et al. London: Luzac & Co., 1957.

Pandit, Sneh. *An Approach to the Indian Theory of Art and Aesthetics.* New Delhi: Sterling Publishers, 1977.

Paul, Diana. *Women in Buddhism*. London: University of California Press, 1985.

Peri, N. "Hārīti, la Mère-de-Démons." *Bulletin de l'École française d'Extrême-Orient* 17, 3 (1917).

Petavatthu. Sacred Books of the Buddhists, vol. 34. Translated by U Ba Kyaw. Edited by Peter Masefield. London: Pali Text Society, 1980.

Philpot, Mrs. J. H. *The Sacred Tree or The Tree in Religion and Myth*. London: Macmillan and Co., 1897.

Popular Hinduism and Hindu Mythology: An Annotated Bibliography. Compiled by Barron Holland. Westport, Connecticut: Greenwood Press, 1979.

Prakash, Om. "The Problem of the First Traditional King." *Purāṇa* 7. 1 (January 1965):129.

Presler, Henry H. *Primitive Religions in India*. Bangalore: The Christian Literature Society Press, 1971.

Propp, Vladimir. *Morphology of the Folktale*. Philadelphia: American Folklore Society, 1958.

Przyluski, Jean. *La Légende de l'Empereur Aśoka* (*Aśoka-Avadāna*) *dans les textes indiens et chinois*. Paris: Ernest Lerous, 1908.

______. "La Princess à L'odeur de Poison et la Nāgī dans Les Tradition de l'Asie Orientale." *Études Asiatique* 2 (1925):265–84.

______. "The Three Factors of Vedic Culture." *Indian Culture*. 1 (1934–35):379 ff.

______. "Totémisme et végétalisme dans l'Inde." *Revue des l'histoire des religions* 96 (November-December, 1927):347–64.

______. "Varuṇa, God of the Sea and the Sky." *JRAS* (1931):613–22.

Rabkin, Eric S. *The Fantastic in Literature*. Princeton, New Jersey: Princeton University Press, 1976.

Ramanujan, A. K. "Indian Poetics." In *The Literature of India: An Introduction*. Edited by Edward Dimock et al. Chicago: University of Chicago Press, 1974.

Randhowa, M. S. *The Cult of Trees and Tree-Worship in Buddhist-Hindu Sculpture*. New Delhi: All India Fine Arts and Crafts Society, 1964.

Rao, T. A. G. *Elements of Hindu Iconography*. 2 vols. New Delhi: Motilal Banarsidas, 1968.

Rawson, Philip. *Indian Sculpture*. London: Studio Vista Limited. New York: E. P. Dutton and Co., 1966.

Ray, N. R. *Theravāda Buddhism in Burma*. Calcutta: University of Calcutta, 1946.

Redfield, Robert, and Milton Singer. "Comparison of Cultures: The Indian Village." Chicago: Department of Anthropology, University of Chicago. Hectographed.

______. *The Little Community and Peasant Society and Culture*. Chicago: University of Chicago Press, 1965.

Regmi, D. R. *Ancient and Medieval Nepal*. Lucknow: Prem Printing Press, 1952.

______. *Ancient Nepal*. Calcutta: Firma K. L. Mukhopadhyay, 1969.

The Reversible World: Symbolic Inversion in Art and Society. Edited by Barbara A. Babcock. Ithaca: Cornell University Press, 1978.

Reynolds, Frank E. "The Several Bodies of the Buddha: Reflections on a Neglected Aspect of Theravada Tradition." *History of Religions* 16: 374.

______. "The Two Wheels of Dharma: A Study of Early Buddhism." In *The Two Wheels of Dharma*. AAR Studies in Religion, no. 3. Edited by Bardwell L. Smith. Chambersburg, Pennsylvania: American Academy of Religion, 1972.

Richman, Paula. "Religious Rhetoric in Manimekalai." Ph.D. dissertation, University of Chicago, 1983.

Ricoeur, Paul. "Language and Image in Psychoanalysis." *Psychiatry and the Humanities III*. New Haven, Connecticut: Yale University Press, 1978.

______. "Psychoanalysis and the Work of Art." *Psychiatry and the Humanities*, vol. 1. Edited by Joseph H. Smith, M.D. New Haven and London: Yale University Press, 1976.

______. *The Symbolism of Evil*. Translated by Emerson Buchanan. Boston: Beacon Press, 1969.

The Rig Veda: An Anthology. Edited, translated, and annotated by Wendy Doniger O'Flaherty. England: Penguin Books, 1981.

Rigvedic Brāhmaṇas: The Aitareya and Kauṣītaki Brāhmaṇas of the Rigveda. Translated by Arthur Berriedale Keith. Cambridge, Massachusetts: Harvard University Press, 1920.

Risley, Sir Herbert. *The People of India.* Delhi: Oriental Books Reprint, 1969, reprint of 1915.

Rockhill, W. Woodville. *The Life of the Buddha and the Early History of His Order.* Varanasi: Oriental Indica, 1972.

Rodhe, Sten. *Deliver Us from Evil: Studies on the Vedic Ideas of Salvation.* Lund, Copenhagen: Swedish Society for Missionary Research, 1946.

Roheim, Geza. *Magic and Schizophrenia.* Bloomington and London: Indiana University Press, 1970.

———. *The Panic of the Gods and Other Essays.* Edited by Werner Muensterberger. New York: Harper & Row, 1972.

———. *Psychoanalysis and Anthropology: Culture, Personality and the Unconscious.* New York: International Universities, 1969.

Ross, Mary Ellen. "Object Relations Theory and the Psychoanalytic Theory of Ritual." Ph.D. dissertation, University of Chicago, 1983.

Rowland, Benjamin. "Religious Art East and West." *History of Religions* 2 (Summer 1962): 11.

Roy, Udai Narain. *Śālabhañjikā in Art, Philosophy and Literature.* Allahabad: Lokbharti Publications, 1979.

Ruben, Walter. *Eisenschmiede und Dämonen in Indien.* In *Internationales Archive fur Ethnographie* 37. Leiden: E. J. Brill, 1939.

The Sacred Laws of the Āryas. Sacred Books of the East, vol. 2. Translated by Georg Bühler. New York: The Christian Literature Company, 1898.

Saṁyutta Nikāya. Translated by C. A. F. Rhys Davids and F. L. Woodward, 5 vols. London: Pali Text Society 1917–1936.

Schapiro, Meyer. *Words and Pictures: On the Literal and the Symbolic in the Illustration of a Text.* The Hague. Paris: Mouton, 1973.

Schmidt, R. "Der Lotus in der Sanskrit-literatur." *Zeitschrift der Deutschen Morgenlandischen Gesellschaft* 67 (1913):462.

Schweder, Richard A. and Robert A. LeVine. *Culture Theory: Essays on Mind, Self, and Emotion.* Cambridge: Cambridge University Press, 1984.

Segal, Hanna. *Introduction to the Work of Melanie Klein.* New York: Basic Books, Inc., 1974.

Seligmann, Kurt. *Magic, Supernaturalism and Religion.* New York: Pantheon Books, 1948.

Semeka-Pankratov, Elena. "A Semiotic Approach to the Polysemy of the Symbol, *Nāga* in Indian Mythology." *Semiotica* 27. 1/2 (1979).

Sen Gupta, Sankar. *Tree Symbol Worship in India*. Calcutta: Indian Publications, 1965.

Shah, U. P. "Yakṣa Worship in the Early Jaina Literature." *Journal of the Oriental Institute* 3. 1: 55–71.

Shulman, David Dean. *The King and the Clown in South Indian Myth and Poetry*. Princeton, New Jersey: Princeton University Press, 1986.

______. "The Serpent and the Sacrifice: An Anthill Myth from Tiruvarur." *History of Religions* 18. 2. (November 1978).

______. *Tamil Temple Myths: Sacrifice and Divine Marriage in the South Indian Śaiva Tradition*. Princeton, New Jersey: Princeton University Press, 1980.

Siegel, Lee. *Fires of Love: Waters of Peace*. Honolulu: University of Hawaii Press, 1983.

Sierksma, P. *Tibet's Terrifying Deities: Sex and Aggression in Religious Acculturation*. Translated by Mrs. G. E. van Baaren-Pape. The Hague. Paris: Mouton & Co., 1966.

Singer, Milton B. *Traditional India: Structure and Change*. Philadelphia. American Folklore Society, 1959.

______. *When a Great Tradition Modernizes: An Anthropological Approach to Indian Civilization*. New York: Praeger Publishers, 1972.

Skorupski, John. *Symbol and Theory: A Philosophical Study of Theories of Religion in Social Anthropology*. Cambridge: Cambridge University Press, 1976.

Slater, R. H. *Paradox and Nirvāṇa*. Chicago: University of Chicago Press, 1951.

Smith, Brian K. "Gods and Men in Vedic Ritualism: Toward a Hierarchy of Resemblance." *History of Religions* 24, no. 4 (May 1985):291–307.

Smith, Vincent A. *A History of Fine Art in India & Ceylon*. Bombay: D. B. Taraporevala Sons & Co., 1969.

Snellgrove, David L. *The Image of the Buddha*. New Delhi: Vikas Publishing House, 1978.

Spiro, Melford E. *Burmese Supernaturalism: A Study in the Explanation and Reduction of Suffering*. Philadelphia: Institute for the Study of Human Issues, 1978, reprint of 1967.

______. *Oedipus in the Trobriands.* Chicago: University of Chicago Press, 1982.

Spratt, P. *Hindu Culture and Personality: A Psycho-analytic Study.* Bombay: P. C. Manaktala & Sons, 1966.

Śrimad Vālmīki-Rāmāyaṇa. 3 Vols. Gorakhpur: Gita Press, 1974.

Srinivasan, Doris. "The Religious Significance of Multiple Body Parts to Denote the Divine: Findings from the Ṛg Veda." *Asian Survey* 29. 2 (1975).

Sthavirāvalī Charitra. Edited by Hermann Jacobi. Calcutta: Bib. Ind., 1891.

Strohl, George Ralph. "The Image of the Hero in Jainism: Ṛsabha, Bhārata and Bahubāli in The Ādipurāṇa of Jīnasena." Ph.D. Dissertation, University of Chicago, 1984.

Strong, John. "Making Merit in the Aśokāvadāna: A Study of Buddhist Acts of Offering in the Post-Parinirvana Age." Ph.D. dissertation, University of Chicago, 1977.

Stutley, Margaret. *The Illustrated Dictionary of Hindu Iconography.* London, Boston, Melbourne, Henley: Routledge & Kegan Paul, 1985.

Stutterheim, W. F. "Le jālalakṣana de l'Image du Bouddha." *Acta Orientalia* 7 (1928).

______. "The Meaning of the Kāla-Makara Ornament." *Indian Art and Letters,* N. S. 3 (1929): 27.

Sullivan, Herbert P. "A Re-Examination of the Religion of the Indus Civilization." *History of Religions* 4 (Summer 1964): 115.

Sutta Nipāta or Dialogues and Discourses of Gotama Buddha. Translated by Sir. M. Coomara Swamy. London: Trubner & Co., 1874.

Sūtralaṃkara. Translated and edited by Huber. Paris: Ernest Leroux, 1908.

Tambiah, Stanley, J. *Buddhism and the Spirit Cults in North-east Thailand.* Cambridge: Cambridge University Press, 1970.

______. "The Ideology of Merit and the Social Correlates of Buddhism in a Thai Village." In *Dialectics in Practical Religion.* Edited by Edmund R. Leach. Cambridge: Cambridge University Press, 1968.

______. "A Performative Approach to Ritual." Radcliffe-Brown Lecture in Social Anthropology. *Proceedings of the British Academy* 65 (1979). London: Oxford University Press, 1981.

______. *World Conqueror and World Renouncer*. Cambridge: Cambridge University Press, 1976.

Taranātha's History of Buddhism in India. Translated by Lama Chimpa and Alaka Chattopadhyaya. Simla: Indian Institute of Advanced Studies, 1970.

Tattvarthādhigama Sūtra. Edited and translated by Pandit Khub Chand. Bombay: 1932.

Thapar, Romila. *A History of India I*. New York: Penguin Books, 1982, reprint of 1966.

Thieme, Paul. "Pūjā." *Journal of Oriental Research* 27 (1957–58):1–16.

Thomas, Edward J. *The Life of the Buddha as Legend and History*. London: Routledge & Kegan Paul, 1949.

Thurston, Edgar. *Castes and Tribes of Southern India*. Madras: Government Press. 1909.

______. *Omens and Superstitions of Southern India*. London: T. Fisher Unwin, 1912.

Tibet's Great Yogi Milarepa: A Biography from the Tibetan. Edited by W. Y. Evans-Wentz. New York: Oxford University Press, 1969.

Todorov, Tzvetan. *The Fantastic: A Structural Approach to a Literary Genre*. Cleveland and London: The Press of Case Western Reserve University, 1973.

Traditional India: Structure and Change. Edited by Milton Singer. Philadelphia: American Folklore Society, 1959.

Turner, Victor. *The Ritual Process: Structure and Anti-structure* Chicago: Aldine Publishing Co., 1969.

The Twelve Deeds of the Buddha: A Mongolian Version of the Lalitavistara. Mongolian text, notes, and English translation by Nicholas Poppe. Seattle: University of Washington Press, 1967.

Tylor, Edward B. *Religion in Primitive Culture*. New York: Harper & Row, 1958.

Uvasagadasāo. Translated by A. F. Rudolph Hoernle. Calcutta: Baptist Mission Press, 1888.

Van Den Bosch, Lourens P. "Yama-The God on the Black Buffalo," in *Visible Religion* vol. 1, eds. H. P. Kippenberg; L. P. Van Den Bosch; L. Leertouwer. Leiden: E. J. Brill, 1982.

The Vedic Experience: Mantramañjarī. Edited and translated by Raimundo Panikkar. Berkeley and Los Angeles: University of California Press, 1977.

Viennot, Odette. *Le Culte de l'Arbre dans L'Inde Ancienne*. Paris: Presses Universitaires de France, 1954.

Village India: Studies in the Little Community. Edited by McKim Marriot. Chicago: University of Chicago Press, 1956.

Vinaya Piṭaka. In *Mahāvagga*. Sacred Books of the East, vol. 13.

Vipradāsa's Manasā-vijaya. Calcutta: Asiatic Society, 1953.

Viṣṇu Purāṇa: A System of Hindu Mythology and Tradition. Text in Devanāgiri with English translation by H. H. Wilson. Delhi: Nāg Publishers, 1980.

Vogel, Jean Philippe. *Buddhist Art in India, Ceylon and Java*. New Delhi: Oriental Books Reprint Corporation, 1977.

______. *Indian Serpent Lore or The Nāgas in Hindu Legend and Art*. Varanasi: Prithivi Prakashan, 1972.

______. "Le makara dans la sculpture de l'Inde." *Revue des Artes Asiatiques* (1930):133 ff.

______. "Nāga Worship in Ancient Mathura." *Archaeological Survey of India: Annual Report* (1908–9):159–63.

______. "Serpent Worship in Ancient and Modern India." *Acta Orientalia* 1 (1923):279–312.

______. "The Woman and Tree or Śālabhañjikā in Indian Literature and Art." *Acta Orientalia* 7 (1929):201–31.

Waddell, L. A. "Demons and Spirits (Buddhist)." In the *Encyclopedia of Religion and Ethics*. New York: Charles Scribner & Sons.

______. "Evolution of the Buddhist Cult, Its Gods, Images and Art." *Imperial and Asiatic Quarterly Review*. (January 1912):105–60.

Waghorn, Joanne Punzo. "A Body for God: An Interpretation of the Nature of Myth beyond Structuralism." *History of Religions* 21. 1 (August 1981).

Warder, A. K. *Indian Buddhism*. Delhi: Motilal Banarsidas, 1980, revised edition of 1970.

Warren, H. C. *Buddhism in Translations*. New York: Atheneum, 1973.

Wayman, Alex. "Studies in Yama and Māra." *Indo-Iranian Journal* 3 (1959):112–31.

Weber, Max. *The Religion of India: The Sociology of Hinduism and Buddhism.* Translated and edited by H. Gerth and Don Martindale. Glencoe, Illinois: Free Press, 1958.

Wheelwright, Philip. *Metaphor and Reality.* Bloomington and London: Indiana University Press, 1967.

Whitehead, Right Reverend Henry. *The Village Gods of South India.* Calcutta: The Association Press, 1916.

Wijesekara, O. H. de A. "The Philosophical Import of Vedic Yakṣa and Pāli Yakkha." *University of Ceylon Review* 1: 2 (November 1943).

The Wild Man Within: An Image in Western Thought from the Renaissance to Romanticism. Edited by Edward Dudley and Maximilian E. Novak. Pittsburgh: University of Pittsburgh Press, 1972.

Williams, Joanna. "Sarnāth Gupta Steles of the Buddha's Life." *Ars Orientalis* 10 (1975):181.

Windisch, E. W. O. *Māra und Buddha.* Leipzig: S. Hirzel, 1895.

Winnicott, D. W. *Between Reality and Fantasy: Transitional Objects and Phenomena.* New York: J. Aronson, 1979.

Yazdani, Ghulam. *Ajanta.* 6 vols. Oxford: Oxford University Press, 1930–46.

Zimmer, Heinrich. *The Art of Indian Asia.* 2 vols. Bollingen Series 30. Completed and edited by Joseph Campbell. Princeton, New Jersey: Princeton University Press, 1968.

______. *The King and the Corpse: Tales of the Soul's Conquest of Evil.* Edited by Joseph Campbell. New York: Meridian Books, 1960.

______. *Kunstform und Yoga im Indischen Kultbild.* Berlin: Frankfurter Verlags-Anstalt A. G., 1926.

______. *Myths and Symbols in Indian Art and Civilization.* Bollingen Series 6, Edited by Joseph Campbell. Princeton, New Jersey: Princeton University Press, 1972.

______. *Philosophies of India.* Edited by Joseph Campbell. New York: Meridian Books, 1958.

INDEX

Abhirati, 64, 144
abortion, 122
acosmic, 20
adharma, 50, 160
Adharma, 55, 157
Adiśakti Mahākālī, 188
Aditi, 22
Adityaśarman, 147
Aeschylus, 113
aesthetic theories, 4
agantu, 166–67
Agastya, a *brāhman*, 88
Agastya, son of Varuṇa, 182
Aggana Suttas, 107
agneya, 60
Agni, 23–5, 48, 49, 65, 70, 73, 180, 183
agni beings, 130
agnihotra, 88
agonistic strife, 110
Agrawala, Vasudeva Sharana, 179
ahi, 176
ahiṁsā, 27, 109
ahura, 181
Ahura Mazda, 76
Airāvata, 176
Ajakalaka yakkha, 106
Ajanta, 106
Ajjunae, 128
Alakā, 147, 150, 151
Āḷavaka, 116–17
Āḷavaka Sutta, 116, 184
Āḷavī, 184
alivantin, 145
amara, 66
Amarāvatī, 35, 66, 106, 173
amṛta, 21–2, 39, 48, 172
Anderson, Hans Christian, 187
Andhra Pradesh, 187
Aṅgāraparṇa, 60
Aṅgiras, 67, 96, 97
Aṅgulimāla, 119
aniconic: stage of Buddhist art, 9, 17
Antagaḍa Dasão, 128, 132, 180, 186
antarikṣa, 74, 179
Anuradhapura, 123
Anuttarovavaiya-Dasão, 186
āpah, 79
apsaras, 29, 46, 54, 60, 61, 97, 137, 138, 162, 186, 187
Arabian Nights, 130
Āraṇya Kāṇḍa (*Rāmāyaṇa*), 182
Araṇya Parvan (*Mahābhārata*), 52
ardha sama, 29
Arjuna, 60, 89, 91, 96
Arthurian legend, 33
Āryan, 54, 59
Aṣādha, 150
asat, 79
ascetical: ideals, 9; stage of power, 2, 3, 115, 128, 133, 184; monism, 3
asceticism, 108, 139
aśoka tree, 28

Aśoka, King, 28, 43
Aśokāvadāna, 26
āśramas, 149
assamukhī, 141
assimilation, 163–65
aṣṭamaṅgala, 33
asuras, 48, 49–50, 64, 75, 77, 79, 80, 90, 110, 130, 158, 166, 181
Aśvaghoṣa, 29, 139, 172
Āśvalāyana Śrauta Sūtra, 179, 181
aśvamedha, 47
aśvattha tree, 26, 27
Aśvins, 22, 67
Āṭānātiya Suttānta, 42
Atharva Veda, 21, 24, 70–1, 80, 166, 171, 172, 178, 179, 180, 190
Athena, 174
ātman, 74
Auboyer, Jeannine, 183
Aupapātika Sūtra, 180
avatāras, of Viṣṇu, 7, 45, 184
Avestan, 76, 176
avyakta, 23, 32, 157
Ayācitabhatta Jātaka, 27
Ayakūṭa Jātaka, 111, 184
Azhi, 176

Bahuputrikā, 64, 144–45
Bailey, Greg, 171
Baka, 60
bakoyakṣa, 75
Bāladeva, 65
bali, 66
Bāṇa, 25
banyan tree, 20
Batanmara yakkhī, 106
Benares, 123, 138, 163, 174
Bergaigne, Abel, 172
Besnagar, 11, 14
Bhadrā, wife of Kubera, 64, 144
Bhadrā, daughter of Soma, 97–8
Bhadraghata Jātaka, 33
Bhāgavata Purāṇa, 45, 176, 190
Bhagīratha, 47–8
bhakti, 45, 58, 68, 121; stage of power, 2, 53, 134, 165, 184
Bhārata, 90
Bhārhut, 9, 27, 29, 33, 106, 137, 173, 181, 183
Bhaumeyikas, 130
bhikku, 108
bhiksha, 146
Bhīma, 52, 86–8, 89, 91
Bhola, 130
Bhūridatta Jātaka, 110
bhūta, 75, 131
Bhūtadamaratantra, 188
Bhuteśar, 14
Bihar, 173
bimba fruit, 152
blood, 174
Bloomfield, Maurice, 172
Bloss, Lowell, 41, 102–3, 171, 175, 183, 185, 186
boar, 36
Bodh Gāya, 29
Bodhi tree, 14, 27, 28
bodhicitta, 112
bodhisatta, birth of, 26; births of, 112, 114, 182; encounters yakkinīs, 138, 139, 141; as *devatā*, 27; embodies *dhamma*, 135–36; as Indra, 33; as Nāga, 110–11; as prince, 28, 35, 109, 126; and yakkha, 85–6, 93–6, 102, 108, 109, 110, 111, 115, 118–19, 120–27, 135–36, 142–43
Bosch, F.D.K., 8, 9, 29, 169, 171, 172
Bosch, Hieronymus, 134
Brahmā, 23–4, 32, 48, 50, 56, 69, 71, 107, 117, 182, 190
Brahmā Purāṇa, 190

brāhma rākṣasa, 164, 167
Brahmadatta, 123
brahman: linked with the yakṣa, 23–4, 71–4
*brāhman*s, 28, 57, 58, 82, 86, 87, 88, 91, 96, 98, 100, 101, 117, 119, 121, 125, 133, 141, 147, 159, 161, 182, 189, 190
*Brāhmaṇa*s, 44, 45, 59, 72, 80, 81, 159
*brāhman*ical: literature, 110; religion, 129, 136
Bṛhadāraṇyaka Upaniṣad, 108, 178, 181
Bṛhaspati, 180, 183
Buddha, 7, 17, 110, 111, 112, 120, 121, 134, 139, 144–45; aniconic representations of, 9–10, 14, 17; *avatāra* of Viṣṇu, 115, 184; conquers and converts yakṣas and *nāga*s, 41–3, 93–6, 114, 115–18, 123; deceased body of, 18; demonic heresy of, 115; iconic representation of, 17; enlightenment of, 27, 28; linked with kings, 17; magic bowl of, 35; and Māra, 3; and the *nāga*s, 26, 102, 135; power of, 114–15; his triumph over *saṁsāra*, 18; as world renouncer, 9; like the yakkha, 135, 175; and the yakṣas, 26–9, 102. *See also* Gautama Buddha, Siddhārtha Gautama, and Śākyamuni.
Buddhacarita, 29, 139, 172
buddhapāda, 14
Buddhi, 130
Buddhism, 3
Buddhist: art, 5, 9–20, 49, 66, 106, 114, 115; cosmology, 5, 105–15, 160; Dharma, 29, 102, 109, 110, 111, 113, 116, 117, 119, 120, 124, 134–36, 160; literature, 164; *lokapāla*s, 66; nature deities, 9, 23, 26–9; trees, 26–9; vegetarianism, 125 Buddhist-Hindu comparison, 2, 5, 85–103, 105, 112, 120–21, 126- 27, 135, 160
Buddhists: as demons, 115
Burgess, James, 172
Burrow, Thomas, 181
Bushamon (Kubera), 63, 66

caitya, 95, 120, 122, 128, 132, 185
Cakavaka, 106
cakravartin, 120–21, 122
Calypso, 140, 187
Campbell, Joseph, 171
Canda yakkhī, 106
Candrā (Cadā), 137
cannibals, 5, 110
cannibalism, 54, 108, 118–19, 124–25, 142, 159
caraka, 153
Cāraka Saṁhitā, 166, 190
Caraṇas, 189
caste, 2, 3, 163–65
caurī, 17, 18; bearer from Didarganj, 11; c. bearing yakṣas, 17
Cetiya, 123
Ceylon, 139
Chāndogya Upaniṣad, 178
Chandra, Moti, 189
China, 66
Chinese *Tripiṭaka*, 144
choli, 154
Christ, 18
Christians, 163–64
chudail, 145
churail, 145
churel, 145
Citraratha, 60
Cittaraja, 123
clouds, 175

Cloud Messenger: See *Meghadūta*
Cocteau, Jean, 19
codependent origination, 107
conversion: to Buddhism, 109, 114, 135, 144, 159, 160; to Jainism, 128, 160
Coomaraswamy, Ananda Kentish, 1, 4, 7, 20, 22, 25, 27, 35, 42, 70, 123, 146, 169, 170, 171, 172, 173, 175, 176, 178, 179, 180, 181, 185, 186, 187, 188
cosmic, 20; egg, 31
cosmology: Buddhist, 5, 105–15; Jain, 131–34
Cowell, E.B., 184
crane yakṣa, 75, 89, 92
crocodile, 35, 173
Culakoka, 106
Cunningham, Alexander, 63
Cupid, 152

daimon, 181
Daitya, 51, 56, 182, 186, 190
dakarakkha, 93
Dākinīs, 146
dānava, 86
Dānavī, 186
Daniel, E. Valentine, 189
Davids, C.A.F. Rhys, 51
dayamalu, 162
death, 80–1, 159
Deccan, 145
defilement: danger of, 2; sin of, 78
Dehejia, Vidya, 188
deluge, 23
demigod, 188; Kubera as, 5; Buddha and, 115; Varuṇa as, 76, 78; yakṣa associated with, 1; yakṣī as, 146
demiurge, 23, 49, 69, 79, 107, 171
demons, 181; ascetical power of, 55–8, 158; assimilation of, 136, 163–65; ethical function of, 2, 4, 113–15, 119–20, 134, 136, 157–59; family of, 49–61, 157; like gods, 3, 115, 133, 134–35, 158; fluid form of, 110, 112–15, 119–20, 158; and gods, and humans, 2–3, 112–15, 133, 160; humans as, 124, 160; in the Jātakas, 105, 108–27, 135; Māra as, 3, 134–35; and *māyā*, 165; popular, 5; psychological function of, 3, 136, 160; responsible for disease, 166–67; Tantric, 75, 146; taxonomy of, 162–65; as threat to sacrifice, 158; yakṣa as, 1, 2, 5, 49–69, 108–20, 122–27
demoness: yakṣī as, 5, 137–46
demonic: conception of, 2, 105, 108, 176
Deogarh, 188
*deva*s, 117, 130, 164, 181; and *asura*s, 48, 49–50, 110, 134, 158, 159; radiance of, 18; yakṣas as, 132–33
Deva, Krishna, 189
Devadaha, 26
devadhamma, 93
Devadhamma Jātaka, 93, 101, 102
devatā, 10, 58, 106, 127, 159; *bodhisatta* portrayed as, 27–8, 49, 113, 124; worship of, 28, 111, 124, 126
dhamma, 29, 109, 110, 111, 113, 116, 119, 120, 124, 134, 135–36, 145
Dhammapādatthakathā, 26
Dhanādhipa (Kubera), 63
Dhanapati (Kubera), 63, 152
Dhanvantari, 172
dharma: order and righteousness, 48, 50, 55, 82, 98, 101, 129, 133, 136, 158, 160, 161; Bud-

dhist, 29, 102, 109, 110, 111, 113, 116, 117, 119, 120, 124, 134–36, 160; of demons, 108, 55–8, 158; and kingship, 82, 88, 91, 92, 99–103, 120–27; obscured by *māyā*, 2, 134, 158; as prescribed behavior, 55–7; and Varuṇa, 98; Vedic, 109
Dharma, the deity, 45, 81, 83, 85, 92, 101, 121, 122
dharmacakra, 17, 18
Dhonasakha Jātaka, 113, 184
Dhṛtarāśtra, 66
Dhumarakka mountain, 123
diachronic, 105
Didarganj, 11, 14
diet: and demonism, 159
*diggaja*s, 40, 67, 175
Dīgha Nikāya, 107, 186, 190
*dikpāla*s, 65
Dimock, Edward C., 174
*dinnaga*s: *See diggaja*s.
Dionysian, 171
Dīpavaṁsa, 26, 41, 116, 121, 175
disease, 166–67
Divyāvadāna, 26
dohada, 29
dolphin, 35
Douglas, Mary, 3, 19, 169, 170
dragon, 176
Draupadī, 52, 53
droit de seigneur, 181
dualism, 3; within Buddhism, 109, 135
dualistic: worldview of Vedic traditions, 3
Dummedha Jātaka, 28, 126, 185
Durgā, 144
Duryodhana, 64
*dvārapāla*s, 121, 122, 159
dvīpa beings, 130
Eck, Diana L., 174, 177
elephant, 36, 40, 43, 67, 164, 175, 176, 189
Eliade, Mircea, 77, 170, 171, 181
enlightenment, 112
Epics, 1, 40, 44, 46, 48, 49, 50, 52, 53, 54, 55, 59, 63, 69, 79, 80, 81, 85, 103, 121, 129, 158, 159, 160, 161, 176
epistemological theories, 4
epistemology, 4
eros, 185
eroticism: yakṣa a symbol of, 5
ethical: ambiguity of yakṣa, 2, 5, 51, 157; dualism, 48, 53; monism, 160; necessity of pollution, 3, 161; paradigms, 2; paradoxes, 2, 103, 162; transformations, 8, 99–103, 134, 160
ethics: of humans, 114–15
etymology: of "*rākṣasa*s," and "yakṣas," 69
Eumenides, 113
evil: definition of, 157–59; inherent in the world, 165

fairy tales, 130
Falk, Nancy E., 182
Fausboll, V., 183, 187
fertility: symbols of, 24–6; yakṣa as symbol of, 1, 157
Fischer, Eberhard, 186
fish, 43–6
The Five Hundred Merchants, 140
flood, 44–6
flowers, 17
folk tales, 107, 129, 143

Gaṁgīta yakkha, 106
gaṇa, 56, 75, 149
gaṇapati, 122

Gandhamādana, 64
gandharva, 46, 49, 52, 53, 54, 59–61, 64, 66, 67, 75, 87, 90, 106, 131, 149, 157, 166, 167, 189
Gaṇeśa, 33
Gaṅgā, the river, 44, 46, 60, 68, 113, 117, 151, 152, 176, 177
Gaṅgā, the goddess, 46–8
Ganges. *See*: Gaṅgā, the river.
Gautama Buddha, 114, 116. *See also:* Buddha, Śākyamuni, and Siddhārtha Gautama.
Geiger, William, 175
Geldner, Ernst, 70
genii, 130, 147
genius loci, 21, 46, 47
ghanika beings, 131
ghosts, 67, 145, 161–62, 167
Gibson, A.C., 172
Gilgit MSS, 178
gnosis, 2
Gobhila Gṛhya Sūtra, 181
God, 75
gods: and demons and humans, 2–3, 112–15, 133; similarity to demons, 3, 133, 134–35; Vedic, 5, 21
Godāvarī river, 177
The Goddess, 7, 144, 146
goddess: yakṣī as, 5
goddesses, 162, 190
Gopatha Brāhmaṇa, 181
graha, 166
grail vessel, 33, 35
great and little traditions, 4, 7
Great Chain of Being, 112
Great Renunciation, 66
Gṛhya Sūtras, 66, 75, 76, 159
Grimm, the Brothers, 130
Grunwedel, Albert, 172
guggula, 146
guhyakas, 54, 56, 63, 67, 189
guṇas, 164
Gupta, 173
guru, 149

haṁsa, 71, 81
Hanuman, 52, 170
Harikeśa, 55–6, 57, 158
Hāritā, 187. *See also* Hārīti.
Hārīti, 64, 143–45, 187
Hastings, James, 187
Hausman, Carl, 170
Hellenistic: influence on sculpture, 36
Hemacandra, 130
Hemavata, 116
Hemavatasutta, 116
heterodox, 133
Hiebert, Paul, 162, 189
hierarchy of beings, 136, 162–65
Himālayas, 182
Himavat, 74, 89
Hindu: myths, 23, 48; sculpture, 1, 66; tradition, 129
Hindu-Buddhist comparison, 2, 5, 85–103, 105, 112, 120–21, 126–27, 135, 160
Hinduism: animal sacrifice in, 126–27; caste taboos of, 3; popular, 4, 165; yakṣa in, 69–83
hiraṇyagarbha, 23–4, 171
historical theories, 4
Hitopadeśa, 190
Hopkins, Edward Washburn, 51, 58, 175, 177, 178
Horner, I.B., 184
horse faced yakkhī. *See assamukhī.*
Horse Sacrifice, 122
horses, 164, 189
Huansi, 143. *See also* Hārīti.
humans: as demons, 124, 160; and gods and demons, 2–3, 112–15, 133, 160

ichor, 152
iconic: representations of the Buddha, 9, 17; sculpture, 7
iconography, 1, 19; Buddhist, 17; early, 8
illusion: of all obstacles, 2; Buddha battles with, 3; sin of, 2
India, 114
Indra, 25, 33, 43, 61, 65, 66, 73, 79, 99, 100, 111, 133, 171, 176, 180, 182, 184, 185
Indus Valley, 26
Īśāna, 63. *See also* Śiva.
island of the sirens, 139
*iṣṭadevatā*s, 146

Jain: art, 5, 146; cosmology, 131–34; sculpture, 1
Jain, Jyotindra, 186
*Jaina Sūtra*s, 186
Jainism: monism of, 3; *nāga*s in, 40; yakṣas in, 5, 9, 105, 127–36; yakṣīs in, 146, 188
jakkha, 128
Jakhin, 145
jama, 154
Jambhala, 144
jaṅgiḍa tree, 25
Japan, 66
Jarā, 187
Jātakamāla, 51, 125, 177
Jātakas, 1, 27, 85, 93–6, 105, 107, 108, 109, 110, 111, 112, 116, 129, 134, 135, 140, 178, 179, 183; demigods and demons in, 26, 39, 49, 61; encode Buddhist concepts, 5, 28; Kubera in, 76; yakkhīs in, 138–46
Jātasura, 53
jāti, 163
Jayaddisa Jātaka, 142, 144, 187
Jayakhya Saṁhitā, 188
Jhallas, 189
Judeo-Christian God, 167
Jyeṣṭha, 187
Jyotiṣkas, 131

Kadamba tree, 186
Kadambari, 25
Kakṣivat, 122
Kailāsa, 67, 153
kālakūṭa, 22
Kālīdāsa, 5, 19, 149, 150, 154
kalpa vṛkṣa, 25, 152
Kaluvela, 123
Kāma, 25, 152, 171
Kāmadeva, 132
kamalā, 32
Kāmamāra, 134. *See also* Māra.
kāmarūpa, 183
Kanthaka, 66
kāpālika, 146
Kapferer, Bruce, 189
Kapila, 47
Kapilavatthu, 26
Karkotaka Vapi, 174
Kārlī, 106
kamma, 113. *See also karma.*
karma, 22, 113, 133, 160–63
Karpūramañjarī, 146
Kāśi Khanda, 174
Kāśi, 56, 174
Kathāsaritsāgara, 33, 147
Kāverī river, 177
kāvya, 153, 154
Kena Upaniṣad, 73
Keyes, Charles F., 189
Khara, 63
Khuddakapatha Commentary, 190
*kiṁpuruṣa*s, 61, 64, 131
king: and the Buddha, 17, 120–22, 126; *dharma* of, 88, 99–103, 120–27, 160, 185; as flesh eater, 123–24; and *nāga*, 86–8, 122,

king (*cont.*)
185; testing of, 85–93, 98–102, 121–27; Varuṇa as, 76–7, 81–2, 85–6; and the waters, 47, 85–96, 160; and yakṣa/yakkha, 88–96, 113–14, 118–19, 120–27, 159, 185; Yama as, 81–2, 85–6
kinnāras, 61, 64, 87, 131, 152. *See also kiṁpuruṣas.*
kīrttimukha, 36. *See also siṁhamukha.*
Konduru, 162
Kramrisch, Stella, 178
kṣatriya, 53, 93, 98, 100, 101, 120–21, 124, 189
kṣetrapāla, 56, 80, 121–22
Kubera: brother of Rāvaṇa, 63–5; deity of good fortune and treasure, 33, 40, 59, 63, 64, 81, 144; fertility figure, 61–4, 179; in Jain sources, 180; king of the *vidyadhāras*, 93; king of the yakṣas, 5, 20, 51, 52, 54, 59, 61, 75, 125, 150, 152; as *lokapāla*, 63, 65–8, 79; lord of thieves, 63; as *nāravāhana*, 67; origins of, 63; patron of drunkenness, 65; protects travelers, 65. *See also* Kuvera, Bushamon, Dhanādhipa, Dhanapati, Vaiśravaṇa, Vessavana, Vittapāla, and Vitteśa.
Kuiper, F.B.J., 79, 171, 175, 181
kumāras, 131
Kumbhakarṇa, 63
Kumbhāṇḍas, 66, 106, 111
Kuṇḍalā, 187. *See also* Hārīti.
kuṇḍalas, 137
Kuntī, 89, 90, 91
Kupiro yakkho, 106
kurubaka flowers, 151
Kurudhamma Jātaka, 123
Kuvanna, 140
Kuvera, 63, 106. *See also* Kubera.
Lakhindara, 174
Lakṣmī, 32, 33, 144. *See also* Śrī.
Laṅkā, 41, 63, 64
Law, Bimala Churn, 190
Laws of Manu, 164, 190
Leach, Edmund, 19
Ling, Trevor, 185, 190
lingam, 25, 172
local religion, 120–23, 158–59
lodhra blossoms, 151
loka, 40, 68, 80
lokapālas, 63, 65–8, 79–81, 97, 180
lola, 107
lotus, 29–32, 49
Lomas Rishi, 173
Lumbini Grove, 26

Macdonell, Arthur, 70, 180
mā, 78
Macakruka, 122
Mādhava, 69
madhu, 22
Mādrī, 91
Mahābhārata, 40, 45, 46, 48, 51, 52, 60, 63, 64, 85–93, 96, 98, 101, 102, 103, 166, 171, 176, 177, 178, 179, 180, 181, 182, 186
mahadyakṣa, 32, 43
Makakoka, 106
Mahārāshṭra, 10
Mahāśaṅkha tree, 178
Mahāsutasoma Jātaka: *See Sutasoma Jātaka.*
Mahāvagga, 175, 184
Mahāvaṁsa, 41, 115, 121, 123, 140, 175, 185, 187
Mahāvastu, 26, 139–40, 186, 187
Mahāvīra, 9, 128, 132, 134
mahāvratas, 128
Mahāyāna, 31–2, 134

Mahiṅsāsa, 93–6
mahoragas, 131
Maitri Upaniṣad, 74, 181
Maitribala, 125
Maity, Pradyat Kumar, 174
Majjhima Nikāya, 175, 184, 186
makara, 9, 21, 31, 35–8, 49, 81, 137, 173
Malaya mountains, 89
Mālinī, 63
Mallas, 189
Manasā, 39, 174
Manasāmaṅgal, 174
Mānava Gṛhya Sūtra, 75
mandakrānta meter, 149
maṇḍala, 114, 134, 136
mandāra, 151, 152
Maṇibhadra, 64, 144
Maṇimat, 51
Manimekhalā, a goddess, 35
Manimekhalai, sea maiden and Buddhist goddess, 35, 187
Manimekhalai, Buddhist legend, 35
Mañjuśrī, 41
Mañjuśrīmūlakalpa, 188
Manmatha, 152. *See also* Kāma.
Manu, 55, 87, 179; and the fish, 44–6; lawbook, 63, 164, 190
Māra, 3, 117, 133, 134–35. *See also* Kāmamāra.
Marcuse, Herbert, 185
Marduk, 176
Markandeya Purāṇa, 177
Maruts, 89, 91, 152
Masson, Joseph, 180
Matakabhatta Jātaka, 27
Matali, 40
Mathurā, 14, 35, 106, 137, 173, 183
mātṛkās, 146, 166
mātṛs. *See mātṛkās*.
Matsya Purāṇa, 171, 176, 178
Mauryan period (322–183 B.C.), 14
māyā, 22, 31, 49, 53, 58, 85, 158; ethical ambiguity of, 2, 101, 134, 165; of Varuṇa, 76–9, 83, 85; of yakṣa, 101, 157, 158
(Queen) Māyā, mother of the Buddha, 26
mediation, 19
medieval Hindu texts, 3
Medusa, 174
megha, 175. *See also* cloud.
Meghadūta, 5, 19, 149–55, 189
mekhalā, 137
Meru, 42, 64, 66, 67. *See also* Sumeru.
metaphor, 19, 170
Middle Path, 28
milk, 171, 174, 175
Misra, Ram Nath, 20, 54, 69, 171, 177, 178, 179, 180, 181, 183, 185, 186, 187, 188
Mithra, 76
Mitra, 77
Mitra-Varuṇa, 70, 76
Moggarapāṇi, 128
monarch. *See* king.
monism: balance between pluralism and, 4, 134; functional m. of Buddhism and Jainism, 129; of the Upaniṣads, 3
monistic worldview, 3
Moon Prince, 93–6
moral: ambiguity, 1, 3, 5; economy, 4; yakṣa as m. device, 3
morality: and pollution beliefs, 3
morphological resemblance, 8, 35–8
Moslems, 163–64
Mṛtyu, 107
Mucalinda, 42
Mucilinda. *See* Mucalinda.
Munjavata, 122
Mushussu, 176

mysticism, 129
myth, 19–20, 170
mythos, 82

Nāg Kuan, 174
nāga, 64, 66, 130, 172, 173, 174, 175, 179; in Buddhist art, 9, 106; in Buddhist legends, 26, 39–43, 107, 108, 109, 110–11, 114, 115, 119, 120; demonism of, 40, 86–8, 159; erotic nature of, 38; as fertility symbol, 21, 38–9; as guardian of treasure, 40–1; as genius loci, 46, 85; killed by Sāgara's sons, 47; testing by, 86–8; tree, 137; as tribal, 42; water deity, 21, 38–43, 49, 85–8, 176, 181. *See also* snake.
*nāgakal*s, 39
nāgaloka, 40, 80
nāgapañcamī, 39, 174, 181
nāgī. *See nāginī*.
nāginī, 38, 115, 138, 145
Nahuṣa, 88, 101
*nakṣatra*s, 131
Nākula, 53, 89, 91, 101
Nalakūbara, 63
Nandā, 64
Nandin, 68
Nārada, 22, 67, 97
nāravāhana, 67
Narmadā river, 177
Natas, 189
Nepal, 41, 114
New Testament, 33
nibbana, 113, 134. *See also nirvāṇa*.
Nidānakathā, 66
Nidhipa (Kubera), 63
nigrodha tree, 113
nija, 166
Nīlamāta Purāṇa, 181
Nirṛti, 55
nirvāṇa, 17, 28, 32, 113, 134. *See also nibbana*.

Ocean of Story. *See Kathāsaritsāgara*.
odhani, 154
Odysseus, 140, 187
Odyssey, 140
O'Flaherty, Wendy Doniger, 2, 133, 134, 141, 169, 171, 172, 177, 178, 181, 182, 183, 184, 185, 186, 187, 190
ojohara, 125
Oldenburg, Herman, 175
Oresteia, 113
otherworldly: religion of Buddhism and Jainism, 129
ouranos, 77

Padakusalamāṇava Jātaka, 141, 187
padmā, 32. *See also* lotus.
Palāsa Jātaka, 27
palāsa tree, 27
pallu, 154
pan, 154
Pāncāla, 58, 143
Pāncālika. *See* Pāncāla.
Pañcaviṁśa Brāhmaṇa, 178
Pāñcika, 64, 144
Pāṇḍavas, 52, 60, 86–93, 122, 158
Pandukabhaya, 123
Pāṇini, 65
*paṇi*s, 59
pāpa, 79, 157
Parāskara Gṛhya Sūtra, 181
Pārijāta tree, 172
Pariśādas, 178
Pariśiṣṭaparvan, 129
Pariyātrā mountains, 89
Parkham: yakṣa sculpture from, 10, 173

Pārtha, 90
parvan, 35, 36
Pārvata, 67
Pārvatī, 67
pāśa, 77, 79, 82
Pātāla, 40, 174. *See also rasātala* and underworld.
Patañjali, 174
Pathari, 188
paṭiccasamuppāda. *See codependent origination*.
Patika Suttas, 107
Patna: yakṣa sculptures from, 11, 14, 173
Paṭṭadakal, 178
Peri, N., 144, 187
Pawaya, 173
*peta*s, 164–65
*peti*s, 165
phallic: form of *nāga*, 38; Indra pillar, 171; tree, 25; mother, 141
philosophical theories, 4
pilgrimage, 46
Piṅgala, 143
pipal. *See pippala* tree.
pippala tree, 25, 27
*piśāca*s, 26, 40, 49–51, 54, 59, 60, 63, 67, 75, 86, 111, 131, 133, 157, 164, 166, 167, 178, 189
pitṛ, 75, 81, 159
pluralism, 4
poetic use of myth, 19–20
poison, 171, 174, 175. *See also viṣa* and venom.
polluters: demons as, 2, 158
pollution, 3, 161
popular: Buddhism, 17, 110; demons and demigods, 5, 159; religion, 4, 7, 8, 9, 159
possession, 166–67
power: three stages of, 2, 3, 53, 115, 128, 133, 184
prabhāmaṇḍala, 18
Prajāpati, 23–4, 32, 48, 54–5, 63–4, 69, 71, 107, 127, 178, 179
prajñāpāramitā, 32
pralaya, 22
pṛdaku, 181
pre-Socratic, 21
Psalms of the Elders, 114
psychological: utility of demons, 3; utility of dualism, 3; theories, 4
psychology: Vedic, 3
pūjā, 75, 126, 165
Pulastya, 54, 55, 63–4, 122
Pulinda, 140
punna ghata. See *pūrṇa kalaśa*.
Punnabhadde, 132
Purāṇas, 1, 45, 50, 55, 69, 121, 135, 160, 161
purity: and pollution, 3; ritual, 2
pūrṇa kalaśa, 32–5, 49
Pūrṇabhadra, 55–6, 65
Pururāvas, 187
puruṣa, 107
Puruṣa Sūkta, 107, 176
Puṣpotkatā, 63
*pyjama*s, 122

Rājagṛha, 122, 128, 143, 144
rājas, 189
Rājput, 125
Rākā, 63
rakkhasa, 93, 108, 109, 110, 115, 133, 135. *See also rākṣasa*.
rakkhasī, 111, 115, 135, 140, 143. *See also rākṣasī*.
rākṣasa, 26, 40, 47, 49–59, 63–5, 67, 68, 69, 75, 86, 87, 90, 125, 127, 131, 157, 159, 161, 162, 164, 166, 167, 178, 189. *See also rakkhasa*.
rākṣasī, 65, 138, 145, 186. *See also rakkhasī*.

Rāma, 64, 182
Rāmagiri, 149
Rāmānujan, A.K., 174
Rāmāyaṇa, 46, 48, 64, 69, 93, 96, 127, 177, 182
Randhowa, M.S., 172
rasa, 21, 48
rasātala, 47, 103. *See also* Pātāla and underworld.
ratiphalam, 152
Rāvaṇa, 54, 63–5, 152, 179, 181
Rayagihe, 128
Rayapasenaiyam Sūtra, 180
Ṛddhi, 64
Revati, 187
Ṛg Veda, 48, 50, 59, 70, 72, 76, 80, 107, 166, 180, 181, 183
rhinoceros, 36
Richman, Paula, 187
Ricoeur, Paul, 78, 181
Rilke, Rainer Maria, 19
rivers, 46–8, 176–77
Rorschach, 43
Rowland, Benjamin, 170
Royal Consecration, 122
ṛṣi, 133
ṛta, 76, 78, 81, 82, 85, 103
Rudra, 55
Rudras, 89, 91
rukkhadevatā, 27–8, 49, 113, 124, 125

sacrifice, 110, 111, 126–27
saddha, 117
sādhakas, 187
sādhana: yakṣa or yakṣiṇī, 146
Sādhanamāla, 188
Ṣadviṁśa Brāhmaṇa, 180
Sāgara, 46–7
Sahadeva, 53, 89
Śaiva Siddhānta, 157
Śaivala fish, 89
Śaivite legends, 146
śakti, 32, 146–47
Śākyamuni, 17, 95, 110, 112, 120. *See also* Buddha, Gautama Buddha, and Siddhārtha Gautama.
śāl trees. *See śāla* trees.
śāla trees, 26, 29
śālabhañjikā, 29, 137
salila, 79
samana, 116–17. *See also śramaṇa.*
saṁgha, 95
saṁsāra, 18, 31, 32, 108, 109, 112, 131, 134, 159, 160
saṁskāras, 165
samudra, 79
Saṁyutta Nikāya, 116, 184
sanātana dharma, 55
Sāñcī, 9, 17, 29, 33, 35, 106, 137, 173
Śāṅkhāyana Gṛhya Sūtra, 181
Sanskrit poetry, 153, 154. *See also kāvya.*
śāntapāna, 58
sap, 21, 25, 172
Sarasvatī river, 98, 176, 177
Sarayu river, 176
sāsanadevatās, 146
śāstras, 75
sat, 79
Satagira, 116
Śatapatha Brāhmaṇa, 63, 171, 176, 179, 180, 182
Satī, 58
sattva, 190
Savitṛ, 50; a *lokapāla*, 180
Sāyana, 69, 179
sculpture: Buddhist, 1, 9–20, 106; integral to religion, 7; Hindu, 1; Jain, 1; yakṣa in, 4
scholarship: early South Asian, 7
Seckel, Dietrich, 14, 17, 169
Semeka-Pankratov, Elena, 175

semen, 22, 25–6, 172
serpent. *See nāga* and snake.
Śeṣa, 175. *See also* Shesha.
Seṭhabaḍi, 187–88
Seven Pagodas, 173
sexuality: and demonism, 159
Shah, Umakant P., 189
shaman, 175
Sharma, Priyavrat, 190
Sheed, Rosemary, 171
Shesha, 174. *See also* Śeṣa.
Siddhārtha Gautama, 14, 109, 139. *See also* Buddha, Gautama Buddha, and Śākyamuni.
Siddhi, 130
Sij tree, 39
Śikhandin, 178
siṁhamukha, 36. *See also kīrttimukha*.
Siṁhapur, 188
Sindhu river, 176, 177
Sinhalese Buddhism, 161
sippagahana, 123
śiras-cakra, 18
Sirima, 106
śirīsa flower, 151
Sirisavatthu: a yakkha city, 139
Sītā, 149
Śītalā, 187
Śiva, 7, 25, 46–7, 55–9, 63, 67, 68, 103, 150, 152, 153, 171, 172, 178
Skanda, 178
snake, 38–41, 75, 85–8, 174, 175–76, 181. *See also nāga*.
Snellgrove, David L., 169
Sohagpur, 188
soma, substance, 22, 24, 25, 39, 48
Soma, god, 49, 61, 65, 97, 174, 175, 179, 180, 183
Somadeva, 33
spāśa, 77
Speyer, Edward, 177
Spirit, 75
spirits, 75
śramaṇa, 108, 133, 134. *See also samana*.
Śrī, 172. *See also* Lākṣmī.
stambha, 25
sthaviras, 128
stūpa, 18, 29, 43, 66; at Bhārhut, 27
Suciloma Sutta, 184
Suciloma yakkha, 106, 183
Sudaṁsane, 128
Sudasana yakkhī, 106
śūdras, 75, 164, 189
Sukeśin, 56–8, 158, 178
Sulocanā yakṣī, 147
Sumerian, 176
Sumeru, 66. *See also* Meru.
sun, 18
Sun Prince, 93–6
Sunda, 40
Suparṇas, 189
Supavasa yakkha, 106
sura, 22
Surabhi, 172
Śūrpaṇakhā, 63, 182
Sūrya, 65, 181
Sutana, 118
Sutano Jātaka, 118
Sutasoma, 123
Sutasoma Jātaka, 123, 124, 125
sūtra, 116
Sūtra Kritanga, 186
Sutta Nipāta, 63, 116, 179, 184, 186
Sutudrī river, 176
suvarṇas, 130
sva dharma, 55, 57
svarga, 113
Śvetāśvatara Upaniṣad, 157, 189
symbols: lifecycle of, 19
symbolism: iconographic, 8
synchronic, 105

Taitareya Brāhmaṇa, 181
Takkasila, 138, 139
tamas, 189
Tantric: demons, 75, 146; rites, 146–47; texts, 3, 146
tapas, 72, 98, 100, 108
Tātakā, 182
Tavatiṁsa heaven, 164
taxonomy, 162–65
Telepatta Jātaka, 138, 187
temple, 106
theology: Christian, 4; Vaiṣṇava, 32
Theratherīgāthā, 114. *See also Psalms of the Elders*.
throne, 95. *See also caitya*.
Tiamat, 176
Tibet, 66, 114
ṭikulī, 137
tīrtha, 46, 122, 176–77
Tirthānkaras, 128, 146
toraṇa, 17, 27, 29, 106
tortoise, 31
transformation: of demons, 3
tree: *aśoka*, 28; *aśvattha*, 26, 27; in Buddhist tradition, 26–9; compared to the yakṣa, 21, 24; as fertility symbol, 24–6, 39; fig, 26; Hiraṇyagarbha rises from, 24; *jaṅgiḍa*, 25; *kalpa vṛkṣa*, 25; *nāgas* and, 39; *palāsa*, 27; *pippala*, 25, 27; *śāla*, 26; Sij, 39; *udumbara*, 25; yakṣa and, 49
trial by water, 85–103
Tripuri, 188
tṛṣṇa, 107
tutelary deities, 144, 146

udadhi beings, 130
udumbara tree, 25
Umā, 74
underworld, 80–2, 159. *See also* Pātāla *and rasātala*.
unmada, 58
Untouchable, 120, 190
Upaniṣads, 3, 71, 72–5, 113, 133, 135, 159
upāsakas, 146, 188
upavita, 137
Urvāśī, 187
Utathya, 96–9, 100, 101, 102, 183
Uttaradhyāyana Sūtra, 186
Uvasagadasāo, 132, 186

vāhanas, 14, 67, 81, 106, 137, 176
Vaimānika gods, 131, 189
Vaiṣṇava: iconography, 32; myths, 115; theology, 32
Vaiśravaṇa (Kubera), 63, 66, 67, 75, 93
Valāhassa Jātaka, 139
vaḷavā-mukha/vaḷavā-mukhī, 123, 185
vaḷavā-rūpa, 123. *See also vaḷavā-mukha*.
Vāmakeśvarimatam, 188
Vāmana Purāṇa, 56, 178
Vāmana Saromahātmyam, 189
Van Buitenen, Hans, 52, 177, 179
Van Den Bosch, Lourens, 182
Vana Parvan (*Mahābhārata*), 52, 88
Varuṇa, 76–83; as *asura*, 79; brings death to his son, 182; compared to a serpent/*nāga*, 80, 181; god of the sea, 33, 40, 61, 79–82, 96–101; as king, 185; as *lokapāla*, 65, 79–80, 97, 180, 181; *māyā* of, 76–9, 93; *pāśa* of, 77, 82, 166; and *ṛta/dharma*, 76, 78, 81, 82, 85, 98, 103; *spāśa* of, 77; transformation of, 77–83, 98–103; a Vedic god, 5, 49, 76–9, 83, 103; and the waters, 77–81, 85–6, 96–101, 181; and the yakṣa, 5, 22, 32, 76–7, 82–3, 85–6,

96–103, 159; like Yama, 80–2, 85–6
Varuṇaloka, 182
Varuṇa-*pāncami*, 181
Varuṇī, 172
Vasudeva, 65
Vasudhārā, 144
Vasus, 89, 91
vāta beings, 131
Vāyu, 65, 73
Vedāntic texts, 3
Vedas: yakṣa in, 1, 5, 23–4, 32, 44, 48, 69–79, 83
Vedic: concept of evil, 110, 184; cosmos, 79, 80, 100, 107, 108, 135, 175; demons, 59, 158 (*See also asuras*.); *dharma*, 109; dualistic worldview, 2–3, 48, 159, 160; gods, 5, 23–5, 49–50, 69–79, 85, 99, 133; ritual, 25, 113, 165; rivers, 176; stage of power, 2, 115, 165, 184; yakṣa, 1, 5, 23–4, 32, 44, 48, 69–79, 83, 157
vengeance, 78
venom, 21, 39–40, 48, 171. *See also* poison *and viṣa*.
Vessavana (Kubera), 93
Vibhīṣaṇa, 63, 64
*vidyut*s, 130
Vijaya legends, 114, 121, 134
vijṛmbhaṇa, 58
(Queen) Vilasvatī, 25
vilopaka, 97
vimāna: *deva*s, 164; *peta*s, 164
Vinaya Piṭaka, 143, 184
Vindhya mountains, 89
Vipāka Sūtra, 178
Virāj, 71
Virudhāka, 66, 106.
Virupakṣa, 66, 90, 181; temple, 178
viṣa, 172. *See also* venom and poison.
Viśiṣṭadvaita, 157
Viṣṇu, 7, 22–3, 32, 41, 45–6, 47, 71, 153, 174
Viṣṇu Purāṇa, 171, 172, 177, 184
Viṣṇudharmottara Purāṇa, 81
Visuddhimagga, 178
Viśvāsu, 67, 179
Viśvavāsu, 181
vitāna, 154
Vittapāla (Kubera), 63
Vitteśa (Kubera), 63
Vivasvan, 44
Vogel, Jean Philippe, 172, 175
Vṛṣaparvan (*Mahābhārata*), 52
Vṛtra, 43, 51, 77, 176, 182
vyakta, 157
Vyantara, 130, 131

Waddell, L.A., 66, 180, 183
Warder, A.K., 183
waters: in Buddhist context, 105, 107, 160; king as conduit for, 47, 85–6; local, 46–8; lotus rises from, 31; mythology and symbolism of, 5, 8, 21–6, 105, 175; *nāga* associated with, 38–43,; symbol of the absolute, 48; trial by, 5, 85–103; yakṣa linked with, 1, 5, 7–49, 85–6, 157, 159
wishing cup, 33
wishing tree. *See kalpa vṛkṣa*.
world guardians. *See lokapāla*s.

yaj, 127
Yajur Veda, 180, 185
yakkha: conversion and outwitting of, 102, 115–18; Buddha as, 175; etymology of, 127; Hindu versus Buddhist, 85–6, 105; as human, 142–43, 160; Indra as, 184; in Jātaka Tales, 107–120, 123–27,

yakkha (*cont.*)
142–43; and kings, 123–27; as monster, 118–20; along with other demons, 133, 135; sculptures of, 106, 183; testing of *bodhisatta* by, 93–6; Suciloma y., 106, 183; Supavasa y., 106; use of the term, 169; in the water, 85–6. *See also* yakṣa: Buddhist.
*Yakkha Sutta*s, 116, 184
yakkhī. *See* yakkhinī.
yakkhinī, 106, 115, 135, 138–46; *assamukhī*, 141; devouring tendencies of, 138, 141, 142, 144; horse-faced, 141; in Jātaka Tales, 138–46; Kuvanna y., 140; y. mare, 123, 185; Sudasana y., 106. *See also* yakṣī.
yakṣa: and *apsaras*, 54; bearers of Kubera, 67; benevolent y., 183; as *brahman*, 23–4; like the Buddha, 135, 175; Buddhist, 3, 5, 9, 14, 85–6, 93–6, 103, 105–27, 133, 135, 158, 160; *caitya*s, 95, 120, 122, 128, 132; with *caurī*s, 17; causes disease, 166; conversion of, 41–3, 93–6, 114, 115–18, 123, 158, 160 (*See also* conversion.); cosmic and acosmic, 21; as crane, 75, 89, 92; as demigod, 1, 75; as demiurge, 107; demonism of, 1, 2, 5, 27, 40- 43, 49–61, 75, 76, 78, 93–6, 100–01, 108–20, 122–27, 135–36, 157–60; as *deva*, 131, 132–33, 163; early scholarship about, 1, 4; as erotic symbol, 5, 150–55; ethical ambiguity of, 2, 5, 21, 69, 76, 92, 100–03, 126–27, 157, 159; etymology of, 69, 127; as fertility symbol, 1, 21, 92, 157; and the fish, 44–6; equated with formlessness, 70; and *gandharva*s, 54, 59–61, 157, 178; as genius loci, 21, 46, 92, 121; Harikeśa y., 55–6; Hindu versus Buddhist representations, 2, 5, 88–103, 105, 112, 120–21, 126–27, 135; in Hinduism, 69–83, 121–22; Indra as, 184; in Jainism, 5, 9, 105, 127–36, 158; in the Jātaka Tales, 5, 28, 85–6, 93–6, 102, 105–27, 135; killed by Sāgara's sons, 47; linked with other deities, 5, 20, 22, 32, 48, 49–69, 76, 78, 82–3, 85–6, 92, 157–59, 178; and lotus, 29, 35; Macakruka y., 122; and *makara*, 35, 49; *māyā* of, 101–03, 157, 158; in the *Meghadūta*, 5, 149–55; as metaphor for mystery, 70, 157; on Mount Meru, 66; as moral devices, 3, 113–15, 157–59, 162; mythological and symbolic associations with, 1, 4, 5, 8, 20, 21, 85–6, 157; and *nāga*s, 38–43, 49, 86–93; origins of, 4, 5, 48, 69–76; ornamental use of, 149; as *paśupati*, 71; as prince, 35, 154; as prototype for the Buddha image, 9, 35; and *rākṣasa*s, 54–9, 157- 59; sculptures of, 9–19, 157, 183; and Śikhandin, 178; connected with Śiva, 178; testing by, 45, 83–93, 102, 129, 160, 169; transformations of, 1, 9, 19, 46, 76, 100–03, 158, 159; and trees, 21, 49; as tribal, 42; use of the term, 169; and Varuṇa, 5, 22, 32, 76, 78, 82–3, 85, 92, 96–101; Vedic, 1, 5, 23–4, 32, 44, 48, 69–76, 83, 157; *vyakta* and *avyakta*, 69, 157; and the waters,

1, 5, 7–49, 85–6, 88–103, 157, 159. *See also* yakkha.
Yakṣa Yuddha Parvan (*Mahābhārata*), 52
yakṣam ātmanvat, 24, 71
Yakshadamaram, 188
Yakṣapraśna, 40, 52, 85–6, 88–93, 122
yakṣī: like *apsaras*, 61, 137, 186; Besnagar y., 11, 14; at Bhārhut, 29, 137, 183; at Bodh Gāya, 29; Buddhist, 138–46 (*See also* yakkhi.); Buddhist sculptures of, 49, 137; Candrā (Cadā) y., 137; as demigod, 1, 146; demonism of, 5, 137–46; ethical ambiguity of, 5; as fertility symbol, 1, 9, 33; as genius loci, 46, 122; Hindu versus Buddhist representations of, 5; in Jainism, 146, 188; in Jātakas, 61, 135, 138–46; at Mathurā, 14, 29, 137; as princess, 154; as *śakti*, 146–47, 187–88; as *śālabhañjikās*, 29, 137; at Sāñcī, 137; shifting form of, 138, 140; Sulocanā y., 147; wife of yakṣa in *Meghadūta*, 153. *See also* yakkhī.
yakṣiṇī. *See* yakṣī and yakkhī.
Yakshiṇīkalpa, 188
Yakshiṇīprayogaḥ, 188
Yakshiṇīsādhana Vidhi, 188
Yama, 65, 79, 80–3, 85, 89, 101, 159, 180, 182
Yāmuna (mountain), 86, 97
Yamunā (river), 176, 177
Yaśastilaka, 65
yātu, 54
yātudhāna. *See yātu*.
yaxs, 69
Yeats, William Butler, 19
yoga, 56
yogic texts, 3
Yoginīs: Sixty four, 146
Yudhiṣṭhira, 45, 52, 53, 60, 64, 86–93, 95, 98, 100, 101, 121
yugas, 23
yūpa, 25

Zeus, 77
Zimmer, Heinrich, 22, 65, 169, 171, 172, 173, 175, 180, 183, 184, 186